In Stillness Conquer Fear

Also by Pauline McKinnon:

Help Yourself and Your Child to Happiness, Melbourne: David Lovell Publishing, 1991.

Quiet Magic, Melbourne: David Lovell Publishing, 1990.

Joseph's Secret, Melbourne: Collins Dove, 1989.

Footprints in the Sand, Melbourne: Collins Dove, 1988.

Rainbow's End, Melbourne: Collins Dove, 1987.

CD Recording:

Stillness for Stress Free Living, Pauline McKinnon Life Development, 1999

In Stillness
Conquer Fear

OVERCOMING ANXIETY, PANIC
AND AGORAPHOBIA

Pauline McKinnon

Newleaf

Newleaf
an imprint of
Gill & Macmillan Ltd
Goldenbridge
Dublin 8
with associated companies throughout the world
www.gillmacmillan.ie

First published by Newleaf 1999
© Pauline Gemma McKinnon
1983, 1989, 1994, 1999
0 7171 2920 9
Print origination by
Carrigboy Typesetting Services, County Cork
Printed by ColourBooks Ltd, Dublin

A catalogue record is available for this book from the British Library.

1 3 5 4 2

The information provided in this book is intended for
general information and guidance only and should not be
used as a substitute for consulting a qualified health
practitioner. Neither the author nor the publisher can accept
any responsibility for your health or any side-effects of
treatments described in this book.

To my husband, my friend
To my family, my life

ACKNOWLEDGMENT

I offer heartfelt thanks to all who have aided my journey. Some I have gone out to seek, some have sought me, the others are constant in their presence.

The Soul sits waiting
she is poised, waiting.
Ever patient, she waits for man or woman
to know her truth;
the truth that frees him or her
from all pain wrought by fear.
The Soul never fears.
Strength is her trademark
peace is her presence, wisdom the arrow that flies from her bow.
The Soul is love.
Deep as the core of a precious fruit
she nestles within us.
Yet wide as thunder and wind
her wings of change embrace the world.
All powerful,
all mild,
she is our own —
our whole and special self.

Pauline McKinnon

CONTENTS

FOREWORD – 1983 EDITION

Pauline McKinnon has done it. It is those who have done it, rather than those who theorise about it, that we should listen to. By great courage and persistence, trying one approach and then another, she has overcome a distressing fear. She writes with great naturalness, letting us share her frustrations, despair and inward humiliation. Then comes the joy of relief, and the full participation in the life of her children which her phobia had made difficult.

But this book has a wider significance than simply an account of someone who escaped from eight years of fear. It indirectly expresses her own values — what is worthwhile, what life is all about — with a charming, simple naturalness ringing through and through with sincerity. The book gives hope to those whose lives are crippled by agoraphobia; an equally important aspect of the book is that it gives relatives and friends some idea of the suffering of those afflicted in this way, and what they might do to help.

In the text, Pauline makes several references to me. For this I thank her. As with the rest of the book, these are part of the spontaneous expression of what has been in her mind.

I have not read a better account of the symptoms of agoraphobia than this story, beautiful in its simplicity, and penetrating in its clinical accuracy.

Dr Ainslie Meares
BAgS, MD, BS, DPM
July 1982

FOREWORD — 1994 EDITION

In business, it is the successful people who are studied. Who sold the most fridges? Who achieved the best results? And how did they do it? What did they do differently, what did they learn, what did they develop that produced their success?

It seems curious, then, that in recent times medicine often has appeared to study what on one level would appear to be the 'losers'. In a hospital setting, the person who is studied is usually the one with the most obscure illness, the one who takes the longest to diagnose, the one who takes the longest to recover.

In medicine, the successful ones, the ones who recover quickly, are usually off and out of the hospital or waiting room before anyone even notices. Surely these are the very people we should chase down the road and demand answers from. What did you do? How was it that you recovered? What can we learn from you that will help others? Pauline McKinnon is one of those successful patients who did it. She recovered. She even knows how and why she recovered. More importantly, Pauline has the ability to articulately share her experience and knowledge with others — in a way that can help them directly and effectively.

Reading *In Stillness Conquer Fear* could change your life; free you to live fully — in ease, comfort and joy. It is a pleasure to be able to recommend something that I know works so well.

Dr Ian Gawler
OAM, BVSc
The Gawler Foundation Australia
December 1993

PREFACE

I remember reading somewhere, a long time ago, a quotation that has stayed with me always. It went something like this:

If you want to help me, please don't teach me what you have learned from others. Teach me something you have learned yourself.

These pages summarise many of my learnings and with pleasure I offer this fourth, fully revised edition of *In Stillness Conquer Fear*. Since 1999 marks exactly twenty-five years since I conquered my own fear, this edition takes on the form of a celebration which I can joyfully share with you.

Originally this book was published from the point of view of a lay-person. However, the years have passed, propelling me to undertake training and the development of my work as a practitioner in meditation and counselling. So while I hope that these pages can be enjoyed free of the daunting medical phraseology often found in texts of this nature, what they contain can now be substantiated by extensive professional as well as personal experience. Though my story of course has not changed, I have extended the original text to include a closer look at my personal life together with detailed instructions for readers to practise *stillness meditation*. I have also included other ideas which have evolved from my own long look at the anxiety reaction!

This is a self-help book. To those who have already gained from reading earlier editions, my wish is that this later work will take you a little further up the stairway to success. To new readers, as always, I wish you a speedy return to freedom from fear. I would be pleased to hear your story and learn of your progress.

Pauline McKinnon
PO Box 151, Kew East 3102, Victoria, Australia

INTRODUCTION

What we do not understand, we do not possess.
                                                    Goethe

He was a bachelor of eighty-six, who could well have passed for sixty-eight: a colourful, interesting man with many a tale to tell from his long and varied years of living. We shared a carriage on a country train, and the three-hour journey through endless pastures, green and flood-strewn, went by very quickly in animated conversation. As the train clattered to a halt at our destination, he looked at me earnestly and said very seriously: 'It's been great to have someone to talk to. Usually the others in the carriage hide behind their magazines and pretend you're not there. People are scared, you know! It's a pity . . . but people are scared.'

A few years earlier in my life, that conversation could not have taken place, for I, too, would have been scared — not of conversing with a stranger on a train, but of being on a train. For eight years, my life was suppressed by *agoraphobia*, the paralysing fear of leaving the safety of home.

During that time and in my desire to conquer that haunting fear, I read a great many books dealing with stress, anxiety and tension. I longed for something written by someone who had known agoraphobia, someone with whom I could identify and who really understood my predicament. I never found such a person or such a book. Eventually I was prompted to fill that gap myself and in 1983, some time after overcoming my fear, I first published this story.

More recently, others have ventured into the area of anxiety, panic and agoraphobia, with books bringing their own personal or professional views into being. So there is greater awareness today than before and models of therapy have changed a little. But there remains a pressing need for people in fear to learn of the intimate experience of another person who has known and felt what they themselves are feeling. And so I tell my story of fear, in the hope that by doing so I can help others to understand and overcome their fears and phobias and live a better life.

Today, with the advent of increased interest in this subject it has become popular for health professionals to diagnose conditions known as *anxiety disorders or panic disorder (with or without agoraphobia)*. Since these conditions all follow the progression of *anxiety, panic and agoraphobia*, if you have been diagnosed with *panic disorder*, you will certainly identify with and be helped by what you read here.

Having experienced sufficient anxiety to lead to agoraphobia, I can well appreciate the misery of those enduring other fears, compulsions or phobias. For quite apart from anxiety disorders and quite apart from agoraphobia, which in itself spoils the lives of thousands of people, there are thousands with other phobias and thousands more with other general fears. How often do we hear the casual comment from young or old: 'I hate crowds,' 'Busy roads frighten me,' 'Oh, not a thunderstorm,' 'Don't expect me to make a speech!' The gentleman on the train was certainly right; we are all scared and our fears — even if they are only minor — can take much of the pleasure from life.

Why are people so scared? Why do so many of us, living in civilised and peaceful surroundings, harbour fears and anxieties even though we are not facing obvious danger? Have we, in our modern society, fallen prey to a constant threat in the form of our own anxiety, which can be as distressing as the threat of impending disaster? Fear is a compelling human emotion. At best it serves to protect us from harm. At its worst it can lead to hatred, anger and warfare. But fear, like any dynamic, also carries an opposite response: fear can prevent people from fulfilling their lives, leading them instead to shame, anxiety and the avoidance of normal life.

Anxiety is experienced by all people and it makes its presence felt in varying degrees or at various levels. Imagine a colour wheel of human fears! If we could spin such a fantasy, we would see a spectrum of hues building from the pale dread of the prospect of an injection to the deeper tones of distressing anxiety and finally to black incapacitation, when people become totally consumed by fear. The colour of anxiety, as it occurs in individual lives, will vary according to the many factors that influence each person. The degree or level of the anxiety particularly relates to the stress he or she encounters and the way that stress is managed. Stress is something we frequently hear about. All too often we learn of someone who has become ill as a result of stress and fear that we, too, may suffer the effects of stress.

Even more significantly, the degree of anxiety present depends upon a person's level of tension at any given time. The higher the tension level, the higher the anxiety. Nervous tension — a negative coping strategy — is also familiar in modern society. It is not at all unusual to hear the cry: 'If only I could relax and unwind.' Anxiety and tension are experienced today perhaps more than ever before — maybe because of the pressures and expectations of modern living, together with a general neglect of self-care in this regard.

While stress, anxiety and tension are part of our human nature they can become excessive so at some level many people are searching for relief from these elements. To achieve that relief we need guidance, for unfortunately we are not taught to deal with these matters as students and such information is rarely handed down to us by our elders. When confused, frustrated, frightened and in need of direction, we either fight the situation, hoping we can learn to live with it, or we seek assistance from various supports which can be temporary, often destructive, and filled with the risk of leading to more stress.

A *phobia* is a defence against anxiety. History tells us that phobias have been suffered by people from time immemorial. But phobias seem uncommon because people fear discussing them. None of us likes to admit to fear of any kind, probably because of the fact that we are really afraid to be afraid! If fears and phobias are so widespread, why worry? Let us talk about them. Let us not be too scared to discuss our fears — for only by facing fear openly can we free ourselves from its bondage.

Agoraphobia is a phobia like other phobias — except that its effects are further-reaching and therefore the individual suffers more severe limitations to living. In my opinion, agoraphobia is not a physical or mental illness but an emotional response following an attack of panic. The person involved has usually been under some degree of stress and for some time has been living in a state of excessive anxiety and nervous tension.

A panic attack, experienced for the first time, can be extremely alarming. Panic is a greatly magnified experience of anxiety in which the physical symptoms of fear become intensified and, of course, the person usually does not understand what is happening. These symptoms may include trembling, sweating, nausea, dizziness, chest pain, rapid breathing, palpitations, numbness and tingling, sensations of de-personalisation or physical imbalance, and perhaps episodes of fainting.

After the first attack of panic, in most instances, with some degree of reassurance and the passing of time, the intense anxiety decreases and the individual goes on, outwardly at least, living a normal life. But anxiety begets anxiety, which in turn increases tension. And so other symptoms may develop, including repetitive worry, insecurity, insomnia, headaches and depression. The obstinacy of these symptoms and the recurrence of niggling 'reminder symptoms' similar to those which accompanied the first panic attack then give rise to doubts and further fears. So the person concerned begins a defence against the possibility of these symptoms occurring again — and the imagined risk of becoming overwhelmed by them. The defence then becomes a habit, which remains in the form of a phobia, and the inner misery of living with this phobia is immense. There is great loneliness attached to this fear and, since 'cure' seems so elusive, there is also a strong sense of hopelessness.

It appears that this particular type of fear has only been acknowledged as a common condition in the last twenty years or so. This is perhaps due to people's reticence to openly discuss what they are experiencing out of yet another fear — that of appearing foolish by admitting to something which he or she feels is solely their own. Should you still feel alone in this, I would like to assure those of you with agoraphobia that your problem is known to a great many others and it is not a hopeless state.

After my personal eight-year struggle, I overcame agoraphobia very quickly and easily by learning to relax *physically and mentally* in a unique form of meditation. Within my liberation from fear, I found that in itself this phobia is a very simple problem. It is the lack of understanding and the endless and often fruitless search to overcome it which transforms it into a stubborn obstacle that people may suffer indefinitely unless they have the means to do otherwise. *Stillness meditation*, by which I overcame agoraphobia, will provide that means and positively assist people with that condition to find freedom from fear.

At this point, I would like to note something of importance. Some people with agoraphobia may also be experiencing a form of mental illness. This is rather like saying that some people with agoraphobia may also have a broken leg or glandular fever; they are separate problems. So also are those illnesses where, among other symptoms, people withdraw completely from society. Such illness ought not be confused with agoraphobia. However, ill health, along with other disruptions to life, is usually accompanied by stress and anxiety to which the skills I offer in this book can make a remarkable difference.

Those who are curious about agoraphobia, or who themselves experience fears of another form or recognise tension and stress in their daily lives, can also gain from what I have learned. For the practice of *stillness* can positively improve the life of anyone who wishes to live more easily, cope with stress and reduce anxiety, tension and other negative emotional reactions.

My most earnest reason, then, for relating my story is to demonstrate to others (not only those who suffer panic or agoraphobia) the importance of finding tranquillity *in true relaxation* and how greatly we can benefit from the changes tranquillity can bring. But my greatest motivation in this work is to reach and reassure those who are trapped by fear. Often they are unwilling prisoners in their homes, or live a life which is restricted to a secure environment. Many of these courageous people are unable to seek help because they find it impossible to leave their security to do so. Perhaps my own experience will touch them with the message: *know and believe that you can conquer this fear and be free to enjoy life to the full.*

My story, I know, reflects the stories of others. While many have contacted me over the years to thank me for what they have gained from it, some people have admitted they feared reading this book because they saw themselves mirrored there. Like the problem of agoraphobia (or panic disorder) itself, it seems easier to avoid or run from anything that incites fear. Such can be our human vulnerability — and inevitably such can be our loss. For there is no doubt that a substantial part of the overcoming of fear involves facing it, but free of tension. So I would like to gently encourage those who feel apprehensive to read on, trusting that the story and the message will lead you to the ease you hope for.

I hope too, that this book will bring understanding to the spouses, families and friends who support the agoraphobic person out of love and loyalty, often without realising just how desperately needed they are.

I want to speak also to those who do not understand another's human fear and will make statements such as 'stop feeling sorry for yourself' or 'pull yourself together', advice that is useless and insensitive. The person concerned has no wish to be distressed by fear, and if 'pulling anything together' were the solution, he or she would willingly do so.

As panic and its accompanying symptoms are manifested in the form of physical distress, the obvious course of action is to seek medical help. Consequently, I ask for the attention of the many doctors who hear the plea of the person in fear, yet do not really answer. Sometimes they do not understand; all too often they are too busy, and occasionally some may respond with indifference or impatience. Unfortunately, the inclination in these circumstances is to prescribe tranquillisers and offer little hope or alternative solution. There is a message here as well for those who really want to help but don't always know how to. To health professionals I would like to say: there is a better and more enriching way to solve this problem.

It is also important that the public be kept aware of the influence of anxiety problems and the tension surrounding them as a concern within the community. At great cost to society, much productivity is lost because of these negative elements. Sympathetic awareness can make it easier to help should the need arise. And just as importantly, general awareness can inspire others to contribute to a more relaxed society by minimising unnecessary tension in their own lives.

My interpretation of anxiety, panic and agoraphobia is that these are not illnesses to be cured, but rather problems to be *understood* and solved. I have deliberately avoided using words such as 'cure' or 'recover', for I think that these terms often give cause for more anxiety. For purposes of identification in the written word, I have found it necessary to use certain descriptive expressions which may amount to the use of a label, such as 'sufferer', or 'victim'. Whilst I may have had to write such descriptions, I do not agree with their general use. So please read these as descriptions only! I do not like labels. A person who experiences anxiety, panic or agoraphobia is a person — with a particular fear. To attach certain words or diagnostic labels such as 'disorder' to these responses can be limiting and can also encourage a sense of personal diminishment which, instead of serving positively, may exacerbate the condition through negative implication.

The story I am about to tell is the unembroidered recollection of how fear invaded my life at a time of stress, the effects of that fear, and how I unwittingly used the weapon of nervous tension to prolong fear and blind me from certain truths within my own life. My story demonstrates that in the skill of *stillness* there is a simple and natural way by which we can more easily handle the challenges of life and possibly avoid unfortunate consequences. In adopting this lifeskill, our fears can be subdued. We can be more relaxed in ourselves. Our tasks in life become less arduous and problems become less worrying because of the serenity distilled by this means. That serenity — or tranquillity — can also bring special strength and the enlightenment which leads to the fulfilment of our dreams.

The telling of my story gives meaning to my own unpleasant encounter and I present it with the conviction that from all that seems bad, good will eventually emerge. Life is not a dress rehearsal. If there is something one can offer to others, it must be done now. I hope this book may also contribute in some way to greater understanding and generosity between people — a drop in the ocean of humanity.

One

MY INTRODUCTION TO STRESS

*A man who fears suffering is already
suffering what he fears.*

Michel de Montaigne

When I was a very small girl, from the time I could walk falteringly on two-year-old legs, I belonged to Nessa. She was the lady next door, middle-aged, childless and lonely. I filled a large part of her life, and she gave me treasures to cherish in my memory that only a child can receive. Together we lived in a dream world where the sun always shone and all stories had happy endings. We shared many things, and I was her pride and joy for as long as my mother and father lent me to her. But the greatest treasure we shared was her garden. She grew everything beautifully: neat rows of vegetables, separated by paths upon which I could walk if I was careful not to overstep and squash the lettuces; crisp little carrots and the peas nibbled straight from their fresh green pods. She cooked baby beet especially for me; and I remember well the pungent scent of runner beans as we picked them by the basketful. These all grew from seeds which she planted in trays covered with glass; she showed me the minute shoots and we watched their daily progress in those tiny hothouses.

There was an enormous fig tree which always seemed to be laden with fruit, and by the age of three I was familiar with the soft sweetness of ripe yellow loquats and the substance of their grotesque and silken stone. Her peach tree produced perfect fruit; so large, so ripe, soft creamy green on one side and blushing pink on the other. When one or two would fall into the cascade of ferns near the veranda, she used to tell me that the little people had dropped them there for me; and I believed her.

In front of the house she amassed all the annuals as each paraded in turn; heady perfumed purple stocks, brilliant orange soldier flowers, masses of starry forget-me-nots, sapphire irises and golden daffodils. Then, I even knew their botanical names. She introduced me to the habits of spiders and insects, and I learned to identify all the garden birds and the call each one made. Every birthday she presented me with a posy of my favourites, the Cecile Brunner roses; tightly bunched buds, coral pink in the centre, unfurling gently to the soft hue of a sea-shell. I still melt when I see 'fairy roses'.

But the best place in the garden was under my mayflower tree. Merely a bush, the mayflower seemed to me then like a huge tree! This was our special spot, its welcoming arms sheltering a cave of soft green grass, where the sandwiches were eaten and the stories were told. Heavily perfumed, my mayflower boasted a myriad of tiny petalled flowers which, when Nessa shook the branches, would cover us both in a shower of miniature white confetti. And under that tree was security, joy and quiet stillness, interrupted only by our special conversations and the distant droning of summer bees.

Such was the tranquillity of Nessa's garden — without fear.

By the ripe old age of six or seven, my visits to the garden became less and less frequent as I became involved with being a schoolgirl, and outgrew my fantasy land. In those years I, like all children, began to experience fear: fears of the dark, of ghosts and 'bogey men'; fear of school teachers, of being alone. It was fears like those that would prompt me to go and visit Nessa. We would have a chat and some fresh cake and go out to the garden. And always I returned home free and happy.

We learn from fear, and we also learn to overcome those childish fears by a basic will to do so and, more significantly, by other distractions. Over and above my school work, I had a passion for painting and drawing and play-acting imaginative games, together with my young sister and as many of the neighbouring children as I could persuade to co-operate with me. Such activities readily dispel fear. So my childhood fears diminished and became only vague memories, later to be laughed about.

But fear is a human instinct, the first of the three great emotions: fear, love and anger. As we develop, our basic instinct of fear is replaced by the intellectual response of *anxiety*, which covers a multitude of human worries.

I had no fears from childhood, and my anxieties in the pseudo-sophistication of the teenage years varied from concern that one or both of my parents would die, to the state of the world in general. After leaving school, I embarked upon a secretarial career which led me into secure and responsible positions. I enjoyed my work, and my home life was secure and happy. So, if I had any real anxiety at all in those years, it was typical enough, I think, of the anxious moments of immaturity.

In those years and into my twenties, I was very much involved with creative ambitions in the field of singing and the theatre. Such interests, I believe, have the effect of counteracting anxiety to a rather large extent. So the security I had known from Nessa's garden was transferred to the security of creativity, and the security that is born of friendships, camaraderie, sharing that creativity.

Of stress in life I knew very little. Then, a few months after my marriage, my father died suddenly of a heart attack. This was my first close encounter with death. I recall feeling at the time that I was not reacting as I would have predicted, had I ever stopped to think about it. It is interesting how one remembers things that are said in times of stress. I recall vividly how I answered the telephone and my mother, in distress, told me the bad news. Then she added: 'I'm sorry to bother you.' What a strange thing for her to say — why should she have been sorry to bother me? And I remember how it seemed that the people I passed in the street as I went to her were in another world — an unfeeling world — when my world had been stricken with the initial unreality of grief. It was many hours before I shed any tears.

As I was more or less available to take much of the responsibility for my mother, I found I was rather leant upon. I had to be strong for her, talk to people, make and drink endless cups of tea, help her with the necessary arrangements and think about her future. When I finally realised that my father had left our midst, it was with an even greater sadness, because only a few days before we had told him that I was pregnant. His longing for the grandchild that he was never to see was very great.

Life, as always, goes on. After the initial shock and disturbance, new patterns formed. But my husband and I now had my widowed mother to consider. To our shock and dismay, about one month later my father-in-law died after a brief illness. Here was more stress for us as a young couple, and another lonely mother to console.

Since our marriage, my husband had resumed a course of study and was attending many lectures each week. Both of us were also working at night in a small restaurant we had at the time. Although this arrangement worked fairly satisfactorily, it involved a great deal of hard work, long hours and lack of rest and relaxation. So we decided we should change this lifestyle by selling that business, and embarking upon another closely related to his new profession. We began to take steps in this direction and had some extra stress and worry when things did not go exactly according to plan.

Then came the worst shock of all. At three o'clock one morning, we received a message that my husband's brother-in-law, in his thirties, had suffered a heart attack and died immediately, leaving a young wife and six very young children. It simply seemed unbelievable. We felt terribly inadequate. We were surrounded by suffering and it was impossible to give enough help to those who needed it. If I had been spared stressful experiences in my earlier life, I was certainly being given them now and in no small doses. I was very shocked by it all. Our personal joy, the baby that was due in four months time, was about the furthest thing from our minds.

Within the next two months, an uncle also died suddenly of a heart attack; my husband contracted a serious eye disease and for some time there was a risk that he would lost his sight; and my mother had a stroke and was hospitalised. And I still hadn't had time to buy a dozen nappies for the expected baby.

When November finally came and our son was born, it seemed that we had lived through a lifetime of change. In those last weeks we had even managed to sell the restaurant and move to a flat, and at last we felt liberated from all that had recently occurred: our baby son was a herald of happier times ahead. He certainly was; but at the same time, suddenly I was a mother. That fact brought new responsibilities, a busier life and, although of an exhilarating kind, some new and additional stress. Nevertheless, for the next few months we led a reasonably normal life.

However, probably triggered by the responsibility of mother-hood, general fatigue and the experience of real anxiety, I recall that I began to over-worry about certain things; vague things, which I had not thought of before, and which I can't even put into words now. But I know that behind those worries were the sudden deaths — the loss without warning — and new fears of illness and death.

I also remember feeling that the peace and happiness we had looked forward to in married life seemed continually to be threat-ened by something beyond our control. I felt very insecure. Because we respond to happenings in our life in our own indi-vidual way, for me, the negative events which punctuated our early married life were stressful and were increasing my anxiety. The pace of my life had been mounting in that stressful manner and I was not equipped to handle it.

Before our daughter was born eighteen months later, two more close relatives had died suddenly; my mother-in-law had been taken ill; and, when our baby girl was only three weeks old, my own mother was incapacitated, and once more needed me.

I remember feeling very tired all the time, and always rushed and edgy, but I didn't have time to stop to think about it. Older relatives were inclined to suggest occasionally that I was 'doing too much' and other vague statements, but I really didn't know what they meant by those remarks — and there was no alter-native anyway. In any case, I believe that opting out will never overcome any burden that responsibilities may bring.

Through all these disruptions, I was still trying to settle into married life. Although many people do it, coping with two infants is hard work in itself, without all the preceding and accompanying worries we seemed to have had. There were constantly things to be done, and apart from filling the role of wife, mother and daughter, I was helping in our business, which meant that I had a pretty constant part-time job as well.

It seemed that pieces of me were required by many people and I felt a great personal burden of responsibility. The suddenness and substance of the demands with which I was faced cast a giant shadow on life at that time. It was no longer the 'bowl of cherries' that I had known before and a sense of threat and precariousness continually haunted me. I do not recall these activities with resentment; they were things that just simply had to be done, and to achieve it all I was living on hardly any sleep and lots of nervous energy. Unfortunately, I accepted that mounting tension as being normal — the only way to live. Many of us do, and it is a great mistake.

I had made another mistake. I had abandoned something which meant a great deal to me; my ambition in the world of the arts. It seemed that with so much happening, there just wasn't enough time, and other priorities came first. So I had no escape from anxiety in the form of creative relaxation.

This account seems to paint a rather sombre picture of our marriage in those early years. That is not necessarily so. In between the worries were times of much happiness. But for me, personally, the anxiety was there — a cloud of uncertainty — of something lost or never found; and the sudden knowledge of too much stress and the inability to deal with it. Life had become difficult, and stress was taking its toll.

The statement made so long ago by Michel de Montaigne probably sums up exactly the way I felt at that time, as I began to experience the adverse effects of stress. I was afraid of suffering, but I didn't realise that I was in fact, right then, suffering what I feared. If de Montaigne made this observation as long ago as the sixteenth century, it would seem that we haven't progressed very quickly in learning to overcome such suffering during the last 400 years! For much of the suffering of life in today's world can be summarised in that one well-known word: stress.

To be alive is to have demands placed upon us. Stress is the effect of those demands, whether they are pleasant demands or the demands of suffering. We cannot prevent stress. As humans we are fragile and we must suffer; that is a fact of life. But without understanding, guidance and assistance, such suffering can be harder to endure.

Dr Hans Selye, who first used the word 'stress' in the 1940s to describe the wear and tear caused by life, writes:

> The soldier who sustains wounds in battle, the mother who worries about her soldier son, the gambler who watches the races, the horse and the jockey he bets on: they are all under stress.
>
> The beggar who suffers from hunger and the glutton who overeats, the little shopkeeper with his constant fears of bankruptcy and the rich merchant struggling for yet another million: they are also all under stress.
>
> No-one can live without experiencing some degree of stress all the time. You may think that only serious disease or intensive physical or mental injury can cause stress. This is false. Crossing a busy intersection, exposure to a draft, or even sheer joy are enough to activate the body's stress mechanism to some extent. Stress is not even necessarily bad for you; it is also the spice of life, for any emotion, any activity causes stress. But, of course, your system must be prepared to take it.

In layperson's language, I think we can understand the effect of stress through the parallel meaning of stress as it has always been used by engineers to describe the interaction of force and resistance. An engineering student is taught that a piece of steel will change shape under stress, and when that stress is removed the piece of steel will resume its original shape. When again subjected to a greater stress, it will react to that stress by stretching or bending more than it did the first time, but will return perfectly to its natural form when the stress is removed. And so on it goes, giving way and stretching under the stress in a perfectly elastic manner, always returning to its original form, until the point of stress is reached where the steel yields; it goes beyond its *elastic limit* and its form is changed and will not return to the original. It could be said that the steel is then permanently deformed. However, the essence of the material is unchanged, and with heat and human skill the steel can be reconstituted and brought back to its original shape, to perform in the same resilient manner as it did before it was stressed beyond its limit.

While we people are far removed from steel, we too have an elastic limit — and an enormous ability to cope with many demands of life before reaching that limit. But if we are not handling those demands with ease, stress will begin to have adverse effects upon us. However, the *way* stress will affect us, or the degree of stress required before we reach our elastic limit, will depend upon each individual's ability to cope with the demands placed upon him or her. What is stressful for one may not be so for another. Something that is an exciting challenge to one person may be a massive problem to the next. A busy life to one may be a very easy life to someone else.

Many people suffer severe stress from the effects of devastating illness, bereavement or personal heartbreak and withstand it very well. Others experience tragedy, disaster or violence. Many more know the stress that comes of poverty, deprivation, broken homes, unemployment. These are major problems, and strangely, taken singly, they are often the problems that we cope with best.

We can also know stress resulting from lesser demands. Stress can mean something as minor as a new day beginning with the milk boiling over on the stove; to pressure from advertising, personal decision making, conflicts within relationships, dissatisfaction at work, poor communication, peer-group pressure, expectations of women (liberated or otherwise, there are still expectations), pressure on men as a result of this; the manipulative rivalry of the business world and the abandonment of former traditions, representative of security. The list is endless.

Many of these demands are from external influences over which we have no control. In these times, we also have to contend with many elements that can aggravate the stress of life: traffic, telephones, aeroplane travel, computerisation, novel appliances and the commotion of city life. All these facilities are marvellous to possess, but if we are not easily handling what is asked of us personally, our modern conveniences will add fuel to the fire of stress.

When stress begins to cause us unease, our anxiety level increases and we begin to fight back with tension. We are living in fear of suffering and we begin to suffer what we fear as we reach our elastic limit.

The most common reactions to stress are the familiar symptoms of anxiety: fatigue, edginess and irritability, insomnia, headaches, palpitations and the many vague complaints which are generalised as 'only nervous tension'. Then there are more dramatic reactions. Sarah, who was involved in a severe motor accident where someone was killed, developed asthma, later attributed to the stress of that ordeal. Bill, who nursed his sick wife for several years developed severe depression — more than grief — after her death.

People seem to be more susceptible to infectious illnesses when under stress; it is said that their resistance is lowered. And these days it is widely held that stress is a precipitating factor in catastrophic illnesses such as cancer, heart attacks and strokes.

When under stress we can feel fragile and fatigued and thus we *fear* an inability to cope with all we have to do. So, again, we suffer what we fear as anxiety rises. So stress could be said to be the forerunner of fear itself.

As it happened, one day in 1967, just as my husband and I had settled once more after having moved our little family into our own home, I experienced for the first time in my life an attack of panic. It seemed that this was what I had been anticipating. Something that alarmed me greatly and something that could not be explained, had finally struck. It was as if my worst fears had been realised. I felt that I was next on the threatened list!

Two

THE RESULT OF THAT STRESS

Life is made up of marble and mud.

Nathaniel Hawthorne

It was a hot, steamy and overcast day, my head was aching and I was very tired. I remember it well. My daughter, who was only seven months old at the time, had cried all night, supposedly teething. My small boy, not yet two and rather adventurous, as most little boys are, had already been bathed twice before mid-day — once for covering himself and his baby sister in the black sandy soil from around the camellias and a second time for polishing the floor with the contents of a packet of cocoa while I was bathing the mud off the baby.

I was watching the clock, as I had to be at the doctor's surgery at a particular time to have stitches removed from my leg, where I had been bitten by a dog a week or so before. Then I had two business phone calls to delay me. I left the children to be minded, visited the doctor's rooms and then rushed back to collect the children, for the person minding them was only available for that hour. I remember thinking that I should have stopped to eat lunch, because the children had been given theirs earlier and it was by now close to the middle of the afternoon. But I had some business at the bank in the next suburb and had to be there before they closed. So, thinking that I would eat later, I organised the little ones into the car again, settled with the babysitter and rushed off once more.

It was as I was driving in rather heavy traffic that I suddenly experienced an unpleasant feeling of unreality. I felt a surge of alarm at this new experience. I remember vaguely thinking that perhaps I had not been concentrating very well on my driving, and almost wanted to pinch myself to see if I was dreaming.

This feeling of unreality, I know now, is quite common and is caused by nervous tension. However, I did not know that then, and I became more tense and therefore very anxious, in an attempt to overcome that unpleasant feeling. I then realised that I was feeling extremely unwell. I was giddy and nauseated, my head was pounding, my vision was blurred and my heart was thumping in my throat — and I was still driving the car. I managed to park it and sat there for a few minutes, terribly aware of the fact that I was ill and away from home and I had two very young children with me.

By then, I was also feeling weak and faint, hot and cold and gasping for breath — *hyperventilating*, so I learned much later. Excessive over-breathing in fright will cause numbness in the hands and limbs, and I then experienced what is medically known as a *tetanic spasm* which, I thought then, was the sudden onset of paralysis. With all those dramatic sensations happening and the predicament of being responsible for my children, I was convinced that I was dying or certainly being stricken with some dreadful disease.

The memory of the sudden deaths and illness in our family flooded my mind and somehow I stumbled, panic stricken, into a shop nearby. All I could say was that I needed help, and quickly, as my head swam with dark patches of fading consciousness. I must also have been the colour of a sheet, for I certainly caused some concern amongst the shopkeepers. I had alarmed them as well as myself, as they confirmed a couple of weeks later when I returned to say 'thank you'.

I didn't actually lose consciousness as many people do in such circumstances, but my mind was swamped with panic and I was terrified. Panic is a word we have come to use fairly loosely in our vocabulary, but the real meaning of the word can only be appreciated by someone who has been through a complete *panic attack*. At that time what I was experiencing was a mystery to me — but I remember feeling threatened by a sense of urgency, and all my responsibilities seemed to crowd into my thoughts, in particular the two little children still out there in the car. It was a sensational and very frightening experience and I felt, in my confusion, that if I wasn't dying, I was about to lose control of my reason and actions.

As being in control is a very important aspect of well-being to human nature, a panic attack is a very unpleasant experience. No one likes to feel threatened in any way, least of all to have their composure threatened. But when one feels threatened by something one cannot even identify, it is doubly hard to accept. I pictured myself in all that confusion, being removed from the scene, with absolutely no control over the situation, even to the extent of not being able to communicate, and therefore losing my identity.

The people in the shop kindly came to my rescue, and to my relief the effects of the attack gradually passed. They also insisted upon taking me home and I was made to promise to have a thorough medical examination. The local doctor assured me that there was nothing seriously wrong, and that I was over-tired and run down. As he knew the stresses we had been under within the family during those years, he emphasised those and said that I just needed a good rest. He was inclined to insist jovially that my experience was just a simple faint due to fatigue, and he did not seem able to explain any of the unpleasant sensations I had experienced. The word 'panic' was not mentioned at all. Panic is defined by many as 'runaway anxiety'. I guess I had just been lucky until that time, for I had never experienced even *mild* panic, as many people do when under pressure. This was something new to me, and it was more than mild panic, so despite his reassurance I could not help worrying about my misadventure. The responsibility for my two young children increased this concern.

If the doctor, or anyone whose knowledge I trusted, had been able to explain those strange feelings properly to me, I possibly would have not thought any more about the attack. But explanation was lacking, definition was vague, and the memory of that feeling of impending loss of control seemed to be imprinted on my memory with electrifying reality.

I wanted to know what had caused such an attack so that it could be prevented from happening again. The only answer forthcoming was the repeated phrase that I had nothing to worry about and that I was simply 'on edge'. I found this difficult to accept. How could being 'on edge' cause such a dreadful physical feeling of illness? I had never fainted in my life, nor had any illness apart from the usual illnesses of childhood. There didn't seem to be any guarantee that 'it' would not happen again, and I began to dread the possibility of another attack.

Anyone will react slightly to a strange or new sensation, and I now know that if a person is tense, those reactions will be magnified. The person overreacts in alarm within the stressful situation, which then increases tension, which therefore produces more and more feelings of fear, and so he or she embarks upon a merry-go-round of fear-tension-fear-tension.

That is how I reacted then. Without realising that I was doing so, I became very watchful for any sign of the attack occurring again and became more tense. Therefore, within a few days, I experienced another attack; not so severe, but of the same pattern. That seemed to be confirmation of the fact that my 'illness', whatever it was, had come to stay.

The doctor's opinion was sought again. This time I really expected him to find some physical cause — it would almost have been some sort of relief if he had — but again his reply was: 'You are overtired.' He prescribed Amytal tablets and told me to rest for a few days. I would have taken any course of action he suggested in order to prevent those unpleasant sensations so I took the tablets as directed and rested. The medication made me lethargic and the rest only gave me time to dwell upon what was happening to me. The memory of those attacks, particularly the fact that the first one had occurred in such a vulnerable situation, was there to stay. I tried to forget it, but it haunted me. I was a very conscientious mother — what if it should occur out in the street again? What would happen to the children?

As well as these worries, I still had an underlying fear that the doctor had missed something and that I might well have some serious illness. Modern living has, unfortunately I think, conditioned us to taking medicine immediately we feel unwell. Unless there is something very seriously wrong with us, we soon feel better. This is partly because the medication aids recovery, and partly because time heals and the illness disappears. Although I was taking the prescribed tablets my symptoms kept reappearing. What I didn't realise at the time was that those symptoms were in fact symptoms of anxiety and its accompanying tension. While admitting that I was undoubtedly overtired and 'on edge', I was quite oblivious to that tension. I simply tensed myself more and more against whatever it was that was happening to me.

Many people have become used to tensing or holding on to themselves as they attempt to allay discomfort of any kind. I, for one, was determined to fight and beat this, for I certainly did not want any more of those attacks, whatever they were. So to fight it I used, or rather misused, tension, and thereby did nothing to reduce my symptoms; in fact I only aggravated them.

As well as worrying about the situation, I had great difficulty describing my feelings. It seemed as if neither my husband nor the doctor, nor anyone in the family to whom I spoke, could really understand why I was worried. I felt apprehensive about going out of the house alone, and all the time I didn't know that it was the tension within me that was causing all my trouble. In fact, I was causing all those sensations myself!

My dear mother, who was not a relaxed person and whose health was not good at that time, offered her help while I rested. Unfortunately, she appeared to have no idea of the worry I was experiencing and only wished to disregard it. In doing so, she was inclined to reprimand me, pointing out the abundance of good things in my life — in truth I was far better off than many others! Though regretful in doing so, I began to avoid *her* company too, and the help she offered.

For everyone's sake, my husband arranged for a housekeeper for the rest of the week. That lady was at least eighty years old. She arrived enveloped in an enormous overcoat and her determined expression was only the more emphasised by the flat straw hat she wore firmly pinned to the prim knot of grey hair on top of her head. These garments were shed as she swept through to my kitchen with intimidating efficiency, while at the same time appraising the situation.

'What's the matter with you?' she asked disbelievingly. I mumbled something vague about being told to take it easy and I could see that she was not impressed. For when you are in your twenties, unless you've just had a baby or a miscarriage, you are not of very great interest to most members of that brigade of housekeepers.

'It's probably sunstroke,' she concluded with an air of finality, wielding a broom.

She didn't drink tea or coffee or eat lunch, and rather reluctantly prepared something for me and the children, whom she obviously terrified. And she'd never been ill — in fact she'd never had a day off work in sixty years. I remember feeling slightly amused at the situation as I watched an eighty-year-old lady beating my rugs against the veranda post with as much vigour as if she had been driving a stake through the heart of a vampire. I didn't think I could stand this for a week.

Yes, perhaps she was right — maybe it was sunstroke! I decided I could get by without her. Such is life. The best way to have things the way you want them is to do them yourself and this ridiculous resting was certainly getting me nowhere.

I decided that the most practical thing to do was to ask my doctor to refer me to a specialist for a second medical opinion, and thereby, hopefully, alleviate all my worries. My doctor's philosophy was: 'It takes a long time to become run-down, so naturally it will take a long time before you feel yourself again.' I felt confused and rather angry that he could seem to treat this so lightly. Only a week or so before, I was — I thought — completely carefree, and now I felt that my security had crumbled. After all, what is a 'long time'? At twenty-six years old, I felt he seemed to be speaking of the rest of my life.

I was sent to a city physician. I remember that visit with great clarity. Because I was feeling so insecure and I would not go alone, my husband accompanied me there, and patiently read a wearied *National Geographic* in the waiting room. The doctor was a rather supercilious man who wore a dark pin-striped suit in the heat of the Melbourne summer. His disdainful attitude had the effect of making me feel exceedingly foolish and inferior. We probably suffered a personality clash. In other words, there was no line of communication and certainly no empathy between us as doctor and patient. But he was supposed to be an expert, and I needed his advice.

I related my story, and his answers to my questions were directed at me as though I were about ten years old. His final diagnosis, after a thorough medical examination and much vague discussion, was that there was nothing the matter with me, and I had nothing to worry about, but it would probably be a good idea to continue to take medication for a while. He handed me a prescription for the Amytal I had already been prescribed. I was ready to accept any advice to be free of this 'illness', but real explanation was still lacking. I was still none the wiser as to what was causing the wretched symptoms or why I really needed Amytal.

Even then, as he showed me out the door and saw my husband waiting for me, he commented: 'Well, you really didn't need protection; we're not such ogres, you know.'

I think my mouth fell open in amazement. This was the very reason I had come! Could nobody understand?

It is curious how circumstance alone can tip the scales of life one way or another. It is often amazing how an opinion expressed by the right person at the right time, or the wrong person at the wrong time, can influence our lives so much. At this point of my life, a set of circumstances arose without which I might never have developed agoraphobia.

After my visit to the physician, I made up my mind to forget the whole thing and get on with living. At least his opinion had put to rest any fear of serious illness, and without that worry and with the continuing medication, the symptoms — and my apprehension — subsided. I began to get back into the swing of life.

I took my mother and my two children on a short holiday while my husband remained at home, so I had no fear then of being away from home. While my mother found the small children a little too tiring, we got on well and it was relaxing; a complete change. I enjoyed it and benefited from it without any symptoms of my former problem.

A few weeks later, my husband and I drove interstate to attend a wedding at which he was to be best man. At this stage, as I very much disliked taking tablets of any kind, and as I felt the whole matter was behind me, I discarded the medication. We left the children with relatives and it should have been a marvellous holiday. Instead, it was a disaster.

Apparently my state of tension increased again. During the wedding, while seated separately from my husband, I once again began to experience the unpleasant feelings which had formerly threatened me. Not only was 'it' happening again, but 500 miles away from home. My mind was racing frantically with fear of another of those attacks occurring here, of all places, in the middle of somebody's wedding. Thankfully, the sensation passed without that happening but, of course, once more I began to be afraid. Because I was afraid, naturally I was tense, and throughout the rest of the holiday I was pursued by 'reminder symptoms' which were, to say the least, spoiling the holiday for both of us.

In desperation, I foolishly consulted a doctor in the city in which we were staying. This was the contretemps. I made a bad choice, for he was the type of man, as I later learned, who had the mentality of 'operating first and finding out what was wrong later'. With that in mind I'm only pleased that I didn't go to him with severe pain anywhere! However, he became very excited about the fact that, in his opinion, the symptoms I described — pounding heart, giddiness, and faintness — were consistent with those of a serious kidney ailment. At the same time, he more or less derided any treatment I had already received. In all, that was an opinion I could have done without, for yet another relative was, at that time, hospitalised with a terminal kidney disease.

All this brought about a sea of confusion and was utterly the last straw. I was a very worried young woman. I could not wait to get back home. The holiday had been an absolute waste of time and I began to miss my children dreadfully.

My husband, probably in a final attempt to add some interest to an otherwise incredibly boring holiday, decided he would distract me from my worries by taking an alternative route home to show me a part of outback Australia. Now, I'm a dreadful navigator at the best of times, but in my state of tension and worry I read the map upside down and it wasn't long before we were well and truly lost on an unmade road, somewhere beyond the proverbial 'black stump'. Naturally the car, which was not too young, broke down and could only be driven at the walking pace of a snail, until we eventually found either a person or a sheep (I can't recall which came first) who was able to give us some directions. We were then forced to spend two days in that remote place while the car was repaired. I was absolutely sick with worry and was sure I would never see my children again.

When we eventually arrived home, I immediately went to my own doctor again and told him of my experience while on holiday, and the opinion of the doctor whom I had consulted there. His response was: 'Rubbish.' Once again I went through the whole medical examination routine. Once again I was proclaimed completely fit, and told not to worry. Unfortunately, that is often easier said than done.

Now I was really in a dilemma. My confidence was shaken; I wanted to believe my own doctor, but I was being pursued by those mysterious symptoms which I believed would culminate in that dreadful attack. And no-one seemed able to explain why.

Without fail, every time I began to venture out of the house, especially unescorted, and sometimes when with my husband, the symptoms would arise. As soon as I found myself alone in someone else's home, in the shopping centre, or driving from one place to another, I would begin to notice what I believed to be the onset of 'the attack'. Suddenly and unaccountably my heart would begin to pound, my palms would sweat, I would begin to feel lightheaded and fear that I might faint; and the feeling of panic (as yet un-named) would begin to well up within me. That would be the moment when I would rush to my car, or out of the shop, or abandon the purpose for which I was away from home, and make for home and safety. Each time this happened, of course, I unknowingly gave in to fear. Now that I understand panic and the effect that tension has upon us, I can see how those symptoms of fear had me completely bluffed. I felt then as though I was being followed by some unidentifiable illness which overtook me when I was out of the house.

I began to dread having to go out where the whole frightening experience would be repeated. I was very much afraid of those attacks, whatever they were. As no-one else seemed to be able to control this recurring 'illness' for me, I somehow felt that by avoiding the situations which apparently caused those attacks, I, myself, had to control it in this way. So I began to remain at home — seeking avoidance as a coping strategy.

As the symptoms of the attack I dreaded could occur anywhere at all beyond my front gate, I began to avoid *any* situation in which I felt an attack would occur. The more I tried to forget it, the more the memory of the first occasion seemed to persist in my mind. And each time I anticipated an attack, I felt certain that this would be the time when it would engulf me finally, one way or another.

Without *knowing* that I was doing so, without being aware then that I was even tense, I was gradually increasing my tension all the time in order to avert any sign of the symptoms. I was constantly apprehensive, waiting for 'it' to pounce on me. I was, without understanding it, afraid to go into a fear-producing situation where I would risk being struck down by fear. With this attitude pervading my life, it was understandable that I preferred to remain safely at home.

As time went on and I remained tense and worried about this unknown ailment, the *habit* of avoiding the fear situation became more firmly fixed. And sure enough, the unpleasant symptoms of fear which I thought to be symptoms of illness would strike whenever I ventured out, because I had become conditioned, like the famous Pavlov's dogs, to expecting them to occur. In fact, sometimes the symptoms would be provoked simply by the knowledge that I had to leave the house.

I felt ashamed of myself for what seemed to be a preoccupation with my health, and I was very embarrassed about being afraid to leave the house. Also, I felt very much alone. To try to explain such a senseless fear to anyone seemed impossible. My doctor was unable to adequately explain the recurring symptoms, and no-one in whom I confided seemed to comprehend that I had any reason to be afraid.

Therefore, as well as fighting the symptoms, I increased my nervous tension still more to *hide* my fear. And all the time that tension was multiplying the symptoms, causing me greater distress. I was caught in that vicious circle of fear, followed by tension, followed by fear, followed by tension, followed by fear, and so on.

Stress had caused me anxiety, which led me to become acquainted with the symptoms of fear — those feelings of fight or flight which are the body's preparation to meet some emergency. The only emergency, had I known it then, was my fear of being overwhelmed by my own natural response to fear, and as I continued to fight with tension I was absolutely trapped by my own reactions.

If anyone had suggested to me before that time that I would ever develop a phobia I would have believed they were joking. As for being afraid to leave my home and thereby be deprived of so many of the things I enjoyed in life, that would have seemed to me impossible.

How little I understood then of fear, of people, of life!

Three

FEAR AND PEOPLE

Why do we feel embarrassed, impatient, fretful, ill at ease,
Assembled like amateur actors who have not been
assigned their parts?

T.S. Eliot

W hat a magnificent description of all our human insecurities
and how scared we are.

'Embarrassed': when so many of us are so sensitive to the
complications of life we encounter that we overreact too often in
a state of confusion and distress. We worry that we have said or
done something wrong, or that we do not reach the standards we
set ourselves in our efforts to please other people. Or we feel we
fall short of that mark and retreat in fear, encased by our protective defences. Or if we are children, we can be embarrassed by
the continual criticisms or, on the other hand, praise and the
admiring expectations of our parents, which perhaps cannot be
satisfied. Self-conscious and often defeated before even trying,
many consequently become haunted by a sense of failure.

'Impatient': we seem to live in a world of impatience. One of
the most frequent statements made by people today is: 'There isn't
enough time.' We can all be guilty of this pressure which tends to
become a marvellous excuse for rushing around a lot and achieving
very little. The pace of modern life becomes faster with every
passing year and the emphasis of success is often heavily laid on
how quickly we can achieve things; from worldwide communication in an instant down to soft boiled eggs in the microwave. So
we find it is not easy to sit still, difficult to pause for quiet
conversation, hard to listen when others are speaking, impossible

to bear solitude and even more impossible to relax. Then, perhaps because we are not really achieving to our satisfaction — and yet we are running like mad and working later and longer hours — we become more and more edgy. Our impatience can cause us to opt out of things or only participate in those things which are of direct importance to us, so then we feel guilty. And because we feel continually rushed, it becomes increasingly difficult to endure events in life with composure. How can we cope with it all?

'Fretful': all the negative feelings promoted and experienced by so many people: irritation, anger, aggression, suspicion, discontent, despair, worry, distress, pride, shyness, intolerance, guilt, obsession, disillusionment . . . all of these are facets of fear and can create anxiety.

'Ill at ease': so very easily understood when we are tensed up and life is wearying and burdened with all those fretful emotions.

These reactions, familiar to all people, are, I think, largely based on the one question we all want answered: 'What do you think of me?'

We all want the answer to be positive, and continually *fear* that it will not be. We all want to be well thought of by others, and to give an appearance of capability and harmony with life, but so often our content is clouded by fear and the negative emotions it engenders that we never quite get our act together. In striving to exist — like Eliot's actors — all too often people wait, assembled, wondering who and what we are.

Although we wear our masks quite well, insecurity is expressed in many subtle ways and is evident in some of us more than in others by the way we react to people and to situations. We all have our own defences. Some will retreat, feeling threatened; others adopt an obviously defensive manner; some of us cover our feelings with an effusive personality, others will calculatingly put people down to build their own egos, while still others will react with indifference or aggression. To a very large extent we are all insecure; therefore we are all afraid.

There is no person who has ever lived who can say that they have no fear at all, and no person is any the less for feeling fear.

The more we discuss fear with others, the more we realise just how inadequate we all feel. Very few of us will express our fears and insecurities openly, for we are inclined to believe that fear is something we should not feel, possibly out of fear of rejection by others. What an entanglement!

Moreover, most of us do not know how to deal with fear other than to conceal it. This is not a new observation, I know. However, it is always refreshingly reassuring to know that we are not alone in this. Consequently, it is probable that those whom we often envy for their apparent confidence are struggling with inner fears, just as we are ourselves.

In primitive times, parents had to teach children to be on guard for wild animals, enemy tribes and similar dangers. They would also have been taught which food was safe to eat and which was not, how to defend themselves, places that were safe and unsafe to venture into, and countless other aspects of self-preservation. Doubtless only those who respected fear were the survivors, so life would have been filled with fear. The human race, therefore, has probably survived through the asset of its innate fear.

As civilised people, while we no longer have to feel afraid of an oncoming attack by wild animals, we still need our instinctive fear. If confronted by a madman with a gun, we would be very much afraid, and rightly so. Our fear would cause us to respond with a rush of adrenaline and consequent thumping heart, as our body prepared us either to fight the situation or flee from it. We might be able to scream. Or we might try to defend ourselves, physically or by verbally reasoning a way out of our plight. Or we might run from the situation or contrive another escape. But there is a third choice: we might panic — and remain immobilised, anxiously trapped, not knowing what to do.

Our innermost fears, those we are unable to clearly identify, cause us anxiety which is expressed symptomatically, just as we would experience if faced with obvious danger. But as there is no outward, visible danger, the symptoms alarm us. Everyone experiences anxiety — our self-preservation against the hazards of modern life — if feeling helpless. We are complicated beings and we become anxious about a great many things. But when there is no outward foe to meet, we are often perplexed by our reactions and find anxiety difficult to manage.

Probably that first fear of 'what do others think of me?' causes us the most trouble, and because we never really know, our feelings of insecurity are increased and so more fears arise. We fear rejection — said to be the greatest human fear of all. We fear openness and contact with others and the closeness of relationships, and yet we fear the misery of loneliness. Failure can mean different things to different people, and we fear the devastation and shame of failure, whatever it means to us.

Some even fear success, and will back off when just about to reach their goals. We fear being hurt, either emotionally or physically, and we fear the vulnerability of mutual trust. Many people fear responsibility, particularly the responsibility of parenthood. Others, who are parents, will fear that their children will be less than what they regard as perfect, and so fear failure or disappointment in that regard. People, particularly young people, fear that if they do not conform to the modes of behaviour set by their peers, they will no longer be accepted — another form of rejection. We fear appearing foolish to others, and many are shy and afraid even to cross a floor or venture into a social situation unfamiliar to them. We fear loss of worldly possessions and fear that somehow others can take what we have from us. Some will fear taking any kind of risk. And people have the sad fear of growing older, a privilege denied to many.

We are not born with these fears; like all our learning, they come with our environment. Many people carry for a lifetime the fears of their parents. In cases taken to extremes, if a child in primitive times were told not to dive into a pool to fish for food in case he or she drowned, the child could perish from lack of food for fear of drowning. While the likelihood of that happening today is remote, people can metaphorically perish inwardly from lack of living, due to fears imposed upon them by overprotective parents or elders. Fears are transferred almost without our knowing, such as in the case of women who dread childbearing for fear of pain. Many modern women (and indeed men) become burdened by fear as their new role dispenses with precedents which spelled security. People carry with them the fears of their parents in fear of germs, of animals and insects, of drowning or injury from the elements of nature. Others express their fear in superstitions regarding colours, numbers and so on, or become reliant upon lucky charms, rituals or other crutches to lessen their uneasiness. Even the least of these nagging fears can be restrictive to living.

There are also those fears possessed by individuals which can amaze others. A friend confided that she would prefer to spend a day in loneliness rather than contact someone for company — she is afraid of intruding. Another such instance is that of an elderly lady with a fear of using the telephone; it is a modern device and she fears it. Yet she has proved on several occasions that she has no fear of tackling a burglar.

Most of us have an underlying fear of unpredictable threats such as war or disaster. Most people fear the possibility of serious illness. And certainly the consideration of one's death and the unknown is cause for many to fear. People commonly experience moments of fear for no apparent reason at all — in some instances we are simply afraid to truly face ourselves. And fear is frequently found among the elderly, who can feel threatened by the pace of living, and dread responsibilities they believe are beyond them as their own lives draw towards evening. If we are at ease within our life, most of these fears do not linger, disappearing with satisfying occupation and rational thinking. But if we are not at ease, anxiety will rise.

Anxiety grows from fear and is an emotion, I think, of two parts: 1. primitive fear, that is, our basic instinct of fear for purposes of survival; and 2. intellectual fear, our more sophisticated reaction to instinctive fear. As can be clearly understood, fear can serve a useful purpose. But when *anxiety* develops from basic fear to intrude into the wholesomeness of our life, fear becomes a destructive element.

Fear and anxiety affect us all. And anxiety circulates within society. Unless informed otherwise, we give it to ourselves, we give it to others and we receive it back from others. This contagious effect of anxiety upon society is accentuated through the ready availability of sensationalism. Today's technology opens doors to information never known before and the media rely heavily upon dramatic stories to sell their wares, popular themes being those of tragedy or illness. Thus people's anxiety can be raised. Artists and creators express the signs of culture and a history of the society they represent. Unfortunately in these times too many of our songs, poetry and prose reflect issues of sadness, loneliness, isolation and *fear* — contributing to worry, introspection and therefore increased anxiety among many people. Other than the fortunate who have discovered peace of mind through personal transformation, only those who are naturally relaxed, especially placid or far less sensitive can avoid the negative influences of the times and therefore avoid the consequences of anxiety.

All this anxiety produces the symptoms of nervous tension. And there is a great deal of nervous tension evident in contemporary society. Nervous tension appears in the habits which cause us to smoke or drink too much in order to relax. We see tension in impatient or agitated behaviour, an inability to slow down, or ever-increasing irritability which might send us to the doctor for tranquillisers. People will say that they're always tired, can't cope, can't sleep, feel tense all the time and are always in a hurry. Tension causes overreactions to happenings in life where people feel edgy, distracted and generally ill-at-ease. Or the symptoms of tension are often experienced in physical sensations when we become involved in a particular incident — a heated argument at home or in business, or a close encounter with a motor accident. Our hearts will thump and we will feel weak and say that we are shaken or that our nerves are on edge, while reaching for another whisky!

When stress comes along, people's anxiety is naturally increased and so they generate more nervous tension. The more tension is generated the more the symptoms of underlying anxiety will increase. For some, this will result in physical ailments such as high blood pressure or an ulcer. Nervous rashes, allergic reactions, tension headaches and psychosomatic illnesses can all be related to stress and anxiety. And for some, the effect of stress, anxiety and tension may precipitate the ambiguous 'breakdown'. It is also at such a time of stress that a phobia is likely to arise.

We all have neurotic trends that we learn along the way; likes and dislikes, habits and quirks that help us to feel easier in ourselves. And our phobias, too, are learned. A phobia, it seems, arises from fear experienced under stressful circumstances when the anxiety level is higher than usual. By developing a phobia, which is an avoidance reaction to the situation that is feared, the individual is provided with a defence against what is feared. But fear feeds upon fear, and as humans instinctively fight fear with nervous tension, it is not long before the phobic reaction is no longer useful but detrimental to a state of well-being.

Some therapists maintain the opinion that a phobia always represents anxiety experienced in early childhood; possibly the hurt of being punished for an offence not committed, jealousy at the arrival of another sibling, anger at being left alone, or possibly some deeper more traumatic experience. This can be one explanation for the phobic reaction, and certainly the influences of early life are extremely powerful and *can* provide valuable insight into adult responses. But from the very large number of people who have phobias, obviously the incident which may initially have caused anxiety in early childhood does not have to be of great significance. Suffice to say that every child knows anxiety at some time. Any one of a thousand childhood incidents could potentially trigger panic in adult life — making the search to identify a single such incident rather like looking for a needle in a haystack.

As fears and phobias are learned, so they can be unlearned, in a simple and uncomplicated manner.

There is nothing unnatural about fears and phobias. Fear is not a sign of psychological weakness or lack of physical stamina.

Again, fear is our natural human protection from danger. But it is the way our intellect has adapted in the form of *anxiety* that makes our fears unpleasant to live with and inhibiting to our lives. We all know of big strong men who dread a visit to the dentist or who will faint at the sight of a hypodermic needle; or the much-caricatured women who faint when they see a mouse. These people experience the physical response to intense anxiety each time they are confronted with the phobic situation: sweating palms, nausea and weakness, thumping heart. The person will feel greatly alarmed and panicky and quickly have to get out of the situation of fear; at this point many people faint.

Probably the most well-known of all phobias is claustrophobia, in which the individual feels trapped or closed in by his or her surroundings. Someone I know very well experiences claustro-phobia in theatres; another friend is claustrophobic in crowded elevators or large crowds of people. Others cannot face going into a church, or taking a trip on an underground train. Some avoid all types of transport because they fear being confined. Coupled with the closed-in feeling in such circumstances comes the panicky feeling of lack of control. Once that elevator door has closed there is no escape until it reopens, one hopes on the right floor! I recall a visit with my husband to a large hospital. The elevator doors closed and the right buttons were pushed, but instead of going up, to the concern of two others in the lift, our journey ended abruptly in the basement of the building. Many other buttons were pushed but to no avail. Even the automatic doors did not release us until they chose to do so. Apparently that lift was going 'off duty', and we had to transfer to another. At that point our companions chose the long walk up the back stairs.

Acrophobia is another common phobia, in which people cannot tolerate heights, and discussion with a man who has this phobia revealed his dread of tall buildings. Just to imagine himself in such a situation is sufficient to make him shiver and show anxiety and tension. He says he fears an impulse, when in a high place, that might make him throw himself over the edge. The common fear of flying in aeroplanes reaches phobic proportions with many people, and is usually expressed as a combination of claustrophobia and acrophobia. The fear experienced in a phobic situation is so great that it is likely that the real danger, the possibility that the plane might crash, will not enter the victim's mind.

Most fears can become phobias and can upset a person's equilibrium: phobias about animals, snakes, spiders; phobias about eating in public for fear of choking; eating anything away from home for fear of germs, and many more.

While some people cannot remember exactly how, why, or when their phobia began, there is a story with a touch of pathos told to me by an old lady. Hers was a phobia about taking a bath. She would only use a shower. Apparently, as a young woman back in the 1930s, she was in hospital awaiting the birth of her first child. She was forced, for some reason, by the nursing staff into a hot and very deep bath; as she said, 'right up to my neck'. With the imminence of the birth and her general anxiety about it, she was terrified. She recalled it almost fifty years later with as much fear and aversion as if the incident had been only yesterday.

Another woman recalled how as a very little girl she put out her hand to 'pat the kitten'. This kitten was really no longer a kitten, but a rather snarly ageing cat, whose general reactions were far from friendly. It hissed, bared its teeth and flung out a paw with claws released, ready to fend off this human nuisance intruding into its life. The child screamed in fright and stood riveted to the spot in fear as the tears streamed down her cheeks. Her mother overreacted, leaping from her chair on the other side of the room and rushing to the child to save her, while old puss went back to sleep. After all that commotion, the girl had a lasting memory of fear in association with cats. It developed into a phobia which has lasted a lifetime.

While some phobias are more rare than others, and people do not readily speak of them, many are known and accepted. Each person finds his or her own phobia inconvenient at times, and life can be complicated by it. However, most can be lived with and 'got around' by avoiding the phobic situation. In most cases this is not too difficult to do.

My friend with a fear of theatres avoids her fear by never going to see a film or a stage show. She doesn't like avoiding theatres, because she misses out on entertainment, but this is her adjustment to her phobia and she has learned to live with it. Similarly, the woman who feels claustrophobic in lifts or crowds avoids such situations. The same adjustment is made by the man who fears heights, even to the point where he employs someone to clean out the gutterings of his house, or to change the globes in his light fittings. These phobic reactions occur after an unfavourable incident of mesmeric proportion is imprinted on the anxious mind. The phobia of my own experience is agoraphobia.

Agoraphobia gives its victim a paralysing fear of leaving the safety of home, especially when alone. I am not entirely happy with the word 'agoraphobia' to describe this state of fear, however. My dictionary defines agoraphobia as 'a morbid fear of being in open or public spaces'. This definition is not completely accurate; for while the person with agoraphobia may well dread open spaces, most will also dread closed areas or restriction of any kind. Really, agoraphobia is in my opinion an extreme expression of situational anxiety.

Agoraphobia is not as easily understood as most other phobias, and I think I can safely say that no other fear can so vastly affect the normal life of the individual as can agoraphobia. Agoraphobia comes about like all other phobias, with the victim experiencing something which alarms him or her to the point of panic. However, the difference between this phobia and phobias of other kinds is that the fearful situation which triggers the phobia is not any one tangible object or situation, but an attack of *panic itself*, just as I have described in my own case. The individual has usually been under some degree of stress and, as a result of this, the level of anxiety and tension is high. But the panic attack will be quite unexpected.

The common story is that one day, away from home and in some public place, the person begins to feel faint for no serious reason, becoming alarmed about being unwell. Quite naturally, symptoms of anxiety begin to manifest, to which the person responds with increased tension; this creates more symptoms and therefore a greater sensation of illness. The body is responding to the instinct of fear with the response *to* fear. But there is nothing visible to be feared. Feeling overwhelmed, the physical symptoms of fear (or anxiety) increase even more. The victim of this attack will think that he or she is being stricken with some devastating illness, or fear that he or she will lose all reason, or that death is imminent. This is panic. And as panic reaches its peak the sufferer may faint, just as a man may faint when panicked by the sight of a hypodermic needle.

Anyone can have an attack of panic. But to someone who has no knowledge of the effects of panic, it is an alarming experience, and gives its victim cause to fear that he or she *no longer has control of life*. This, then, is the great underlying dread: what *is* going to happen to me? He or she will literally be the last person to understand that frightening experience. 'It couldn't possibly be only fear or nerves that made me feel so ill; there was nothing there for me to be afraid of.' It is impossible to believe that the body was only responding to the fear of the feelings taking place. So, in a nutshell, what he or she fears is within themselves: the victim of agoraphobia is *afraid of fear.*

A person who can identify his or her phobia, such as fear of an injection, can accept it and live with it. The person who cannot identify the phobia, fear of fear, cannot accept it and so feels constantly threatened by something unknown. The closest he or she can come to identifying the fear is that what is feared occurs away from home, so the best thing to do is to avoid being overwhelmed again by the invisible, and to stay at home. This person can then be said to be suffering from agoraphobia.

It must be understood that being agoraphobic does not mean that the victim is afraid of 'a shop' or 'a street' or 'a lift'. There is no single identifiable situation or object of which the agoraphobic person is afraid, as there is with other phobias. Panic is the ultimate result of all phobic situations, but because those who have specific phobias know what it is that they are afraid of, they are able to escape or avoid the situation before panic *completely* overwhelms them. In agoraphobia, it is the *ultimate* that is feared, so the fear can arise in any one of a million different situations; and as the object of fear is fear itself, which is within the victim, the phobic situation is impossible to avoid completely.

Because it is our natural instinct to fight when we feel threatened, the person with agoraphobia tries to fight those symptoms when they arise. But there is nothing to scream at or run from; no matter how hard he or she fights, the symptoms continue. While fighting against fear with ever-increasing tension, that vicious circle of fear and tension develops as I have described in Chapter 2. This and the avoidance then become habitual; and because the need to leave the house is ever-present, the agoraphobic person is facing fear almost permanently.

Those who cannot comprehend the agoraphobic reaction may understand more clearly from the following example. Most of us have heard of someone who will no longer drive their own car or attempt car travel at all after having been involved in a motor accident. The accident caused much stress, the memory of it is too real and the person concerned cannot face the situation again without experiencing high anxiety. The anxiety suffered in an instance such as this is obvious to the observer 'because of the circumstances surrounding the dreadful accident'. But the fright and subsequent anxiety contained within an unexpected attack of panic can be as severe as the fright one may experience from a traffic accident. Our feelings and our reactions are part of our individuality and so the outcome of any encounter will be relative to individual response.

Since it adversely affects normal functioning so dramatically, agoraphobia is considered the most severe of all phobias. The impact of anxiety and agoraphobia on the community can be seen in the following figures from the Australian Bureau of Statistics. Samplings of Australian women in 1996 show that sixteen per cent had a panic disorder, twelve per cent were agoraphobic and in all, thirty-one per cent suffered from generalised anxiety disorder. In the male population, eight per cent recorded panic disorder and ten per cent were agoraphobic. However, a massive thirty-three per cent admitted to some general anxiety disorder.

Anyone, male or female, of any age and in any role or rank in life, can become agoraphobic. However, it occurs more often in young to middle-aged adults, and there seems to be a higher proportion of women sufferers than men. Any concession to fear arising within an individual is dependent upon the degree of vulnerability of that person at a given time. If anxiety and tension are high and stressful circumstances occur to provoke alarm, fear can overwhelm anyone.

Since overcoming this phobia myself, and having wide experience with other sufferers, I have found people whose lives have been impaired by agoraphobia for up to forty years. The state of fear varies in severity from total enclosure to a life of limitations. In very severe cases, the victim will remain totally within the home, never going anywhere. Then there are those sufferers who can perhaps go as far as a next-door neighbour's house alone, but cannot cross a street, go to a shop or attempt to travel any distance. Many others can venture short distances to limited destinations and can only go further afield in the company of another person in whom they have confided. Some can drive a car, others cannot, and most dread public transport.

People with this fear who work are often able to get to and from their job without too much panic, but cannot go anywhere else or divert from that routine. Many more, particularly those within secure relationships, can easily keep secret their fear, providing their partner is always with them and preferably always within sight.

All these people are superficially living a normal life, but concealed from the rest of the world is their overwhelming fear. Learning to live with it in this way causes them to endure, to say the least, a second-class lifestyle. And there are thousands of people with varying degrees of agoraphobia.

Sometimes an observer may be inclined to accuse an agoraphobic person of being 'only a hypochondriac, worrying all the time about how he or she is feeling'. The fact is that the fear is difficult for the sufferer to understand, so naturally it must be even more difficult for those around to understand. In secure surroundings, the fear is apparently totally forgotten, and the victim is completely at ease, until, having to face the prospect of stepping outside that door, he or she can begin to feel very ill indeed.

Worse still, the person may be categorised by others as being 'just neurotic', an unfortunate label which covers a multitude of human idiosyncrasies. This is an unfair judgment, because his or her fear, and the accompanying symptoms, are very real and very debilitating. Yet it is difficult for people with agoraphobia to describe their predicament adequately; and when they do try, what they are saying sounds, to them, terribly futile and they feel ashamed. Agoraphobia is never an escape from things its victims do not wish to accomplish, and anyone who suggests this would only have to encounter this type of fear once to know that their idea is incorrect.

Most people with agoraphobia do not accept their condition. They are constantly striving to overcome it and to live as fully as they did before fear began to dominate their lives. This striving builds strength and discipline. Such a person is very likely to be the one who will act very responsibly in a crisis, and is well prepared to withstand with great wisdom and acceptance any troubles that life may deliver. But because the fear of leaving the safety of home is so restricting, and because the person concerned becomes an unwilling servant to it, life is virtually no longer their own. This puts a great strain on family, friends and colleagues. A great deal of patience and understanding is required.

The victim of agoraphobia is just like anyone else, 'embarrassed, impatient, fretful, ill-at-ease', while at the same time trying to live and enjoy their existence to the best of their ability. There is just one difference: that person has now been alerted to their fear and wants to overcome it, ever fighting, and unwittingly prolonging their misery indefinitely.

That's how I found myself in that summer of the 1960s. I should have been at a peak of happiness and security. Instead, I seemed to be very much like one of Eliot's amateur actors — on the stage of life waiting for guidance, wanting to understand and terrified to make a move.

Four

TO FIGHT MY FEAR

Habit, if not resisted, soon becomes necessity.

St Augustine

The telephone woke the entire household one night and the clock read 2.30 a.m. The strident bell had penetrated everyone's dreams, but when it was answered the caller hung up. Each of us looked at the others helplessly. The surge of alarm that filled our hearts in those few minutes of awakening was far from pleasant; the thoughts and fears and questions as to why someone should be telephoning at that hour caused temporary anxiety. And I momentarily experienced a stab of fear reminiscent of many years before.

Everyone has experienced at some time the piercing fear that hits us and then sweeps through us when faced with something alarming or something we dread having to do. In my years of agoraphobia, those moments were with me every time I was faced with leaving the house. And from that first flush of fear would arise all the other unpleasant symptoms of fear: pounding heart, giddiness and weakness. As those symptoms mounted in intensity, the anticipation of loss of control of the situation was there, and with that came the even greater fear of how, or if, I would cope if that occurred. I use the words 'loss of control' because it was not until many years later that I learned that the feeling I lived in dread of was, in fact, panic.

The more I remained at home in my attempt to avoid the possibility of those attacks and in trying to control the persistent symptoms which, as yet, I didn't understand, the more difficult it was to go out. I could still force myself to leave the house sometimes. When I was with my husband the symptoms would not be so severe and I would not be so afraid. But as my existence was dominated by the prospect of that fear in each new day, the lifestyle of our little family began to become rather complicated. I was no longer free. Where once I would have bundled the children into the car and, if necessary, left them in someone else's care while I pursued some need or interest of my own, now every move I made was calculated, for fear of being caught unawares by fear.

Memories in most instances are merciful. When they are of fear, they are invincible, and fear is therefore perpetuated. There is great wisdom in the old adage that if a child falls off a bicycle, he or she must be helped to get straight back on and ride again, otherwise the memory of the fall will dominate the will to ride. In the case of those who are victims of agoraphobia, our memory of the first attack of panic is very strong, and each subsequent one or impending one adds another layer of anxiety to the original. We feel terribly vulnerable. We do not understand our situation, we cannot control it, and our total security is shaken. If only that fear were as easily dealt with as a fall from a bicycle!

The house in which we lived in those years was situated close to all necessary facilities. To some extent I blamed my car (or driving alone) for helping to produce those unpleasant feelings, and I was not at all keen to drive alone for that reason, so I persuaded my husband that a car was not essential to my day-to-day requirements and we sold it. Having no car was a perfect excuse not to have to participate in trips away from home alone and, if necessary, at that stage of my fear, I could still take a bus or tram. I secretly hoped that by disposing of the car I would also dispose of my symptoms. (One agoraphobic man I know actually gave his car away, so great was his desire to be free of the threat of having to drive it.)

As I was rather obviously tied to the house because of our young children, my husband patiently suggested that I try to achieve at least one small trip out of the house each day. His philosophy was that if I could force myself out of the house each day, even if only for a short while, I would eventually overcome my apprehension. He also insisted that it was better to continue to try and succeed just a little than not to try at all. I could see what he meant, so I tried to persevere, hoping that one day I would find myself miraculously free again. However hard I tried, my successes became fewer and fewer and I would always experience some of the unpleasant sensations and frequently return home in fear.

I would take the children for walks within the block in which we lived, or to the small shopping centre nearby. I always avoided open areas or parks, where my active little boy would want to stop for ages on the swings, or simply just run in open space. The agoraphobic feels extremely alone and open to threat in spacious areas, whether it be the local park, streets or motorways, the vastness of a beach or the seemingly oppressive atmosphere of the mountains. There appears to be no hope of gathering oneself for escape in an open area if the feelings of panic begin to arise, so I stuck firmly to a very restricted walk.

At the same time, friends in the neighbourhood with children the same age as mine offered mutual companionship for the little ones. But, much as I desired it, I began to find it difficult to visit their homes. Different from open space, but bringing the same intensity of fear, is the confinement of closed areas, so great is the tension against which we are fighting. Of course, we do not understand this at the time. Under those conditions, the response of fear can be precipitated by the mere closing of a door in an unfamiliar house; a similar feeling of being trapped occurs while waiting to be served in a shop. So I felt really secure only in my own home and I was very happy to have a constant stream of small visitors to play with my children there. What was more, I didn't have to go far afield to provide my little boy with company. Our street was pleasant and safe. The houses were not too far apart and the neighbourhood was well endowed with small children to play together. I was also fortunate that compromise was easily reached — I didn't have to go much further than my front gate to call my little boy home.

I can easily understand how our forbears, with less compli- cated minds than we have today, earnestly believed in odd superstitions to soothe their fears. In trying to banish this fear from my life I remember, as well as parting from my car, impulsively doing other things which I felt might help. Ridiculous really, but desperate. One day, my husband arrived home to find his wife, who had had quite long hair that morning, now had a very short and expensive haircut. I was afraid to go out of the house, yet obviously I had spent quite a sum of money on a hair style, which meant a visit to a good hairdresser. To him, that must have seemed very inconsistent, to say the least, especially as I might well have asked him to buy the meat for dinner.

Women very often change their hairstyle, or its colour, to lift their spirits. But in this instance there was more to it than that. I really hoped that a 'new start' would somehow blot out the past months and announce the arrival of freedom. I had managed to force myself past fear to achieve this. For the remainder of that day the magic worked, but disappointment struck me again when I woke next day in dread of having to leave the house to keep a dental appointment. Unlike Samson who lost his massive strength when he lost his hair, fortunately my mediocre strength continued, but the symptoms I had hoped to lose on the way remained with me as before.

An agoraphobic person will dread a visit to the dentist. It is bad enough having to leave the house to go there, but then one will possibly have to endure a long wait in the waiting room. And when finally admitted to the surgery, one will be trapped in the chair. As any comedian will demonstrate, the dentist will fill one's mouth with cotton wool and plastic, while the nurse encloses the patient in the chair with a tray of implements jammed under the chin and a vacuum cleaning device ready for action. Virtually a prisoner, one wants to say: 'I don't like this situation at all.' But it seems too foolish, so the patient tenses up and wills it to be over quickly. The dentist sees the fear and automatically chants: 'Just relax and open wide. Where did you go for the holidays?' It's simply not possible to 'just relax', open any wider, answer the question and feel at all comfortable, so tension is increased and makes the situation twice as bad. This can bother anyone, but the person afraid of panic really wants to leap from the chair and run like mad. In those days, I dreaded that situation; yet I had no fear of dentists or any work they may have had to do. It was simply fear of being trapped — with the possibility of panic occurring.

I understand now the significance of the dentist's words to the patient. But I wonder how many dentists, and certainly how many patients, really realise the significance and importance of what is being said? Many such situations can be improved by the patient's understanding of what it means to relax. The feeling of being unable to endure events such as that with ease has little directly to do with agoraphobia. It is caused by the tension used to fight the agoraphobia — the vicious circle again — and is a common problem to anyone who is tense.

In the months that followed that visit to the dentist, I continually tried to leave the house, and my failures far outnumbered my successes.

Among other things, I forced myself to attend a course for women, glorying under a very grand title — something like 'Creative Living in Today's World'. It turned out to be a very boring series of talks given by a well-meaning but uninteresting lady on 'how to be a homemaker', a fairly typical presentation of the Sixties. I managed to attend four out of six of those sessions. I learned nothing I didn't already know, and the strain of forcing myself to get there and endure it was far too great for the scant reward. Such endeavours frustrated me terribly, for that was not the sort of thing I wanted to participate in from choice. Projects like this were merely something I could make myself do because the venue happened to be on the direct bus route from my home.

It seems that agoraphobia is suffered by a greater number of women than men. A possible explanation for this is that in our society the male is still primarily the major income earner, and when a man is stricken by agoraphobia, he more or less has to keep going to work, difficult though it may be. As long as he can keep going, it helps him with his fear, and he may even overcome it before avoidance becomes a habit. But as soon as he succumbs and relinquishes his work because of agoraphobia, he has been defeated by fear, with the possibility of losing his career as well. The same, of course, would occur in similar circumstances with a working woman.

I think it is also possible that fewer men than women will admit to agoraphobia and therefore fewer males would be recorded as having sought help. It takes great courage for anyone — especially a man — to admit to fear, particularly if he only feels secure when supported by a woman. He runs the risk of ridicule. Interestingly, I have heard one authority state that it is possible that agoraphobia is more common in men than in women. But while the female will remain securely at home because of fear, the male tends to seek respite from fear by more and more visits to the local hotel. Because of agoraphobia, many men have been forced to ignore or refuse promotion or business opportunities in order to avoid leaving their existing work situation, where they feel safe. Such disappointments are a great blow to morale, and a further cause for anxiety.

When agoraphobia develops in a woman, it is often, as it was with me, because her first experience of panic occurred when she was alone and responsible for young children. The dependency of those children can reinforce her fear until she becomes agoraphobic. Without the responsibility of children, perhaps many women who experience panic would conquer the fear before it reached the proportion of a phobia. And as society still has a far greater number of women than men at home looking after small children, perhaps this explains, to some extent, why agoraphobia could appear to be more common in women than in men. So it was with me. As I only felt safe at home, and I knew my children were safe at home, home was where I preferred to stay.

In forcing myself to make those trips to the Creative Living course, I had begun to experience the symptoms I feared while travelling on the bus and while enduring the talks. 'It' was following me everywhere, and I now began to avoid trips on public transport and became increasingly edgy about walking even as far as the local shops or around the well-worn block. I expected the symptoms in any situation, and I retreated again in defeat. I had tried and I had failed.

So I arranged to telephone my orders for the week's shopping, and they were delivered to me. Anything over and above essentials had to wait for a time when my husband was free to shop with me, and even then I didn't greatly enjoy being out. From that time, I became expert at catering for most of the needs of my family by that wonderful invention, the telephone. It is surprising just how much shopping one can do by this means! Today of course, in the advancement of technology, people are being *encouraged* to shop by computer. Although this facility may be convenient at times, as a long-recovered agoraphobic who knows the misery of personal isolation, I am concerned that such a lifestyle may become common practice. Should such a dehumanising way of life eventuate, I can predict many future social problems within the community.

Thankfully, I was well occupied. I was still involved in our business, working from home by means of the telephone, and that provided interest and contact with the business world. From day to day there was plenty of contact with other mothers of small children, plenty to do with the children themselves and the two grandmothers, who were constant visitors. Other friends called on me, not knowing my plight, and when invitations were reciprocated I found some reason to decline.

As well as those activities, I threw myself wholeheartedly into home renovation, cookery (which I enjoyed and cultivated as a hobby), gardening (also enjoyable to me) and dressmaking (which I detested and still do). I should have tried to retrace my steps and find again my Thespian interests, but in those years I had no piano, and to be involved otherwise meant leaving the house, which was as good as impossible. The idea only hurt and frustrated me. As a compromise I played around with brushes and paints, but without proper training achieved little that satisfied me and, again, felt cheated and frustrated.

At other times, social contact was available through activities with my husband. The fear was always with me, but at least when he was present I could see each occasion through without dashing home in fear. So I gave the appearance of leading a life like anyone else and enjoying it to the full. But underneath I was in constant dread of any reason arising for me to have to leave the house alone. Because of this I had to fabricate endless excuses for not participating, which saddened me. And if I had not also been able to entertain at home for any reason, many friends would no doubt have been lost.

I felt hurt and angry at my predicament, and wondered whatever had happened to the person I used to be. Firm decision-making now became difficult, as I was afraid to make a commitment. Something I could force myself to do on one day might be impossible to face on another. I began to feel very guilty, as these contradictory or inconsistent reactions were not true to my nature, and were not easy for the family (or me) to live with.

I can see now how one thing complicated another; fear growing from fear and more anxiety growing from the negative results of fear such as guilt and anger. But none of this was clear to me then; I was trapped in a tangled web of feelings which I didn't understand. Had I understood it all then with the clarity with which I can view the problem now, agoraphobia would never have arisen. *C'est la vie.*

The time was approaching when my little boy was to start kindergarten. I wondered how I was going to face the commitment of taking him there and collecting him again each day. The constant fear of being suddenly overwhelmed by the dreaded attack worried me more than ever. Despite continued enquiries, I still had no understanding as to why I continually met with the mysterious symptoms. There seemed to be no way of losing 'it' and no assurance that it would disappear of its own volition.

Worse than all that, my confidence was broken. I had never been a particularly nervous or highly-strung person; in fact quite the contrary: I was the one on whom people tended to lean, and I greatly disliked this feeling of vulnerability. I was confused and unhappy; I couldn't find a solution, and I was beginning to think that I was destined to spend the rest of my life within the confines of my home.

Something had to be done. As any medical practitioner I had consulted to date had been unable to supply an answer to my riddle, I sought the advice of a Catholic priest. He was a psychologist and social worker who had no doubt dealt with many, varied problems.

To see him I had to force myself to take a tram trip to his office. That day also marked my last excursion on public transport for many years. The symptoms were intense and the subsequent fear was very great on my way to keep the appointment. Yet when I related my story to him it sounded, to me, extremely trivial and unimportant. To my amazement, he showed understanding. Apart from my husband, with his continued and loving tolerance, this priest was the first person to whom I spoke about my fear who could at least comprehend my difficulty. To the embarrassment of both of us, I wept uncontrollably simply from the fact that somebody *listened*. He had not buried my problem under a pile of prescriptions!

He suggested that, as fear is an emotion, I should discuss the matter with a psychiatrist who, he said, 'would be more capable of helping you to fight it than I am'. I really believed that the symptoms which followed me around could only be caused by some obscure physical ailment, and that if only someone could discover what that was and cure it, I would no longer have anything to fear. It seemed impossible to me that such persistent symptoms of illness could have an emotional basis. At that time, I only associated psychiatry with mental illness, so his suggestion was inclined to alarm me further still.

I believe now that psychology is probably the most significant aspect of medical knowledge, and that an informed understanding of human behaviour by general practitioners is of great importance. For it seems that most human ills, if not caused by, are certainly complicated by, our emotions, and anything we learn or any way we can better understand our response to living can only be beneficial to all. In this age, our science and technology have helped our progress in many significant ways, but it can be easy to forget that people are still people, with worries and needs, hopes and dreams.

All those years ago I wasn't so sure, but although confused by the priest's recommendation, I would have done anything to overcome my symptoms and fear of leaving the house, so I agreed. He gave me a letter of introduction to, as he put it, 'a wise old doctor whom I know quite well'. I arranged a taxi to take me home, which somehow I safely reached once more, clutching proverbially at another straw.

Later that week I visited the psychiatrist. He was long-retired, seeing a few patients at his home. He was very correct, very kind, very understanding and very, very old. Once more, the whole story was told.

'My dear,' he whispered in the velvet tones unique to gentlemen of that generation, 'the persistent and unpleasant feelings you are experiencing are only symptoms of anxiety. You have been under stress and the symptoms of anxiety have increased and persisted. They will pass with time.'

He seemed to understand what was puzzling me, and I had no reason nor any choice other than to believe in what he told me. But there was still no satisfactory conclusion to the problem of my fear of leaving the house. The prospect of having to put up with those symptoms of anxiety for an indefinite length of time, until they chose to leave me, was not something that pleased me at all.

I had several discussions with the elderly psychiatrist over a few weeks, most of which were fruitful, if a little irrelevant to the situation that bothered me. But, although I respected his knowledge, he seemed to be part of another era. I felt that he was too old, too out of touch with the world to which I belonged to really help me. So, tactfully, I disengaged myself from further appointments.

As we parted, he gave me some advice, the kind of advice that can only come from the mass of wisdom gained from longevity. He said, and I have never forgotten a word: 'Never let your children see you distressed in any way. Never try to run a perfect house; be firm, but let the children be free. They must experience the feel of earth on their hands and feet — and let them have lots of animals for pets. And, my dear, never try to change the course of destiny.'

At least my talks with that inspirational man had given me a little hope. I was not imagining my uneasiness; it was something real, and surely something could be done about it. With a fragment of renewed courage, I went back to my local doctor and said firmly: 'Please refer me to the best psychiatrist you know of. I need someone to show me the way out of this maze of fear.'

Five

SEARCHING FOR A CAUSE

I count Life just a stuff to try the soul's strength on.

Robert Browning

The psychiatrist I was sent to was a sincere and gentle man with great patience. He showed understanding of my fear. Like those before him, but more convincingly, he assured me that my recurring symptoms were not those of any serious ailment, reaffirming that they were caused by increased anxiety. He explained that everyone's level of anxiety increases under stress, and we discussed to some extent the stresses I had encountered before that fateful day in the shopping centre. The phobia I had developed — an avoidance strategy — was apparently my personal adjustment in an attempt to control the symptoms I feared. He suggested that the cause of my elevated anxiety was due either to a suppressed or long-forgotten childhood experience that had caused me alarm, or an unresolved conflict from my past of which I had been unconsciously reminded while under stress. He said that the symptoms which bothered me would disappear when such a conflict was discovered and freely discussed. To achieve this, he recommended psychoanalysis. In the meantime he prescribed medication, updating the Amytal to the more popular Valium, which I could take if I wished to reduce the symptoms.

He also stated that I was an intelligent, articulate and attractive woman with a strong and stable personality and good qualities to contribute to life. I found this summing-up reassuring and felt a little less embarrassed about my fear. My ever-dwindling confidence and somewhat crushed ego was therefore slightly revitalised. On the strength of this summarisation, the doctor indicated that there seemed to be no reason why I should not overcome my fear with little delay.

I was grateful for his reassurance and, as he seemed confident of success, I was willing to co-operate with analysis in order to be free again. If something in my life was revealed that was causing me anxiety, the symptoms would then disappear and obviously so would my fear of leaving the safety of home. However, the idea didn't make a great deal of sense to me, as I couldn't understand why I had suddenly developed these symptoms and the subsequent fear following that first attack in the shopping centre. My life held no unpleasant memories and had been generally secure and happy; I was not weighed with any major disturbance from the past. So what kind of quest were we undertaking?

Fear of leaving the house (the word 'agoraphobia' was still not used) for fear of further 'attacks' (the fact that those attacks were panic was not clearly stated either) was my difficulty. It seemed now to be a chicken-and-egg situation; was I afraid to leave the house because I was experiencing anxiety from something in my past? Or was I experiencing anxiety simply because I was afraid to leave the house? I seemed to be getting into deep water. But how else to overcome my fear?

Recollecting all the stressful events in the first months of my marriage made it clear to me that certainly stress had increased my level of anxiety and must obviously have contributed to that initial attack of panic.

Over subsequent years, in discussing stress with others who suffer agoraphobia, it seems to me that the type of stress and the amount of stress necessary to increase anxiety, and therefore set up the chain reaction of panic, varies greatly with the individual. The aftermath of an operation, the birth of a baby, a death in the family, a broken relationship or the loss of a job are recalled by many as the stressful incidents which preceded the onset of agoraphobia. Some have mentioned pressure of work and others, like myself, a build-up of many shocks and disruptions over a period of time.

Jane, a single girl, was in a car accident. Although she was not severely injured, she was deeply upset by the injuries sustained by another person. Shortly after the accident she became chronically ill, and after many months her illness was finally diagnosed as a thyroid condition and she was operated on. She had become extremely worried while awaiting the diagnosis and during the preceding months of illness, and therefore did not make a good recovery after the operation. She continued to feel unwell after returning to work, and experienced anxiety symptoms and panic at work. She finally gave up her job. This, she claims, was her big mistake, for once she was not pressed to leave for work each day, she began to find it difficult to leave the house at all, and soon developed agoraphobia.

When I first met Judith, a youthful married woman with three adult children, she had been agoraphobic for twenty years. She was not totally confined to home and held a responsible position, but was unable to venture far from her own locality without her husband close at hand. Her fear developed after the birth of her first child, as a result of the stress of what she describes as 'the overwhelming responsibility of motherhood'. It became increasingly difficult for her to leave her home, as she continually experienced panic when out of the house, and she spent many years as a prisoner of fear when her family was younger.

Lynne's agoraphobia began after a severe panic attack in the local butcher's shop. She was a nurse in the children's wing of a major hospital. She recalled that she took her responsibilities very seriously, and was under considerable stress as she became emotionally involved with the young patients.

Rod was a Navy man and obviously worked for many years out of doors. He then joined an airline company, working his way up to a senior position of responsibility, involving long hours and shift work. His stress centred on worry about his work, and after repeated attacks of panic at work, he blamed the fact that he was working indoors. He left that job, hoping that his symptoms would go once he was working in the open again. Of course, that was not the solution, and he subsequently lost three other jobs through agoraphobia, thus ending his professional life.

Helen, an agoraphobic for twenty-six years, became so after a panic attack combined with a severe migraine headache while out shopping with her young baby. The stress which preceded the attack began with blood pressure problems during her pregnancy, and the fact that when the baby was born her husband became ill with a viral infection and was not permitted to visit her or the baby for two weeks. She added: 'Then I had no sleep for six weeks, as the baby did not stop crying. I was exhausted.'

Eighteen-year-old Michael developed agoraphobia in Year 11 at high school. When he was eleven, due to failing eyesight, he was prescribed glasses, but was too shy to wear them to school, a stressful situation at that age. Because he couldn't see the blackboard he became more and more anxious and panicky that he wouldn't get a seat in the front row. Consequently his anxiety increased with the years, until he found himself experiencing panic out in the street and began to stay home more and more after leaving school.

Maureen was agoraphobic for eight years following panic while suffering severe depression. For eleven years preceding that depression, she was under stress, nursing her sick mother, and also, for part of that time, a close friend who was terminally ill. Both died within a very short time of each other and Maureen felt their loss with devastation and loneliness.

Neville, a bachelor, has had agoraphobia for nearly twenty years. He went for a regular medical check-up when young and was told, incorrectly, that he had high blood pressure. Being a very young man at the time, this concerned him, especially when soon afterwards the father of a friend died of a stroke. Then Neville's mother died. He experienced panicky feelings on and off, and believed it was blood pressure which continued to worry him. Then his sister died, and around the same time he broke off a relationship, all of which added to the stress. He was working hard and decided to 'have a good night out' and play golf the next day. It was during the game that he experienced severe panic. Life has been complicated for him by agoraphobia ever since.

All these people exhibited tension, a response that has been with them for years. The stress that preceded their lasting problem of agoraphobia had been coped with up to the *elastic limit* of each person, and they had fought hard with tension as their anxiety level increased. Interestingly, most spent many years fighting without knowing that what they were fighting was *panic*. I had done likewise, and fear had intruded into my life. It seemed that the only solution to my problem was to commence psycho-analysis in the hope that a cure would be revealed to free me from bondage.

The psychiatrist took my fear seriously and was always kind and, above all, compassionate. He had still put no name to the panic attack and referred to what I feared as 'anxious feelings'. So what I actually dreaded was still, in itself, a mystery to me, which no doubt increased my fear of fear. More importantly, then, I still did not realise or understand the fact that I was also a slave to tension.

Obviously, being afraid to leave home meant that keeping regular appointments for psychoanalysis was very difficult. For analysis to have any chance of success, regular appointments were essential. But to achieve this, I had to leave the house and go to the doctor's rooms. If I did not go, I felt I was denying myself the only hope of overcoming the symptoms and my fear.

This went on for many months. The main benefit of analysis to date was the fact that *having* to keep the appointments at least forced me out of the house on those occasions, and the psy-chiatrist was able to provide some degree of the reassurance necessary to me.

My husband convinced me that I should have a car again, and as being without a car had not negated my symptoms, I agreed. The car soon became a crutch, a form of security, and in it I could venture limited distances in our locality. It was not that I was ever afraid of driving; it was always the fear of being out and away from safety in case I should be overwhelmed by my symptoms. Even though I now accepted that the symptoms were those of anxiety, I was still very much afraid of them and what they might lead to. I was completely in their power. But I was fortunate in being able to drive those short distances, for there are many people who for many years have not left home alone at all.

Sometimes it occurred to me that the psychiatrist himself did not really comprehend the utter misery I was experiencing, for each time he spoke the simple phrase 'come back in two weeks', that very suggestion in itself would send a knife-like shock of fear throughout me. Yet I would bravely agree. So we struggled on, my phobia causing me to dread the appointments with the psychiatrist, changing them often when I simply couldn't face going (which made me feel terribly guilty), begging my husband to accompany me, and all the while, never feeling one bit of improvement. But there was apparently no alternative.

I would wake on the morning of the appointment in an immensely fearful state at the thought of having to leave the house and face a trip to the *city*. If it was one of the days when my husband was not available to take me to the appointment, I knew that I would either have to go alone, or not go at all. I would begin the day by trying to decide whether I would drive my own car, take a taxi or travel by public transport.

Public transport was definitely out. To take a bus, I had first to walk to the bus-stop and wait. The symptoms of fear would certainly arise during that time, and if they didn't then, they would as soon as I had stepped on to the bus. The agoraphobic person feels panicky on public transport, because once inside the vehicle, one feels trapped and not in control of one's own fate, knowing that one has to complete the journey. Or should the symptoms become too intense and close to panic, one might feel driven to get off the bus before the actual destination and probably into some very unfamiliar area. I didn't ever find myself in that particular circumstance, but the idea was distressing so the possibility of this happening was yet another fear to fear. If I went by bus, and assuming I arrived safely at the psychiatrist's rooms, I still had to get home again; so as far as I was concerned, public transport was not a welcome consideration.

To take a taxi every time I had an appointment was usually only one-way security, too. I always felt that while I would get to my destination without the degree of anxiety that would be associated with public transport, I had the added worry of not knowing whether or not a taxi would be readily available to take me home again — and getting back home, to the agoraphobic, is the most important part of any outing. So there arose a secondary problem, as I didn't want to risk being stranded in the city.

One woman in that predicament told me how she became overwhelmed by panic and rushed up to a policeman for help. She must have chosen an understanding policeman, for he was able to assure her while securing a taxi for her safe return home. The agoraphobic needs this security, this feeling of being prevented from 'that attack', so very much that although to some people taking taxis everywhere may seem extravagant, the agoraphobic would pay any price to avoid suffering what he or she fears. Over the years I did take many taxis, and I found this means of transport provided a level of security necessary under such conditions.

My third choice was to drive my own car. That was about the most difficult thing I could face doing. I was able to drive those short distances near home, but even when doing that, I repeatedly experienced the symptoms. I would then immediately turn around and drive home again. To contemplate driving to the city was an impossibility. Distances seem to stretch for a person in a state of tension and fear. The traffic seems more threatening, crowds seem oppressive and finding somewhere to park satis- factorily is an ordeal in itself. Generally, people with agoraphobia don't like large central car-parks. Nor do they relish the prospect of having to park out of the central business district and walk the rest of the way. Again, the sensations of anxiety in relation to unfamiliar or open or crowded places where, hypnotically, metres seem to stretch into kilometres and the threat of being over- whelmed by all these obscurities are very strong.

After considering all three options for getting to the appoint- ment, I would frequently be overpowered by the very thought of having to go through with this, and plead with my husband to alter his programme for the day and accompany me. Then I would be wracked with guilt, while frustration and anger at my encumbrance converted to tears.

Having brought all those worries upon myself, I would then be unable to eat a thing; yet I would fear that if I didn't eat something I might feel weak, which might then precipitate the dreaded attack. And because of the fear of feeling faint and weak, I would then agonise over what to wear. Anxiety generates body heat and being too warmly clad, together with impingent anxiety, might also lead to feeling faint. Such worry — and what a dilemma.

Then there would be babysitting to organise for the children, and I would be worried about leaving them, always afraid deep down that those symptoms would deal their final blow while I was away from home.

After I'd done all this worrying in anticipation of fear, which now seems so futile, I would have to make the decision as to whether or not I could actually keep the appointment that day! I have always been a person with a strict sense of responsibility, and dislike cancelling or changing things. But with all the preliminary worry about going out of the house I would, by now, be feeling decidedly 'wrung out'. The temptation to phone and say that I couldn't keep the appointment was very great, and this would also eliminate immediately all the things I had just spent ages worrying about. But, no treatment, no freedom — or so it seemed. What turmoil. And what a waste of energy. And how aware I was of the irrationality surrounding my entrapment, even then.

Eventually I would find myself on the way to the psychiatrist's rooms, with much apprehension — my constant travelling companion — and anticipating distress all the time. I would then invariably have to wait to see the doctor for anything up to an hour. Waiting, to an agoraphobic, is dreadful. One seems to be in such a state of urgency, only wanting to get home to safety again, so that even the thought of having to wait will stir up symptoms. This is, of course, caused by the continuing tension which makes endurance impossible. But we do not realise this, and go on fighting our reactions, worsening our situation by the minute.

I would try to distract myself by browsing through a magazine, but inevitably there would be some article in it which would not help. Every time a worried person picks up a paper there seems to be something written in it on the symptoms of disease which seem to match the symptoms of anxiety. I sometimes used to think, if I was feeling especially light-hearted, that this was a service from the media to the doctor — to give him some really good symptoms to work on! Eventually it would be my turn for consultation.

I have heard people who have experienced psychoanalysis complain that they have spent every session mercilessly discussing the themes of Freudian sexuality. Thankfully this doctor did not relentlessly pursue themes of that nature; if he had, I think I would have felt that I had succumbed to a living cliché. We examined, nevertheless, my childhood and later years, people who affected my life and the meaning of dreams. It seemed to be important to analysis to relate current situations which produced anxiety symptoms, to any similar experiences of my childhood. But as my mounting sensations of anxiety seemed to occur at any time and in any situation outside the home, this was almost an impossibility. Each visit was the same, and we were not making positive progress. I would make another appointment and go home, only a little more easily than I had come, to resume my agoraphobic life once more until the next appointment.

And still I did not understand that the attack which I lived in fear of was *panic*, the natural response to fear. Over and above the problem of being constantly afraid to leave the house, there was something else that concerned me; and it was something which I knew I didn't understand.

Although reassured by the doctor to a certain degree, possessing those symptoms worried me. I viewed my fear as a problem exclusive to myself, as though I had suddenly sprouted wings or a spare pair of hands. I felt that experiencing anxiety in this way was an indication of weakness or failure, and I felt burdened by something I couldn't dispense with. In my ignorance I did not understand then that anxiety is part of life. It may be reassuring to many at this point to reiterate that there are almost no fears, thoughts or feelings that are not experienced by others. There is no need to feel alone.

Time passed, and after a number of visits the psychiatrist came to the conclusion that my anxiety was caused primarily by suppressed anger. Far later in my story I came to accept this as part of the big picture and to some extent, a contributing factor. But at that time, any fragment of self-awareness that could have been helpful was masked by the dominance of my constant state of anxiety.

On one particular visit, he repeated that deduction somewhat formally and quite emphatically: 'You're very angry, Mrs McKinnon. Your anxiety is caused by so many angry feelings — feelings that you haven't expressed.'

'Nonsense,' said I. 'I'm never angry, and I certainly don't feel angry right now.' I remember he laughed — very kindly.

He went on. 'You're far too "nice". You're making life extremely difficult for yourself by continually being so obliging.'

I had no idea what he was talking about. I just simply lived; the only way I knew how. And I wanted to be free of fear to participate in life as I had once known it.

I thought about this conversation for a few days. It occurred to me that perhaps I was not contributing enough to psychoanalysis and that I should be making a more concerted effort to alter certain aspects of my personality, to release the anger the doctor spoke of, and thereby hasten a remedy for my fear.

The most obvious person to practise on was my husband. I tried very hard to be aggressive, but it only amused him. I tried to be more assertive, but it only irritated him, as it was a false display of assertion. I tried to find an opportunity when he would really make me very angry and I could tell him so. No such opportunity presented itself to my awareness.

Then I remembered that an angry woman is more than capable of serving the evening meal to her partner on a speeding plate, delivered somewhere between nose and knees when the unfortunate male has sauntered in late and with no valid reason to excuse him. Why couldn't I react like that? I wasn't prepared to sacrifice any lengthily prepared dinner for such an exercise, but the next time my husband forgot the time without justification, I risked a dish of summer-soft butter. Of course, one cannot pre-meditate angry reactions, or any emotional reaction for that matter, and naturally the butter missed its object. He just stood there laughing good-naturedly as my plan of self-help went somewhat awry. I spent an hour cleaning a rather greasy kitchen.

'Did you feel any better for having done that?' asked the psychiatrist on my next visit.

Did I feel any better? Of course I didn't feel any better — I had had to clean it all up. And I was still terrified to walk out the front door.

He tried to console me by praising my sense of humour.

Six

ON FRIENDSHIP

*A friend is someone who knows everything
about us and still accepts us.*

St Augustine

One afternoon as I was sitting dejectedly in my garden trying to read a book, and wishing I was taking the children somewhere interesting for all of us, I was called to the side fence by my friend and neighbour. She attracted my attention by waving an unopened bottle of sherry. At that time she had four little children and was leading a busy and stressful life herself, and she obviously understood that all was not entirely well with me. I think she probably assumed that I, like so many women can be, was overwhelmed by the duties and responsibilities of those busy years of mothering. We have since recalled this incident with amusement and it has stayed in my memory because of her insight at that time. She practically forced the bottle of sherry upon me, saying; 'I don't drink at all, but I'm sure you'll cope better if you have some of this.' I took it from her only because I was touched by her concern, and her insistence was great. Actually, I don't like sherry much, which was probably fortunate, or I may have taken her advice too literally, demolished the entire bottle and set myself upon a far worse course than that which I was already following.

But despite the fact that she had reached out with the hand of friendship, I could not bring myself to tell her that fear was disturbing my life. I was greatly ashamed of my fear and I was 'scared' to admit to it. Friends who later learned of my phobia expressed amazement: 'I never would have guessed, you certainly concealed it well.' This is so. Most who endure agoraphobia do conceal the problem very well, and no-one but the closest person to us will ever catch a glimpse of the misery and distress suffered in private as one is confronted with having to leave the house.

As already noted, when submerged by fear, I believed that I was alone with the problem and I carried a self-inflicted stigma because of this. Many others do likewise. Even today, with far greater public consciousness of anxiety disorders, people of all ages and either gender are still reluctant to share their fear openly — out of a sense of shame. So generally, the victim of fear will endeavour to hide their difficulty from all but the chosen confidant and continue to carry the problem primarily on his or her own shoulders. And yet if communication and discussion with trusted friends and relatives could relieve some part of the anxiety, it must be useful to attempt this.

Anxious people are sensitive. In their sensitivity (a gift of their natural temperament), they invariably worry that their fear, while already ruining the normality of their life, if admitted to, will adversely affect their reputation too. Then the anxious person falls prey to imagining what might happen, should they share their story. These speculations, in my opinion, identify a significant element of the agoraphobic condition: the fear of rejection. The shame and humiliation associated with rejection can contribute to agoraphobia itself, and these feelings can also invent a major stumbling block in the individual's progress to freedom.

Because enduring fear fractures confidence and self-esteem, and people are in numerous ways deceived by their fear, those burdened by agoraphobia become adept at protecting themselves from any hurt whatsoever. This is understandable of course, as part of one's need for self-preservation. However, in preserving oneself from rejection, shame, hurt or humiliation, the need to defend oneself is further heightened. Anxiety, at many levels, remains high and substantial energy — and notable tension — is required to maintain this natural, if exaggerated, need.

So even in the matter of friendships, which ought be healing, the agoraphobic is juggling various facets of anxiety. And yet, a problem shared certainly *is* a problem halved. The sharing of the story can help eliminate a portion of that anxiety.

Most people, anxious or otherwise, tread cautiously around the area of personal disclosure. The agoraphobic person treads *very* cautiously. However, if such a person can have the courage to make the first move, he or she can find new support and may indirectly help someone else as well. But there is risk involved, which then raises a choice: should a person with agoraphobia confide in their friends and find loving support? Or, if this step is taken, will tenuous threads of confidence be torn apart should the person so trusted respond with some form of rejection?

It is not easy, I know, for the person with agoraphobia to discuss the problem freely. It seems such a foolish thing for an adult person to be afraid of leaving their own home, particularly when there are so many specific and serious troubles in the world to claim more importance. A person with agoraphobia who might like to confide in others is faced with a difficult decision, for, having spoken, the choice of confidant may have been a poor one, and the risk of regret, alongside the possibility of benefit, is very great. And it is true that there are people who are insensitive or uncaring of others' needs.

In discussing this dilemma with a friend, we talked about the pros and cons of whether people can and should assist one another through emotional difficulties. This was a delicate conversation, for the man I was speaking with was, at the time, under a great deal of stress, caring for his wife who was dying of cancer. I was impressed by one particular comment though, when he observed that it seems to be much easier to help others emotionally when you are in the midst of emotional suffering yourself. One person's suffering seems to make other sufferings acceptable. Therefore, in choosing a new confidant, it may be useful to bear in mind that people of similar sensitivity, and people who have some life experience in personal pain, are more likely to respond in kind.

The person in fear is also cautious around the family. The first time my children knew that I had experienced a fear of this nature was in the early stages of planning this book. I took aside my then teenage son and daughter on separate occasions and explained to them what I had in mind. It came to me as a pleasant surprise when each, independently, gave me great encouragement. With enthusiasm, both said, in their own way: 'Yes, you must write it; it's very important that people understand these things.'

I was greatly relieved by their loving reassurance and friendship. I had expected them to have reacted with frivolity or embarrassment at my story. Since then, I have observed the reactions of other young people to the subject, and to similar matters concerning human emotion. The result has been very much the same.

Perhaps we, of other generations, have something to learn from our children where empathy and communication are concerned. I know, at their age, I would not have been so tolerant — or perhaps even so compassionate. People *can* be insensitive to others' pain. Perhaps some such people have developed in an insular atmosphere. Protected like porcelain in a glass box, it is easy to observe without being touched, until eventually they come to rely upon that glass box to protect them from any kind of fragility. Many of the new generation are educated in acceptance as a general rule, and are therefore more generous in their openness and willingness to communicate better with others. In this way, they have learned to cast aside protective armoury, thus diffusing the aura of mystique — or fear — that can contribute to the need to keep frail or sensitive feelings undercover. In attempting to share these feelings, they are likely to be reasonably safe in the hands of youth.

However, during my years of agoraphobia, I refrained from telling my children. I think when children are very young, that decision is a wise one. It was my feeling then that if a mother admitted fear to her children, they might feel insecure also. I could not allow that to happen. I also worried that, if the children knew, they might mention it to other children, or worse still, in the hearing of other parents. Once again, here was the risk of people knowing my shame.

But keeping such fear from other people is quite a strain, for there are so many situations to be 'got around'. It may seem strange to the reader who has not experienced a phobic reaction that a mother can keep this fear from her children for many years. But the agoraphobic person becomes very adept at 'keeping a stiff upper lip', emanating ease and enjoyment no matter what is felt within, and fabricating that endless repertoire of excuses as to why he or she cannot do this or that. This is not deliberate deception. It is a role, well played by conscientious people, to avoid panic and to save face. Although we don't really know it at the time, it keeps the fire of fear smouldering.

Elizabeth, a middle-aged married woman who had been agoraphobic for twelve years, told me of her worry that one day her aged aunt who lives nearby will become ill or need her help. Because of her phobia, Elizabeth will probably not be able to go to her aunt's assistance. If she could speak of her fear to others, especially to her aunt, Elizabeth would be relieved of worrying about a situation which may never arise.

These days, when I speak openly to others about having been agoraphobic, almost every person to whom I speak knows of someone else who is similarly hiding that fear. And certainly everyone with whom this fear is discussed knows of *some* type of fear, either through their personal experience or that of another.

An interesting question now arises. In my case, is the reaction of the people to whom I have spoken only positive and enthusiastic because I have already overcome the problem? And would people react in the same way if I was saying that I was still agoraphobic? The answer can only be speculative. Unfortunately, greater glory is always handed out to those who can say they have overcome a difficulty. And it seems to be a trait of human nature to be critical of those in the midst of difficulties, even while at the same time possibly trying to help. Personally, I have not met with a rejection: perplexity sometimes, but never a rebuff or an outright rejection. Perhaps this could be because, in over-coming that fear, I have regained my confidence so the reactions of others do not concern me as they would have once before.

In the case of other individuals who are still suffering from agoraphobia, we need a crystal ball to advise us whom to choose to confide in and whom to avoid telling. As one woman put it: 'I've had no success in telling people about agoraphobia. I usually get a blank stare while the person tries to decide whether to back me in the last race or back off in case I'm contagious!' This would certainly indicate that many people do not understand agoraphobia.

Then she added: 'Some may say, "What a shame. Oh, but that's nothing, you just have to forget that and make yourself get over it."' Again, hardly a very sympathetic reply. Perhaps she has just been unlucky, but these responses do tend to make the sufferer want to forget the idea of opening up to others.

After many years of fear, I did eventually confide in several friends, and their reactions were always favourable and helpful. My first experience of sharing this was when I tentatively spoke of my fear to a close woman friend. I had hardly finished speaking when she, with the same sense of relief, told me that she also suffered quite similarly. A professional woman, she worked full time and always found that the commitment of her work helped her cope with her fear. However, driving to and from the office was a particular problem to her. She dealt with it in a very pragmatic manner and always travelled by the same route where she had to pass several chemist shops. If the panic feeling began to occur, as a matter of routine she would immediately park the car, go to the chemist and ask for something to calm her. After she had regained her equilibrium, she was then able to continue her journey. She too, has an understanding husband, and the four of us from time to time went to theatres and restaurants together. Because we each knew how the other might feel at some stage, neither experienced panic in those situations and the occasions were always very enjoyable. I think the peace of mind that came from knowing that we shared the same fear and understood each other gave a sense of ease which prevented panic from occurring.

On the other hand, Marie, a single woman of middle age who lives alone with an agoraphobic history of twelve years, has only told her older sister of the problem. Her sister is apparently a rather overbearing person without much sensitivity and is inclined to force Marie into action. Such an attitude is not at all helpful to a person with fear. The domineering sister's manner creates feelings of inadequacy for Marie, which in turn has the effect of having the dominant person present more capably. Anyone who is tense and embarrassed will fumble, drop things, say things they wouldn't normally say, forget things, and so on. Before one knows what is happening, one has relinquished one's own self-image and allowed the other 'capable' person to take charge of the situation. In Marie's case, when this arises, she gives in and unwillingly allows her sister to manipulate her into doing anything she wishes her to. Sooner or later it all becomes too much, she begins to panic, and then her sister's attitude more or less indicates that Marie is simply a nervous wreck who is incapable of coping with anything. So she dreads her sister's visits — yet she cannot bring herself to tell anyone else.

A good example of friendship strengthened by the capacity to understand is that of Jenny, an agoraphobia sufferer of eleven years. A bubbly woman in her thirties with a good sense of humour, Jenny told this story. The friend in whom she had confided wanted to buy a garment for a special occasion and asked Jenny to accompany her. Jenny was not too keen on department stores, especially when evening wear was on the eighth floor! However, she agreed to go with her friend, but stressed the point that she could only go as long as her friend didn't leave her side. Her friend was sympathetic and seemed to understand Jenny's need. At the same time she herself was feeling on top of the world at the prospect of her purchase, and it wasn't too long before she was in the fitting room and Jenny was left alone.

Jenny recalled: 'I couldn't see her anywhere; she had absolutely disappeared and I was on my own, in an unfamiliar and enormous store, crowded by people and garments and eight floors up in the elevator.' She was able to laugh about it later.

'As panic began to mount, I found a post and hung on to that for support, thinking: someone will find me eventually, even if it's not until the store closes.'

When her friend swept out of the fitting room with her new dress, she did find Jenny, still clutching the post. She was shocked and surprised that in her own light-heartedness she had over-looked the intensity of Jenny's need not to be left. She amended her innocent mistake by linking her arm through Jenny's and promising not to let go until they were safely back at street level. Undoubtedly a greater sense of understanding was reached through that incident between those two women, and she has been of great support to Jenny ever since.

Here is another slant on the various reactions of different people whom agoraphobia sufferers have confided in. A woman who had suffered from agoraphobia for seventeen years eventually told her two daughters who were, by then, young adults. Of course they accepted it very readily, offering encouragement and any kind of help their mother might require. The older girl, who was by that time living away from home, made a special arrangement whereby her mother could always contact her should she feel the need to. The younger daughter was very easily able to understand her mother's fear, as she herself had a great fear of spiders, so they were able to discuss fear openly and objectively together. When these girls were asked by their mother whether, as little children, they had ever wondered why they were never taken out by their mother alone, they said that the thought had never occurred to them. They simply remembered always going everywhere together, as a family. So, for all her effort in keeping her difficulty from her family, the mother was the only one who had endured any deprivation; no-one else had missed out on anything because of her agoraphobia, and now that the family knew, they couldn't do enough to help.

In contrast, Irene, when she finally told her young adult daughters that she was agoraphobic, found that although the girls readily paid lip-service to her problem and gave the appearance of understanding, in the next breath they would say: 'Would you pick up a few things at the sale for me today please, Mum, they'll be closed before I get home'. And 'Mum, perhaps your agora-phobia would go if you slowed down a bit and rested more!'

So Irene, who found it difficult to go into the butcher's shop for the week's meat supply, would endeavour to force herself across the road to the store with the sale. Perhaps she over-indulged her children by giving too much of herself, but this is a small example of how, ironically, people with agoraphobia can force themselves to achieve what is usually impossible, though doing so will be immensely distressful.

But there can be unfortunate negative reactions to the sharing of confidence. Cheryl, who was agoraphobic and with a particular fear of being out at night, confided in a supposedly close friend. Her friend, possibly in a misguided attempt to help, invited Cheryl to spend the day with her, promising to drive her home after-wards. When the time came to leave, Cheryl's friend absolutely refused to drive her home, saying that she was making a fuss about nothing and she must find her own way home like any other sensible adult person. That 'sensible adult person' was quickly reduced to a fearful and tearful state as she was left to her own now weakened resources.

Cheryl said: 'I've never spoken to that person again. She used to be a close friend, but her lack of compassion hurt me so greatly that I can never really forgive her.'

Possibly even worse than total misunderstanding can be the absurdity of misinterpretation. Kath, an agoraphobic for a number of years, was a sweet-natured person, living alone and therefore rather alone with her fear. Eventually she summoned sufficient courage to divulge her secret to a neighbour. That was a huge step for Kath, and that neighbour could have been of tremendous support to her. But in this case it was not to be. Kath's biggest dread was of being in large stores and alone among crowds of people. The prospect of a visit to the local supermarket to buy a few groceries was quite terrifying; so the fact that she found herself alone in that very situation was a small triumph, filled with apprehension. Just as she was tentatively making her way to the checkout, she met the neighbour in whom she had confided. Instead of the thrill of support she hoped to feel, Kath's already ebbing confidence was shattered by the neighbour's exclamation: 'Good Lord, Kath, you shouldn't be shopping in here — you're agoraphobic!'

Those of us listening when this story was recounted were highly entertained as we pictured the neighbour's confusing of agoraphobia with kleptomania! That is about the last thing an agoraphobic person is likely to be. The woman had obviously mistakenly thought that an agoraphobic person *shouldn't*, for some reason, go out into a shop, where she should have understood that the agoraphobic person simply *couldn't* go out.

Until I confided in my friend mentioned previously, my husband had really been my only confidant. The confidence I gained from speaking with another prompted me to tell more of our friends of my fear, one of whom deserves special mention. He is a man gifted with a lively personality and during those years he was of great help to me. We shared the same sense of humour and I was able to laugh, sometimes, at my fear. He kept me in touch with reality and broadened my horizons at a time when it could have been easy to forget what life was about. How grateful I have always been to possess a sense of humour!

This friend would phone me frequently, usually in the morning when I had the tasks of the day ahead of me. I never once put down the receiver after that call without feeling encouraged and optimistic. He was something of an actor and an excellent mimic, and his calls would be lengthy and contain outrageous jokes and stories, nonsense conversations and serious conversations, but he was always positive. He was a lecturer at a university, and on at least three occasions he coerced me into driving there — quite a distance from my home, and an extremely threatening trip for me to tackle. The idea was that I would meet him at an appointed place, we would go on a tour of the university, have coffee together and I would drive home again — a simple enough thing to do, for anyone who is not afraid of leaving home.

I remember the first occasion very clearly and as a very happy memory, although it was a tremendous ordeal for me. I was dreading going through with it, but I had promised I would be there, so I had no choice but to go. Anyway, I *wanted* to do it. It was almost as if the achievement of that small objective was proof of my own capability. So, although I was extremely nervous and anxious, I was also feeling the excitement of anticipation. To allay my fear of leaving the house, I kept telling myself that I was being ridiculous, I would not suffer that attack I dreaded, I would not get lost or become involved in an accident, nothing out there could hurt me, and anyway I would be safely met upon my arrival. If I had been attempting my first overseas flight alone to the most remote corner of the world where nobody spoke my language, I could not have been more apprehensive. I remember arranging to have someone mind the children and felt rather as if I was going to my doom. But I had to do it, and I had to do it with style. I even recall what I wore, and I dressed painstakingly for that little occasion, with attention to every detail; I had to boost every scrap of confidence I could find.

Finally I was on my way. Of course, once I had driven for a while, I calmed down and as no feelings of panic had arisen I began to enjoy the challenge. It helped tremendously to know that the person who in this instance was my security was waiting for me at the end of the journey. However, it was still a rather shaky woman who parked her car in an area that she had not been near for at least six years. Just the same, I was very pleased with myself; the first half of my goal for that day had been achieved and that alone was far more than I had attempted in those years.

For the next hour or two I played the role of tourist with my friend acting as an exaggerated and ridiculous guide. There was much hilarity from both of us at the expense of my predicament, for the agoraphobic never relinquishes that hold on the knowledge that he or she is away from home and safety. Therefore, every so often I would interrupt his description of our surroundings with an exclamation such as:

'What will I do if the car breaks down on the way home?' Or: 'My legs are shaking so much, I can't possibly walk up those stairs!'

My friend was very patient, but he insisted that I had to complete the whole deal. There was to be no opting out and no short cuts. When we finally sat down to coffee, my head was spinning, and my heart was pounding so much with fear that I felt sure it could be heard by people blocks away. It was then that I wanted to run in panic, for I felt I had forced myself as far as I could go and my desire was to be home in familiar surroundings. But I had nowhere to run, except to the car, which I still had to drive home. So somehow I managed to finish my coffee, we completed our tour and I was accompanied back to where I had parked the car. The car, my security, immediately relieved my anxious feelings and so I drove home, elatedly. As I pulled into the drive, my gladness became tinged with regret that it was all over. It had been an occasion of fun — an excuse designed to extract me from the house on my own and throw my fear overboard, and I had survived it; something I thought I could not do.

Over the next few months, we repeated the same outing with a similar mixture of success and failure: success because at least I managed to go through with those excursions, and failure because I couldn't do it unsupported.

The positive attitude of this particular friend made me achieve something which otherwise I would never have attempted. Knowing he knew and could comprehend my plight, that he would be there to meet me and that he would phone to make sure I had arrived home safely afterwards, gave me just enough confidence to go through with it. His help amounted to cognitive behavioural therapy (CBT), which is practised and advocated widely by many health professionals today. The fact that the person supporting me in this instance was also a personal friend made it unique. In other words, I trusted him, and he imposed a discipline on me in the hope that, through it, I would overcome my fear.

Though my husband filled this supportive role tirelessly, one might expect the involvement of a person outside the family to have a greater effect. But the 'treatment' *didn't* solve my problem, for as soon as I had to face leaving the house without his creative support, my paralysing fear rose up once more. However, the generous help of this person certainly kept hope alive and I think that's what friends are for. If he should read this, I trust he will now know my eternal gratitude and thanks for his understanding.

So it *can* be worthwhile to confide in others; it is not so difficult to know upon whom to rely if we choose with care.

The *Desiderata* of the seventeenth century may not be the greatest literary or philosophical work ever preserved, but it is rich in common sense, and I quote:

> As far as possible without surrender be on good terms with all persons.
>
> Speak your truth quietly and clearly; and listen to others, even the dull and ignorant; they too have their story.
>
> Avoid loud and aggressive persons; they are vexations to the spirit.

On two occasions during my life as a single woman I happened to work for two very significant men. The first was an Englishman, resident in Australia, who was internationally honoured and respected in theatrical, military and business circles. I was his secretary for nearly three years. The second was the founder of the company — an empire-builder — who visited his Australian office for a few weeks on a working tour. I was chosen to assist him during his stay. Both these men shared one fine and noticeable quality — true humility. The point of this recollection is that first impressions of people are rarely wrong. We can know someone for only days or we can know someone for many years, but the truth of the inner person shines clearly from the outset of the meeting. We can be sure, then, that the smallest of great people will always respond in a manner true to themselves. Such a person is the one in whom to confide.

It is also true that by looking beyond ourselves and by listening and *hearing* the needs of others (which are usually far deeper than they appear) we can offer our support and possibly be helped in return. In the main, I think, we are only too well aware of the fact that people depend upon each other. If we feel afraid, we should be able to say to another person without shame: 'I am uncomfortable in this situation;' or 'I don't like elevators; would you mind if we took the stairs?' That person should be able to accept the request graciously in the knowledge that he or she one day may feel the same.

And if we do experience an apparent rejection, it is better not to be so deterred that we will not approach someone else — or even try the same person again! People will react differently at different times.

There will always be people in the world who need assistance for the practical things of life. Their form of suffering is easily recognised. But there will also always be people who need assistance and support in less obvious ways, centred within their emotional difficulties. This is an area where others may feel uncomfortable, areas from which others may choose to draw away. Generally, we still have much to learn about human emotion, how we can relate to each other at that level and how we may help each other and relieve at least some of the many complications that emotional problems produce. Yes, for the agoraphobic there is risk involved in opening oneself to our friends. But the rewards of sharing at that level are huge and well worth the risk. Those who intentionally or unintentionally cause hurt to a fear-filled person by their rebuff are possibly feeling equally anxious and ill-at-ease, but for a very different reason.

A friend is someone upon whom we can depend, someone in whom we can confide, someone we can trust and someone who accepts us for who and what we are.

Every person is of value and we each have much to give and much to receive. Who knows, some day someone we care about may need our assistance, and if we haven't learned to share our needs and our feelings, we may be denying ourselves — and our friends — the opportunity to experience a taste of true love.

Seven

THOSE NEGATIVE EMOTIONS

*Pale Anguish keeps the heavy gate and the
warder is Despair.*

Oscar Wilde

B ecause of the fortress of fear which so securely imprisons its
captives, other negative emotions arise within the heart of a
sufferer of agoraphobia, and it is not uncommon for such a
person to relinquish all hope of freedom.

First, it is with something of a jolt that this person will realise
he or she is almost totally dependent once more.

As I write this from my secluded position on the veranda, I am
watching a family of wrens busily searching for food in the soft
grass under some melaleuca bushes. Although the air is close,
muggy with January heat, it is still cool and damp under the trees
from night rain and there is plenty of food for the birds. The
parents are tending to their little ones, all chirping happily. Two
in particular have my attention; the bright male with his blue cap
and shiny black breast and the tiny brown baby, so totally
dependent.

In the beginning, all of us, like the birds, are of necessity
totally dependent. To some extent throughout our lives we are
dependent on others; for companionship, for love, for sharing
joys and sorrows, even for achievements. Our achievements may
largely lack meaning if not accomplished while in interaction with
others. And in practical ways, also, people need each other. We
all know how great it feels to depend occasionally on someone
near to us; the caring if we feel unwell; the task done for us when

time is short. But while this kind of dependence will boost our morale, the feeling of being *absolutely* dependent shatters it.

A friend of mine broke her leg very badly in a skiing accident and was in plaster for months, dependent on others for a great many things. Eventually the break healed, the plaster was removed and, after a time of caution, she was free again. The agoraphobic person becomes psychologically dependent as if there is a plaster cast on their spontaneity, and this is not a happy state. Yet there is no plaster to be seen and the crutch is the husband, wife, or friend upon whom there is immeasurable dependency.

The person with agoraphobia seems to be continually complicating life for those closest, because of the need to have that support person in sight whenever out of the house. If the person depended upon is away for a few minutes, the symptoms of fear will begin to arise. This makes life difficult for the support person, who feels continually obliged to be at the side of the agoraphobic to provide that necessary security. And because the agoraphobic person is so dependent upon the other, though unwillingly, conflicts can arise, together with mutual resentment, and the enjoyment of any situation is lessened for both parties.

It may seem incredible, but a mother can depend upon a young child being with her when away from home. The child may never know of his mother's needs and her dependence upon him, without whom the mother could not venture out of her home to attend to the extended needs of living.

The agoraphobic who works has another kind of dependence: the dependence upon the tolerance and understanding of the employer or associates. If this predicament is not understood and tolerated, he or she no longer has employment.

Teenagers with this fear may often be misunderstood, and they depend upon the love, trust and understanding of their parents, who may take their unwillingness to leave the house as laziness or a lack of interest in life. And while their peers may try to understand, they cannot be *depended* upon too much, for there are too many good things enticing them, a preference indeed to staying at home with their agoraphobic friend.

If the support person is not available, something else will take on the role of a crutch, such as the car that must be parked where it can easily be seen and readily reached. It seems that a car represents an extension of the home and brings with it sufficient security for the individual to be able to venture out a little. A person with agoraphobia will feel an immense relief upon reaching the car, which also brings an immediate means of escaping quickly from any situation of approaching panic.

A woman with agoraphobia will not wish to be parted from her handbag. Therein lies her identity, her sense of security. One woman told me that she always carries an enormous bag which contains anything she could possibly need for practically any emergency: aspirin for a headache, tranquillisers in case she panics, a hat in case the sun comes out, an umbrella in case it rains, scissors, needles and thread and so on. I wouldn't have been surprised if she had added that the bag itself could unfold to make a sleeping bag! Irrational? Perhaps so, but this is her coping strategy and she needs to know that she has it all with her before she can venture into the world. Then there are many people who carry a small bottle, carefully filled with brandy; another form of security. Although the bottle will probably never be opened, the individual depends upon its being there.

And there are other forms of dependence. Those who fear public transport depend on others to drive them here and there. And, in reverse, those who are afraid to drive their car therefore depend upon catching a cab or other forms of public transport. This means they are constantly on edge, watching the clock and organising their activities to fit in with other people or timetables.

The woman who can only shop by telephone depends upon the delivery man to have her groceries there when she needs them. That was one of my dependencies and I became a great improviser — although my family still remind me that rice is no real substitute for potatoes!

As much of the fear of agoraphobia is built upon those memories and failures from previous occasions when fear struck, the ago- raphobic person will also depend upon circumstance. In the anticipation of fear, if the place about to be ventured into does not turn out to be as pictured in the apprehensive mind's eye, he or she will be very uncomfortable there. This dependence upon circumstances being favourable puts a special dread on having to attend a function such as a wedding or a large formal dinner, where the guests' seating will have been prearranged. In such an instance, the individual may then feel very vulnerable seated at a large round table in the centre of a huge room with unfamiliar people — and a long way from the exit.

Now that the fear has long left me, it is difficult to imagine feeling so insecure. But I did experience many dependent reactions, and because agoraphobia prevented me from acting spontaneously or impulsively, everything I wanted to do outside the home depended largely upon my husband's availability.

No matter what life situation a person is in with agoraphobia, a second negative emotion emerges: that of loneliness. With agoraphobia a person can feel very lonely even when surrounded by many. We all experience that feeling at some time in our lives, and my earliest recollection of that type of loneliness comes from a time when as a small child in a big playground I was caught up in a game of 'chasey'. I was 'it' and no matter how hard I tried I could not catch another child to replace me. I felt very lonely indeed until a little friend, recognising my plight with childish intuition, volunteered to take my place. She is still a close friend to this day, and although I'm sure she thought no more of that incident, I will never forget it, for to be rescued from loneliness is a memorable event.

Because in this state of fear a person will only do those things that he or she absolutely can do, the agoraphobic will be lonely in day-to-day life. Fear has drained away spontaneity and it is not easy, sometimes impossible, even to visit the person next door. The agoraphobic will observe the workday routine of neighbours, groups of friends going to golf, people meeting socially or driving freely all over the city and beyond. He or she will feel a tremendous loneliness, and although welcome on countless occasions to join them, unless the support person is there, he or she will graciously decline. After all, one could collapse in panic in any of those situations even while desperately wanting to be part of it all.

In the years when I was a captive of fear, I was very busy, with young children growing up. This is partly an advantage, but it is also a disadvantage. That situation means that a mother has plenty of good reason to stay home, and that time at home was when loneliness touched me as a result of fear. You hear of other mothers making their way again in the workplace, and observe people shopping, playing tennis and freely dropping in here and there. But you know that if you attempt any of those activities you will be preoccupied with fear and elusive ease and enjoyment will be minimal.

Because of that ongoing fear, friendships are hindered, and it prevents the development of new relationships with others through lack of continuous contact. Often during those years I cancelled arrangements with some excuse, because I couldn't force myself to go, only to spend the rest of the day sobbing my heart out and envying bitterly those who had gone. Then, of course, having failed that time, each subsequent occasion becomes more and more difficult to face.

While those with agoraphobia who are part of the workforce are under more strain than the next person, the advantages of occupation — providing he or she is able to manoeuvre the ordeal of travelling — are immensely helpful to the condition. More than the obvious advantages of income and personal satisfaction, within the workplace there is mental stimulus, people to communicate with, a sense of accomplishment and a necessary distraction from the weight of one's own struggle. All these will help dispel loneliness. However, such people are sure to keep rigidly within the confines of the workplace and resist the desire to join colleagues in socialising after hours. There seems to be security in routine, and to step outside of that routine could be to tempt fate and attract that dreaded attack.

The person with agoraphobia living alone with no career or occupation outside the home to inspire any level of motivation can become severely withdrawn. Fear creates a situation where staying at home is the best option. This social isolation exacerbates the existing fear and another vicious circle commences. It is advisable for a person in this kind of situation to invent the necessary motivational need. This advice may sound a little ruthless, but if the situation is to improve, one must be courageous enough to change things. A lonely, middle-aged man living this way took on the responsibility of a puppy. He grew fond of the dog, and since its little life depended upon him, he became more able to go beyond fear to care for his pet. One helped the other as the animal became a kind of 'support figure' giving confidence to its master.

The third persistent negative emotion is that of guilt. Through dependence upon those close to us, we seem to be always inconveniencing other members of the family through the inability to act freely. Even when the children are not aware of their mother's fear, and do not realise that they themselves are not participating in life as other mothers and children, the agoraphobic mother will still feel guilty. We will therefore endeavour to compensate in other ways to appease our guilty feelings. One woman told me that she liked dressmaking, and made so many new clothes for her children that it was almost impossible for them to wear them all. Another told me that her way of compensating her husband for his patience was to mow the lawns, chop the wood and do many other chores for him that he normally would have expected to do himself. Not being as energetic as she, I became a prolific cake baker!

Then on top of guilt we begin to feel angry and frustrated. 'Why did this have to happen to me? Is this what life is all about — constant fear?' People may say you should count your blessings; we do, and we feel all the more guilty. And then we are all the more frustrated because we know that if we were not blocked by that invisible obstacle of fear, we would be out in the world, participating and making a worthwhile contribution to life.

In seeking help or advice for agoraphobia, the sufferer will inevitably be told to 'keep occupied'. In itself this is good and sensible advice, until we stop to consider that in order to do this properly it is usually necessary to leave the house and venture

out into that threatening world which will cause all those unpleasant symptoms. This recommendation feeds the guilt and
increases the frustration. The person concerned knows only too
well all the things in life he or she would be capable of achieving,
if it were not for this stranglehold of fear. The agoraphobic will
probably feel rather angry at this well-meant advice, as it seems
that the person giving it simply has no concept of the mammoth
problem. He or she has been trying, apparently in vain, to explain
it for so long! 'How can they expect me to do that when I am
afraid to leave the house?' Then self-doubt will probably set in, as,
taking with it more hope, despair lurks in the background.

It is at a time such as this that the victim of fear will make a
supreme effort to achieve something alone. Fear has been dominating life for some time; he or she is sustaining many negative
emotions, is beginning to despair that the situation will ever
improve and is finding it necessary to prove him/herself as a
capable and companionable person. While in the state described,
he or she is propelled with increasing tension into the situation
most feared. Usually, instead of proving anything, the person is
overwhelmed by impending panic. The individual will then assume
that instead of any hope of improvement or of overcoming fear,
he or she is getting worse. Once again there arises the vicious
circle of fear.

An incident such as this will be very painful, especially if the
person has managed to get halfway to a destination and then had
to return home. He or she feels terribly foolish and bitterly disappointed — a complete failure. In defeat the person may almost
give up trying, and resume the safe pattern of making excuses or
refusing invitations, or simply just going without doing all those
things most desired.

The irony of continually avoiding situations of fear is that while
all these excuses will allow us freedom for the moment, they are,
of course, only temporary and very soon we will be faced with
another such predicament. Because we are intelligent human
beings we are only too well aware of this and our phobia is
further burdened by old memories of shame and humiliation. Our

doubts, our lack of confidence and loss of self-esteem all grow greater, and we can begin to feel worthless as our pride is hurt more and more. Then come more tears and frustration while observing, incorrectly, that everyone else in the world is so 'normal' — and we ask: 'Why not me?'

In most cases, the person with agoraphobia has very great expectations; standards are high, and what is 'normal' to him or her may well be far above what is normal to others. For all people have failings and the word 'normal' is an overrated mystery. From my observations of others with this fear, I believe generally speaking they are, either by nature or necessity, competent, sensitive and strong people who have always been seen by themselves and others to be self-sufficient, hence, they are not expected to falter.

Because of the ongoing state of fear aggravated by those negative emotions, and the continual tension combating those emotions, it is possible for other symptoms of anxiety to arise which are not necessarily part of agoraphobia. By these I am referring to any of the vague symptoms of nervous tension commonly experienced by people. Again, these can increase general anxiety. The more complicated life becomes through all these negative emotions the greater the anxiety in the individual. So it can easily be seen how some people *can* become totally incapacitated, not by agoraphobia, but by the extra anxiety that has been born of it. But being agoraphobic does not necessarily mean that the victim will have other common phobias such as fear of heights or flying in aeroplanes. In fact, many agoraphobic people to whom I have spoken are less afraid of things which are a source of great fear to others.

An agoraphobic man told this humorous story. He and a friend went on an historical visit to a cemetery. The agoraphobic felt safe because his friend was with him, and in his enthusiastic pursuit of history they became separated. He became alarmed and went to find his friend for support. The agoraphobic man's fear was allayed when he found his support person petrified with fear because he had found an old grave with a lifted slab.

Apparently he was expecting to see a ghost emerge from the tomb. The agoraphobic calmed his friend by saying: 'Don't worry about that, the dead won't hurt you . . . for me it's just being alive that's scary!'

People with agoraphobia will, however, probably experience associated uneasiness from time to time. Two good examples of this would be fear of losing the support person, and fear of agoraphobia and its accompanying difficulties in old age. Such a compelling fear leaves a person feeling extremely vulnerable because of blow after blow of what we deem to be failure, and the overall sensation of insecurity. One of my own worries was that as I seemed to be experiencing fear for a great part of my life and for very little apparent reason, whatever would my reaction be if I were faced with a crisis or a real reason for fear? Because of the continuous buffeting by the fear within, when contemplating other worries in life we begin to wonder just how much we can take.

I used to discuss this with the psychiatrist to ease my concern. He assured me time and again that I had no cause for worry in that regard for, in his opinion, I was a strong and stable person who would always cope well with life. My feeling of greater vulnerability came only from the fact that fear fosters feelings of insecurity . . . and my anxiety, or fear, was then very high.

As time went on I realised that he was right, for many demanding situations arose during those years which, out of respect for the privacy of other people, cannot be recalled here. I always dealt with my part in any of those situations in the way in which I wanted to, or felt was expected of me. In other words, despite agoraphobia (which won't disappear with the onset of other problems) I didn't ever fail myself in other areas of living.

What actually troubled me was the broken confidence and the total frustration of the condition which prevented me from living life fully. So, in the midst of agoraphobia, we have a person who has been used to leading a full and happy life, but who is now terrified to leave the security of home for fear of the consequences of fear, plus the anguish of dependence, loneliness and guilt. And because we believe there is no hope of overcoming the problem which is spoiling our life, we suffer the persistent emotion of near-despair, together with feelings of anger, hurt, frustration, doubt, shame and humiliation. A growing loss of self-esteem only intensifies one's fractured confidence. In summary, fear's victim will think: 'There is so much in life to contribute and to receive, but I cannot shake off the shackles of fear which tie me to my home and so I am bereft of all. I cannot truly live . . . I am trapped, effectively paralysed beyond hope.'

All of this brings about a disenchantment with life that could certainly not be called 'living at the top of the world'.

Eight

LIVING WITH FEAR

Who overcomes by Force hath overcome but half his foe.

Milton

The first time I saw someone paralysed with fear was on a visit to the circus when I was about twelve years old. The show ended and the people began to leave the circus tent. The seating accommodation at such an event then and today is always of a temporary nature and rather precarious in its stability. I was surprised to see a woman nearby who remained sitting high on the stand, completely unable to make herself climb down with the rest of the audience. She was coerced and encouraged by her family, but she was paralysed with fear. I remember that I had great admiration for the practical attendant who, when the tent was almost empty of people and the circus hands had started to dismantle the seating, bounded up to her, took her hand and pulled her down the steps saying loudly: 'Come on lady, you can't stay there all night, we've got to get moving.' No doubt he had come across that problem before!

Strangely, during my eight years of agoraphobia, that incident evaded my memory. It was only in writing about fear that I recalled it and realised that it is a keen example of how the person with fear of leaving the house feels when confronted with the prospect of crossing the threshold. Probably that woman never went to a circus again — but then it is much easier to avoid a circus than it is to avoid buying the week's food supply. How unreasonable that avoidance seems to me now, yet how necessary it was at the time. And because the agoraphobic person is not perched on top of a stand of seating that is about to be dismantled, he or she can continue to hide their fear, negotiating dreaded circumstances, though living a lesser life.

I have wondered what that woman at the circus would have done if the attendant hadn't intervened. Of course she would have eventually had to force herself down the steps somehow — she had no choice. The reader might say now: 'Surely then the person in any fear can force himself to overcome it.' Unfortunately, without proper understanding, it is not so easy to do. The victim is aware that the fear is irrational, but avoiding the situation is his or her self-defence against what is feared — the frightening and persistent symptoms believed to lead to that mysterious and dreaded attack. So discipline alone will not overcome the difficulty, and the effect of forcing him/herself through a situation is only a temporary palliative. The person with agoraphobia is continually practising self-discipline in order to achieve anything outside the home. But as earlier stated, the harder he or she tries to overcome fear, the more tension is generated to fight with and the more symptoms of fear are naturally produced, which in turn increase that fear.

Yet agoraphobic people also have their pride; a natural sense of dignity and self-worth prevents their absolute surrender to fear. Should something be demanded where all excuses have failed and we cannot avoid leaving the house without losing face in the sight of others, somehow we will achieve it.

Gwen, who had been agoraphobic for over thirty years, recalled this story. A neighbour whom she greatly admired was giving a rather important dinner party, and during the evening suddenly realised she had forgotten to buy cream for the dessert. She phoned Gwen (not knowing that she had this phobia) asking her to do her the favour of buying some cream to save her party. Gwen had no choice but to say yes.

Gwen said:

> I certainly didn't want her to know that I was afraid to go to the shop, and I wanted to help her anyway. But I was terrified that I

would fail and be overwhelmed by panic in doing so . . . and although I was shaking with fear every step of the way and to me it was a tremendous ordeal, my friend got her cream!

After an incident such as that (which really can be a huge mission for a person with agoraphobia) the individual will hope that it will mark the beginning of the end of fear, and will feel certain that having forced him/herself through fear, freedom will result. But no! A new day will dawn and all the anxious feelings will be ready and waiting as companions to whatever has to be done, because, through tension, fear is still the master.

We cannot treat this phobia philosophically either. We cannot say to ourselves: 'All right, sometimes I experience these dreadful symptoms that I don't understand. But that's my problem and I'll just have to learn to live with it.' Again, it's not as easy as that, for although we are doing our best to live with it, it affects us and those around us constantly.

As such a great part of life is involved with things outside the home, the agoraphobic person is eternally on guard. Someone has only to mention innocently that there is no milk in the fridge and a stab of fear will strike; and that fear will build. While the victim may be able to force him/herself to go for the milk, in doing so tension will be increased for the remainder of the day. If it happens that there is something else to be faced later, the dread of anticipation will be far greater than usual because of the already increased tension; because we do not understand. *We do not understand our own responses and the fact that if we ignore those symptoms they will pass; that we are simply caught in a chain reaction which has become a habit out of sheer self-defence, that added anxieties grow from fear and that we are always aggravating the condition when we fight with nervous tension.*

Although the fear was always with me, fortunately I never totally succumbed to it. Despite my pain throughout those years, my life held a wealth of achievement, enjoyment and happiness. I must add a sincere word of admiration here to all partners, spouses and families who are sympathetic to the agoraphobic person. My husband was always understanding, helpful and tolerant and I know there are many more husbands, wives and friends whose patience, love and faith in their companion is being tried and proven in this way. Those people who have agoraphobia as well as the misfortune of being misunderstood, or where there is disharmony in the home, where, naturally, existing anxiety is higher for all, must lead a difficult life indeed.

During those years I avoided leaving the house alone whenever possible, and everything I did which involved doing so was still a gigantic ordeal. Yet when the event was over and I was safely home again I would wonder how I could ever be so afraid — until faced with the next occasion. Any attempt to leave the house was always preceded by apprehension; the piercing fear, the overall feeling of weakness, pounding heart and anticipation of the possibility of the dreaded attack. The pattern of the symptoms of the attack was always predictable, but whether or when it would occur was not predictable. So in every situation away from home I was in an increased state of tension, trying to ward off the attack of panic which I feared so greatly, and still did not recognise or truly understand.

Knowing that there were certain events which had to be attended and could not be avoided would cause much worry, and rarely was I at ease in any situation away from home. However, as my husband and I both enjoyed the company of others and participating in as many things as possible, I usually managed to force myself to go anywhere, as long as he was with me and never far out of sight. Occasionally fear would overcome me to the extent that I could not go through with whatever it was we had to do, but this didn't happen too often on occasions where we were both involved.

Unfortunately, it did happen often when I was alone. I was able to travel comfortably for a mere kilometre from home, providing I drove myself, I was out for as short a time as possible and my car was always parked close at hand. To achieve this, I often had to take the prescribed medication, which I greatly disliked having to do. I only ever took very minimal doses and when absolutely necessary. Even then I always, at some stage of my journey, experienced the onset of the symptoms of panic. The complete attack never occurred again (for all my worrying), but the anxiety symptoms were with me like a constant reminder that 'it' had not forgotten me. Those would be the times when I would abandon my purpose for shopping or escape to home from some social situation, relieved that I had survived.

As most of my living was obviously going to take place at home, I found ways to keep occupied. I was still involved in our business, and worked at my part in it from home. I also maintained as many interests as possible without having to leave the house. Having accepted that I could no longer pursue my singing ambitions, I had a yearning to study art seriously, but I could hardly expect my husband to accompany me to classes or lectures. That was out of the question. I did attend ceramic classes close to home and, once I had forced myself to get there, found that potting and moulding is creative and good fun. But, as usual, the build-up of fear before the event was so great that I began to dread each Tuesday night as it approached, so I did not re-enrol for another term.

I investigated correspondence classes in various subjects. The first year of that proved worthwhile. However, I couldn't bear to have completed the course and not to have the achievement of sitting for the examination. But I knew my fear would prevent me from doing so. By requesting special permission, I was able to sit for an exam in my home, under supervision. The results were pleasing, so I pressed on. When examination time came the following year I really didn't feel justified in asking for special consideration a second time, and decided I would force myself to go and sit for the exam like all the other students.

Of course, my husband took me there and promised faithfully that he would not leave the car, parked close by, so I could find him should I need to. Somehow I managed to complete the paper, and I even passed the exam, but I remember feeling that I was putting myself to an extreme test. Surely it was bad enough to be afraid to leave my home, without making myself go through the misery of an examination room as well. Anyway, I survived it — somehow we always do — and I believe it is worthwhile to keep trying and never give in, although now I know there are easier ways of going about it.

The year after that, I attempted another subject by correspondence, but because it was more complex, and really required tutorials and discussion with other students, my progress was halted — because I just couldn't make that kind of commitment. For the person with agoraphobia, nothing in life is simple.

No-one but the agoraphobic knows how difficult it is to make an appointment at the hairdresser's or to drop in to the school with that forgotten lunch; to buy a new dress, to go out to dinner, to see a film or enjoy a cup of coffee with a friend.

A visit to the hairdresser should be a soothing and pleasant experience. To a woman in a state of fear and with the accompanying tension, a visit to the hairdresser is nothing short of an endurance test. First she has to go through the misery of actually getting there and keeping the appointment; having arrived there is sure to be a dreaded wait as the hairdresser is certain to be running behind time. Then there is the trapped feeling while the hairdresser seems to take forever to complete the wash, or trim or style or whatever, during which time the victim is frantically wondering what will happen if she is overwhelmed by the symptoms of panic. She increases her fear by her desire to forget the whole idea and rush from the salon in a state of disrepair with wet or half-cut hair! That, of course, will never happen; somehow we steel ourselves and see it through, possibly promising ourselves that we will never go through this again. So it becomes another unpleasant memory to add to those before it.

The same feelings arise when buying clothes. It is virtually an impossibility for an agoraphobic person to enter a fitting room to try on a garment. I can almost guarantee that many garments have been purchased by people under such conditions and never been worn because there comes a point when the person in fear of panic will buy anything just to escape from the shop and flee home to safety.

Restaurants and theatres hold their own type of dread for the agoraphobic person, as such people prefer to be seated near the door or on an aisle where the exit can be easily reached, which cannot always be arranged. While trying to appear to be enjoying ourselves, we have a continuous monitor on our reactions and are thinking: 'However will I cope if those feelings of panic strike now?' Of course we rarely find out, because at the first appearance of any symptoms we manage either to leave discreetly at some appropriate moment, or to fight it through anyway, thereby saving face. But life is not being fully lived; the occasion has lost its sparkle. And because of the inhibiting fear, the pleasure of the most minor moments in life is lost through lack of spontaneity.

Although during those years I joined committees and attended meetings under great strain, one of my greatest dreads, familiar to most agoraphobics, was of such meetings, or church services or any organised occasion where I felt confined. How often does the well-meaning clergyman or chairperson inadvertently cause misery to 'those people standing at the back — there's plenty of room for you to be comfortable in the front row!' If only such people understood! The back row is preferred, seated right on the aisle. I don't think I ever did leave any such occasion because of panic, but the amount of nervous tension and energy that it took exhausts me, now, to think about it.

The years rolled on. Children were born, people died, there were weddings and christenings and funerals. Christmases and birthdays came and went, we visited old friends, made new ones, took holidays to various places and entertained at home. And during that time our family number increased to five with the birth of another lovely daughter. We encouraged the children in new interests as they grew older, participated in business and family activities, attended Boy Scouts barbecues and all those other activities that come with being a parent, along with the fun and the duties involved. Life changed and developed all the time and I participated in all these things, but not without a great deal of fear and tension.

We moved house again and began another renovation. I vaguely hoped that a different house would dispel my fear, but of course it didn't — how could it when the fear was within me? I was busy, and renovating is a creative hobby to say the least, but I lived for years with wallpaper that I detested because it was chosen in haste and under tension while desiring escape from confinement in the shop.

Because my children did not know of my fear, and because I always wanted to do for them everything I could, to the best of my ability, I constantly forced myself to be involved in everything that affected them. The needs of young children are not easily forecast, and are more immediate and therefore of extra concern. There is always the thought in the back of your mind that illness or accident will occur and you will have to face taking the child to hospital in an emergency. You also know, deep down, that if you have to do it, you will, and very ably. But you go on dreading that it might happen and hoping like mad that it won't. Fortunately for me there was only one such emergency, and a fairly minor one, and of course I dealt with it.

Another woman with the same fear recalled how only once in many years the school phoned to tell her that one of her children was ill. She was saved from having to leave her home in that small emergency by the fact that her husband had happened to come home for something he had forgotten and was able to collect the child. But I believe that, had he not been there, she would have gone.

That is not to say that the fear is inconsistent; it is always there and we suffer much in doing these things, but we *can* force ourselves past it when something of this nature occurs or somebody needs us. The agoraphobic person who wishes to overcome fear is always striving and will rarely give up, but because he or she is going about it the wrong way, it is all very hard work.

In those years, whenever necessary I took the children to the dentist or to the doctor, or to school interviews or any other event which involved their well-being. I became astute at arranging appointments so that we were either first or last to be attended to. At least such organisation would to some extent cut down the dreaded time spent in waiting rooms. These days, if I try to avoid waiting, thankfully it is because there are many other things I would prefer to be doing!

I tried as often as I could to make myself attend those meetings mentioned and participate in any other duties that particularly involved mothers and their children. I remember well when, for a time, I forced myself to help with voluntary assistance in a class-room. Looking back I probably should have had more sense than to torture myself unnecessarily, for such tasks as these were achieved more from a sense of duty than from any reward or personal enjoyment, because of the ever-accompanying build-up of fear. All the time I was terrified that at any moment I would be stricken by the symptoms I dreaded, and worried about what would happen to all those children in my care if I was swallowed up by that attack.

I can look back now and say: 'Why worry? Life is precarious enough anyway and disaster — real disaster — can strike at any time, yet we don't dwell upon it.' But in those years, the fear which I couldn't see or touch or run from haunted me, and the part I played in any situation of responsibility was of great consequence to me.

Should the observer venture to think at this stage that a person with agoraphobia is merely a procrastinator who is totally preoccupied with his or her own well-being, let me hasten to remonstrate. Often it is with thought of the well-being of another that our fear is foremost in our minds; in particular of course, anyone who is dependent upon us — our own children, those children in the classroom, elderly parents, the non-driver whom you are driving home, any task we have in hand for another person. The agoraphobic feels that he or she may fail any of these people if overwhelmed by the dreaded attack which, for all that is known, may progress beyond control.

At the same time, we don't want that person who is relying upon us to feel our insecurity, so we tense up and fight it through. How could I, when in my thirties, 163 cm tall, of proportionate weight and looking extremely healthy, have said to a trainee teacher at the nearby kindergarten (who only looked like a child herself): 'Don't leave me alone and responsible for these little children; I might faint.' Absolutely ridiculous! Yet the fear still hovered.

The fact that I continually forced myself to do these things at least gave me some extra feeling of accomplishment in life, but it was all very difficult and although I fought hard, I was still going about it the wrong way. All these achievements were within that one-kilometre radius of home, and if anything was organised at a venue other than those local ones, unless it was something to which my husband could also go, I would decline. And many times I did just that, when fear won the battle over reason. Often I would have to defer an appointment or ask my husband to fulfil whatever was in hand in my place, or have him accompany me.

Because that constant uneasiness drains and eliminates spontaneity, one of the most displeasing aspects of being agoraphobic is that very lack. We cannot, on impulse, take the dog for a walk, drop in on a friend, fly a kite in the park with the children. Everything must be planned so that fear will not strike. Everything seems to be preceded by the words 'but' or 'if'. Included in that area of lack of spontaneity, for me, was the inability to do my local shopping freely. I still had the essential items delivered, and by this time had perfected the technique of never running out of necessities. (Later, with spontaneity restored, I seemed to be always running out of everything!) However, just occasionally, something would be required that could only be purchased at the supermarket. I had no positive reason to dread those places, though many do; but when one thinks about it, such large stores do generate a great deal of nervous tension. They are brightly lit, with a dazzling array of products, powerfully and competitively advertised to make purchases more confusing and decisions more difficult. There is often loud background music or an insistent voice arresting attention through a microphone, crowds of people, long queues at the checkouts, and once inside, you are usually a long way from the exit! No wonder people who are tense and afraid commonly detest the modern supermarket. And no wonder many a store manager finds the odd can of pet food in the refrigerator or breakfast cereal with the soap powder or even an occasional fully-loaded shopping trolley completely abandoned — some poor shopper, overcome by panic, has fled the store.

So in those years, when something was needed from the supermarket, we either had to manage without it until the next delivery, my husband would buy it, or the older children would go to the small store nearby, while I stayed in the car ready to leave as soon as they reappeared.

That car was always a faithful and supportive servant to me. As long as the car was nearby, I was able to make those brief trips, while at the same time avoiding any particularly dreaded areas. With the car, I could always leave any situation when I wanted to, and it provided the necessary security and independence so that others did not have to know of my discomfort. I believe with hindsight it would have been easier to tell more people and not fight alone, but then of course, I didn't understand fear and its effects; nor did I know how to explain it — I just knew I was afraid.

I faithfully reported to my psychiatrist all the locations where the symptoms arose (which were just about everywhere outside home), wishing all the time that he, or we, would identify some link between the anxiety experienced at that time and some incident of conflict or fear from my childhood. We continued to analyse my life. I made no further attempts to change my personality and as long as I was at home I was happy, relatively at ease. At this stage of my journey no therapeutic discussion had ever brought relief from the recurring symptoms and no great revelation from my past had emerged to dispel my anxiety.

After years with fear lingering like a great grey cloud and nothing worse having happened than the symptoms themselves, one might think it could be somehow accepted, forgotten about and thus overcome. Probably as close as I came to doing that was this: I *had* learned to live with it. But it is indeed second-class living; the overall sense of loss, of missing so much in life and the disappointment of that eternal guard on spontaneous existence . . . You know, however hard you fight or try to forget, that as soon as you reach the threshold, your heart will start to thump, your legs will turn to jelly and you realise that 'it' has not forgotten you.

Nine

PERSEVERANCE

Perseverance, dear my Lord
Keeps honour bright: to have done is to hang
Quite out of fashion, like a rusty mail
In monumental mockery.

Shakespeare

Probably I am a rather determined person, but in all this dreadful maze of fear and the side-effects of it, I had one ambition: to get out of it.

As my life prior to this happening had been spent in doing outgoing things, and my greatest youthful dream then had been the world of music and the stage, my present behaviour was paradoxical. I had never been afraid like this. Why was I so afraid now of something, which I couldn't even identify, that prevented me from living life with freedom? Fear was dominating my life and taking with it all my hopes and ambitions. It annoyed me greatly to think that something could have such power over me, and because of it, I had lost confidence in myself and suffered much loss of self-esteem. So I wanted very much to continue to seek any form of help that was available which might enable me to return to my former self.

However, if agoraphobia had caused me loss of spontaneity and spoiled my life in other ways, I began to realise that the manner by which I was endeavouring to overcome this problem was causing me yet another problem. As this fear represented failure to me, I was prepared to do anything that I deemed to be necessary to overcome that failure and be liberated from fear. With psychoanalysis, however, there is little one can 'do' in the strict sense of the word. Liberation from the problem in hand should apparently just happen, as a result of talking and trying to relate times of anxiety to other situations which have occurred in life. Then, we hope, one day the pieces of the puzzle will fall into place. Some past event of significance will be discussed freely enough to be consciously revealed. From this insight, the inhibiting anxiety symptoms should gradually disappear.

This seemed to me at the time to be a very vague and slow solution to my fear of leaving my home. For my life was happy! I was not living with any major problem or stressful situation to cause anxiety — but there existed a barrier of fear through which I couldn't pass. So, in an attempt to hasten this remedy, I tried very hard to associate the occasions when I felt most afraid with the circumstances in which these occasions occurred. But the answer was always the same: my anxiety symptoms were power-fully connected with having to leave the house or be away from home.

Here then, was my new problem. I found that, added to my loss of spontaneity due to my fear, I also had a guard on my natural emotional reactions. I found myself trying too hard to analyse why I had felt uncomfortable in that particular street, shop or house; or why I did not feel edgy at one particular gathering of a group of friends, yet at another gathering with people from the same party, feelings of panic had arisen. Thus I was constantly on the lookout for symptoms — which of course increased the likeli-hood of such feelings occurring. This also had the effect of pre-venting me from deliberately attempting something where I had experienced fear previously, in case fear arose again under the repeated circumstances. Very complicated!

That was certainly not a good attitude, and while I am sure that the doctor didn't intend me to react in this introspective manner, I was so keen to lose my fear that I would have tried anything in order to pinpoint its cause and therefore hasten my freedom.

As I didn't speak openly about these thoughts, fortunately it was primarily only myself, and occasionally my husband, who suffered the monotony of them. But I would always recall such ideas to the psychiatrist and we would try to relate all these instances to the rest of my life, or he would again raise the subject of my suppressed anger and I would go home more puzzled than ever.

Thus far, neither this expert nor I had been able to access the source of either my supposed anger *or* my ever-present anxiety by means of the usual psychoanalytic/therapeutic discussion. So it was recommended that I participate in a therapy session, accompanied by a sedating, truth-revealing cocktail — a mixture of Amytal and Ritalin administered intravenously. This was a dreary day-long experience in an old and gloomy hospital and no amazing 'truth' came forth. The occasion was made memorable for me only because after the session, I was left to sleep off the drug, waking a little later to find teeming rain hammering through the decrepit ceiling, practically drowning me there in my bed! Once again, my enjoyment of the ridiculous salvaged the moment.

If instead of such measures, a clear explanation had been proffered to help me understand that the symptoms I lived in fear of and the attack I dreaded were largely produced by my own tension — an automatic (though negative) defence — at least I may have begun to see the wood for the trees. But in constantly analysing my feelings and searching for their cause by fair means or foul, I was magnifying my fear and unintentionally keeping *tension* at peak level.

During this period of my life, I read many books on the subject of anxiety, looking for the solution. Most of the material available at that time did not seem to recognise my specific fear and the majority of works were technical and therefore of little support to me. I found clinical books lacked the comfort of intimacy, leaving me, the reader, feeling very much removed from the writer and more mortified and alone than ever. Many books and articles advocated the overcoming of fear by force (in other words, various forms of exposure to fear); these usually had the effect of increasing rather than decreasing my anxiety. Anyway, I had tried this formula already in the kindest way possible and to no avail. When one can be overwrought by the very thought of going out unaccompanied, reading material such as that is of little assistance. I also found little by way of lucid explanation of the condition and never a relatively basic solution to the problem.

Eventually I came across one book in which, although it was written primarily about more severe mental conditions, the author did touch on the initial symptoms of fear. From this book I finally learned that the attack which I spent my life trying to avoid was in fact *panic*. I also learned that the initial symptoms of that attack were caused by the rush of adrenaline which is the body's natural and automatic response to an emergency.

How strange that I had to find this information in this manner, and that no-one had been able to define this for me adequately before. That knowledge at least brought some explanation and a little less dread of the symptoms themselves. But I still didn't understand why I continued to experience the symptoms, and nor could I comprehend from the book how I could prevent them and be free from fear.

Around this time, a friend, in whom I had confided, told me she knew someone else with my fear, and that it was known as 'agoraphobia'. Now at last I could identify my difficulty! Yet, with this information and the continuing search through the past, there still seemed to be little hope of losing either the symptoms or the fear of them.

As a result of my new knowledge, I then forced myself to attend courses run by organisations specialising in human behaviour. These included behaviour therapy, discussion sessions and various relaxation techniques. Nothing changed, and getting out of the house to attend any of these options was, naturally, the ongoing problem.

The treatment had now gone into several years and I was still living in fear, experiencing the same feelings over and over again. The strain of keeping the appointments with the psychiatrist was as great as ever, and no escape was forthcoming. He had long established that my anxiety, although distressing to me because of the persistence of its symptoms, was, in itself, not of an extraordinarily high level. I suppose I should have been encouraged by such a fact, but this knowledge seemed to me only to increase the ridiculousness of the whole situation. All I wanted was to be able to walk out my front door and live freely and naturally without constantly experiencing enough rising panic to justify an approaching herd of wild elephants! How could those symptoms experienced in the local shops, or the thought of boarding a tram, be so dramatically linked to some unrecognised incident from my past? I began to wonder whether there was any point in continuing with this treatment. I had tried what seemed to be everything to overcome agoraphobia. There was apparently nothing beneficial left to try, and I had virtually accepted the problem, at great cost to my personal enjoyment of life.

At this time, the psychiatrist suggested I become part of one of his therapy groups. Again, willing to try anything, I made myself go — with my husband waiting for me in the car, of course, or a taxi there and back again.

The therapy groups were worse. I experienced all the symptoms of panic, all the apprehension of leaving the house to keep the appointments, plus the emotions of several other people as well. Their needs seemed so much more important and their problems much more dramatic than mine. Within that group were discussed issues that included dark depression, sexual deviance, attempted murder and suicide. Within this situation, my eyes were opened a little more to the challenges of the wider world. But my fear of leaving the safety of home paled into insignificance beside the traumatic events that had affected those people. I am sure most had no understanding of my difficulty. I remember those sessions as if one had suddenly landed as an intruder in another world; the atmosphere was filled with intensity and introspection, there was a distinct lack of humour or optimism and there was very little feeling of hope. I felt out of place in that environment and tense from fighting my own constant apprehension. So by the time the session began, I would be preoccupied with my own feelings and unable to contribute greatly to the group as a whole.

No-one in the group seemed to comprehend that I had trouble attending the sessions because of agoraphobia, and that just *being* there was a problem in itself. The final frustration in that phase of treatment came when one of the group members asked me quite aggressively: 'What are you doing here anyway?' I had on several occasions, so I believed, attempted to explain my own predicament. Yet still none of the participants there could see it as an obstacle for concern. I left in a flood of tears, privately vowing never to return.

I decided some time after my experience in group therapy that I had had enough of psychoanalysis, at least for the present.

I was, at this stage, about six months pregnant with our fourth child and could see no way to freedom from agoraphobia. I had lived the last few years accompanied by fear, so apparently I must continue that way.

To some extent analysis had been interesting, as it explored the regions of the past and tried to associate past with present-day life. However, I seemed to be going round and round in circles and making no progress to end the confusion. All in all, I was totally frustrated by this endless and seemingly pointless search that was absorbing much of my energy.

Out of five years of psychiatric assistance came very little, I think. The phobia had lessened only to the extent that my life appeared normal to the rest of the world. However, I'm sure that any improvement was due more to the passing of time and the fact that, although virtually housebound, I had always remained very much involved in life. The psychoanalytic model and the psychiatrist's model for psychotherapy was at no time able to reveal any unresolved issues or significant events, past or present, great enough to justify eight years of anxiety compelling enough to produce agoraphobia.

I made no further appointments with that psychiatrist, more or less accepting this as my lot in life. I believed I would just have to continue to live with it. I have the greatest respect for that doctor, and I appreciate the many hours he spent listening to me and offering reassurance. I do not intend my comments to display a lack of appreciation of his skills or assistance. But I know that psychoanalysis — and indeed, similar psychotherapeutic approaches — are not effective in overcoming this kind of fear. In fact, right then, I *almost* gave up hope of overcoming it at all. I almost accepted that I would live the rest of my life only able to move within that one-kilometre radius of my home, depending in all other instances upon my husband's presence. However, as my older children were approaching their teenage years, I wanted to be able to participate with them in life as a mother of teenage children.

Somewhere, deep inside me, was my faithful friend: perseverance. I knew there had to be an answer.

Ten

THE INTERVENTION OF DESTINY

Happy is the Man that findeth wisdom and the
Man that getteth understanding.

Proverbs

It is certain that the path upon which Destiny leads us is never clearly defined; it is also often bumpy and seems to be leading nowhere. Then suddenly and surprisingly we arrive at an intersection at which point we must make a choice, a choice which may put meaning into all that has gone before. There is indeed, a time for everything.

In those preceding eight years, I had sought the best of help and treatment that I knew to be available to overcome my fear. Now my fourth child was to be born and of course I was dreading leaving home, the stay in hospital and so on, but I had been through that before with my phobia and survived. Our first three children had been delivered very easily, but because of a complicated miscarriage between my third child and this pregnancy, I was apprehensive of the actual birth in a way that I had not experienced on those occasions.

As mentioned earlier, I had read many books dealing with anxiety. Out of all those books the one which impressed me most was *Relief Without Drugs*, the first of many self-help books published by Dr Ainslie Meares, an eminent Melbourne psychiatrist. Now virtually a classic, this book intimates with sincerity the author's profound and sensitive insight into human emotions, and the difficulties people can be confronted with due to the influence of anxiety and tension upon their lives. In this book the author teaches his unique style of 'meditation' — at that time described as 'mental relaxation', a positive and natural life-skill for the relief of pain and tension.

In my search for a particular kind of reassurance at that time, I re-read the section in *Relief Without Drugs* which deals with childbirth. I thought about Meares' ideas a great deal. What was said clearly in black and white somehow made more impression upon me then than did any former relaxation technique that I had been exposed to. I re-read his entire book.

When I had read that book previously in my search to over-come fear, I have to admit that I didn't accept his advice. I did not believe in relaxation of any kind — I had experimented already with a range of similar techniques and no improvement to my state of fear had come from these. And I was still so involved in trying to overcome fear by other means that Dr Meares' ideas seemed altogether too simple to be effective. Also, I felt that I was missing some vital point in his message, and therefore had no hope of achieving what he recommended, or changing in any way by attempting those recommendations.

At this stage, it was the birth of a baby, not so much the agoraphobia, that was foremost in my mind. I was prepared to try to do as described in that chapter to allay my apprehension of the delivery. I practised as described in the book and pictured myself in the situation, all the time telling myself to release tension. When the time for delivery came I very much had the idea of *physical* relaxation, and to my amazement and delight, the birth of our younger son was completely free of distress and without drugs of any kind. This was the first time in my life that I really appreciated what *relaxation* meant — and took it seriously.

The experience impressed me tremendously. If being aware of tension and knowing how to release it could remove the apprehension which contributed to pain in childbirth, then I felt there must be something more in this doctor's idea. I was still desperate to conquer agoraphobia, and yet I was also well aware of the fact that if I investigated his teaching further I could be about to embark upon one more lengthy project which would yet again amount to nothing. Having experienced success with physical relaxation, it seemed sensible at least to take this a step further. As I wanted to understand completely how *mental* relaxation was achieved, I decided to write to Dr Meares. I told him of my recent experience and asked if he could help me to overcome my fear of leaving the safety of home.

Dr Meares' reply invited me to attend one of the large group sessions he was holding at that time to instruct people in the experience of his teaching. I was pleased to receive this ready response, but of course I had all the usual trouble leaving the house, taking a taxi to the city and arranging for one to bring me home again — together with the immense apprehension and insecurity that was my constant companion when out of the house.

However, when I arrived at my destination, I was immediately relieved by the sense of ease — a quiet, almost sacred environment welcomed me, despite there being such a large number of people gathered together. I felt reasonably comfortable there. But I have to admit that my first attempt to experience mental relaxation was not very satisfactory. The fact that I was away from home and alone in new surroundings, together with the experience of something so different, created such concern within me that I found it quite difficult to close my eyes for more than a few moments at a time. I was far from relaxed, so I spent the time wishing the event would soon be over. The prospect of another such visit did not please me, but I felt I should persevere a little more as this appeared to be my last hope of freedom from fear.

I arranged to see Dr Meares privately, which gave me the opportunity to discuss with him personally the fear I had lived with for the past eight years. I needed this personal contact and his reassurance, for I still believed I was the sole possessor of such a ridiculous fear.

As already explained, the task of keeping appointments and waiting for extended periods of time is sheer torture to a person whose anxiety has reached phobic proportions. I remember noting with some relief that I was kept only a very few minutes in his reception area. I also noticed a rare tranquillity in the atmosphere; a pleasant efficient orderliness in mellow surroundings, and a vase of perfumed jasmine on his secretary's desk.

Dr Meares listened to my story. There was no lengthy discussion as to the cause of my constant fear. There was no mention of psychoanalysis or any wandering into the past. Dr Meares had, by this time, separated himself from mainstream psychiatry, working outside the conventional framework of medicine. Therefore he no longer recommended or prescribed medication. While he mentioned that the practice of his method of mental relaxation would replace all need for medication, he did not insist that I either take or not take tablets. There was no suggestion that I must make myself overcome fear or force myself in any way, and there was no dramatic diagnosis. Yet he obviously understood my difficulty and I sensed strongly that he knew exactly what I was experiencing.

In summary, he simply stated: 'You are rather tense.' And he promised me that if I accepted his idea, and learned and practised mental relaxation as he taught it, my anxiety and its accompanying tension would be greatly reduced, the persistent symptoms which caused me to be afraid would disappear, and I would be free of this affliction.

On that occasion I expressed some doubt, saying to Dr Meares: 'And if I should fail?' Having tried so many ways to overcome agoraphobia, this seemed too easy and I was still concerned that freedom would elude me yet. Firmly but gently, he replied — and these are his exact words: 'There is no question of failure. Trust me.' So it was arranged that I would return in two days' time for the first of a series of group sessions in mental relaxation.

When I was home again after that discussion, I wondered about where I had been, what I had learned. I had tried for so long and in so many ways to overcome fear — was this any different? What was this doctor offering to teach me that no-one else had suggested? *Release of tension — and the relief of anxiety through bringing the mind to a state of stillness . . . a kind of meditation.* And if I did learn this meditation, how could it help me overcome that persistent phobia? Surely it was too simple for all my years of misery? Scepticism tugged at me. Was this man genuine? Were his promises to be trusted? Was I being 'taken for a ride'? Was I going to be disappointed again? And yet his attitude was calm, strong and positive and one of absolute hope. I could have wished for nothing more.

It was a glorious spring day and I walked out into the sunshine musing upon these things and wondering whether or not I had made a wise decision by committing myself to this process. As I stood there, a certain fragrance came to me and simultaneously I noticed the swirl of pink and white jasmine on my own fence. And then I remembered Nessa's garden. The peace and serenity; those precious quiet moments where tranquillity could not be shaken. The security and reassurance of that haven without fear stirred in my memory and this was the inspiration I needed to pursue my goal.

Dr Meares' promise was precisely what happened.

Initially I attended meditation sessions with Dr Meares twice weekly for about four to six weeks. I was taught to sit in slight discomfort, and to experience *without trying to do so*, a complete physical relaxation leading to, more importantly, the experience of *stillness of mind*. The first few sessions were difficult. I had believed that I could not learn to relax. I had not seen any point in relaxation of any kind, nor could I accept that pausing to relax could benefit the task of living. This was a prejudice and a mistake.

Because of that prejudice, now I had to overcome a tendency to resist the idea of 'letting go'. I was being taught to 'go with' rather than fight against disturbing thoughts and feelings. To allow this approach to occur, it was necessary during my early sessions *consciously* to let go of physical tension. Dr Meares explained that the release of physical tension must come first; ease within the body would lead to ease within the mind. This too, was to be simple in its execution. There was none of the usual progressive muscle relaxation, just the simple awareness of the natural ability to relax.

He also indicated that release of tension is particularly important where the muscles of the face are concerned and especially the muscles of the forehead, as 'the smoothing out of the forehead has a stilling effect on the mind itself'. I could understand the significance of that and was soon surprised to discover just how many areas of my body were holding tension. Even more importantly, I began to recognise how greatly my whole being had been dominated by tension.

After a few sessions, it became easier for me to release physical tension but it was to be some time before I would experience similar release within my mind. At first I was trying to achieve this, trying too hard. I suppose I could say I over-applied myself in endeavouring to rest my mind. Utter simplicity was all that was required, without effort. But within myself I questioned myself; my thoughts and reactions as I sat there; the anxiety that welled up within me at intervals during the experience; the eerie absence of any kind of stimulus as my mind grew used to letting go. I wondered whether others found this experience the same as I did, and at times I became quite afraid. But I persevered. And over time I learned and accepted that, contrary to my former belief, there is nothing difficult about relaxation and that no harm can come from letting go of tension — in the body or in the mind. In fact, I began to acknowledge that mental rest was a natural and spontaneous function of the mind.

Dr Meares insisted that for complete effectiveness, as well as attending sessions with him, I had to practise this myself, setting aside time to deliberately re-create the experience at home a couple of times each day. Like anything that is worthwhile, the more we are prepared to put into it, the greater the result. I began to find the regular meditative experience a pleasant and rewarding addition to my daily routine. The effect of the frequent visits and my home practice was dramatic, to say the least. I was experiencing something that was most definitely new to my adult life: two hours each week of absolute stillness, as well as the times I took for daily practice. And gradually, and unbelievably, something was changing.

I began to see how ready I had always been to fight off my symptoms when they arose, becoming more and more tense in an effort to keep such mounting sensations at bay. I developed an increased awareness of unnecessary tension within me at any time, during any day. With this awareness I was able to consistently release that tension, thus gently breaking down the defences which I now began to identify as being no longer useful to me.

Supported by the repeated experience of stillness, I reminded myself to let tension go all the time: walking, talking, driving, leaving the house — even thinking about leaving the house! The symptoms of fear were becoming less intense and occurring less frequently.

Questioning myself again, I wondered whether these changes were occurring just because I was spending time in deliberate relaxation. For I was not doing anything else to subdue fear . . . the improvement was just happening, almost without any intervention. If that was the case, it had taken apparently very little by way of relaxation to reverse that fear of so many years. Why then, had the other forms of relaxation that I had attempted been ineffective?

I realised that I *was* experiencing the sense of stillness in the right way; and it *was* that experience of *stillness meditation* that was so effective, not merely the practice of physical relaxation. But while I was disputing the source of my success, the subtlety of *stillness* was being overlooked. So relaxation was the answer! But not just *any* attempt at relaxation, for I had not found relief by that means before. It was the acceptance of simplicity and the *meditative element* — the mental relaxation — that was the secret.

Time went by and more changes were noticeable, many of which were as subtle as the stillness itself. My first observation of these changes was quite special and here is an odd little anecdote.

Being animal lovers ourselves, our children grew up surrounded by pets. At the top of the list was the dog, in those years a standard poodle. He was a beautiful animal, chocolate brown with golden eyes. He had been part of the family for some years by then and, each morning after the older children had gone to school, Kimba would sit faithfully on the floor beside me as I read the morning paper.

On one particular morning, a few weeks after my commence-ment of meditation, we were sitting together as usual and Kimba snuggled closer to me and put his head on my lap. I remember looking down at him — and for the first time, I truly looked into his eyes. As if my own vision had been blind to his deeper existence, for the first time in years I *saw* the life within him. Tears sprang forth as in a surprising and curious way I was filled with a kind of compassion for all of life in this tender exchange of love between myself and our dog. This serendipitous moment seemed to confirm the beginning of my own transformation — as if until that instant I had been somehow lost to existence and had now been found again.

Following that experience other things came into sharper focus. It seemed that within this new capacity to be relaxed I was also experiencing a spontaneous kind of growing, coupling the ability to perceive my surroundings differently with a fresh appre-ciation of my own participation in life and a richer sense of existence. I noticed my thinking had become clearer and my concentration improved, while ideas, memories and insights blos-somed into my awareness, bringing an understanding that had until now been absent. As if in answer to a line from one of my favourite Sondheim songs today, it then became easier for me to become 'more adaptive'. It was easier to be more accommodating of change, or of events and situations, to be more open-minded and to be more optimistic.

Around this time I also became aware of the renewal of the gift of trust and I realised that trust was not something that had always been present to me. Doubt, somewhere so fittingly des-cribed as 'the tail of the snake', had slithered into my awareness, imposing its negative influence upon me. In this new turn of events, I had had to trust Dr Meares and his method — in fact he had asked for my trust. And, after consideration, I had given it. Now, within the experience of meditative stillness, I began to see that I had in recent years lost trust in myself. In learning now how to relax and let go into stillness, I was indirectly learning to relax into my own capability . . . to trust and let go a little in daily living. Rather like the person who must now abandon his crutches after relying upon them to walk, I was learning to abandon the doubts and crutches of my dependency.

Within the repetition of *stillness* my fatigue of many years vanished. For a long time all my energies had been drawn into coping with fear and managing my responsibilities as best I could. In place of exhaustion, I began to notice new energy. Young children keep their mothers very busy but the fatigue I felt was more than that of busyness. I was not really coping well with all I had to do. Now, with my energy restored, increased stamina and a zest for life, maintaining order was less of a chore. And there *was* more order in my life. I wasn't doing anything differently to create this — it just began to happen that I could achieve more in any day in a calm manner and with far less effort.

As I experienced and practised meditation *more* and questioned it *less*, I began to glimpse the right idea, and the experience itself became freer: the letting go of tension, the letting go of happenings around me, the pleasant feeling of deliberate effortless *being*, inwardly removed from distracting sounds, thoughts or memories. Soon, during meditation, I began to encounter a velvety stillness and an at-one-ness with my self and my surroundings, very calm, very natural, a feeling which transcended discomfort of any kind. And an inner 'knowing' of the essence of the stillness and strength of life — something that had not been part of my everyday expectation.

On one occasion during a meditation session at Dr Meares' rooms, I experienced feelings of panic arising. Having tasted sweet success and believing such feelings to have deserted me, this seemed like a setback and alarmed me. Dr Meares explained the incident as transient anxiety, a normal enough occurrence, which was of no consequence.

He reassured me by explaining that occasionally something like that might happen when learning meditation, because:

> We sit quietly and allow ourselves to let the tension go. As we let go, old defences alert our subconscious mind. This alert can trigger alarm bells, causing adrenaline to be released within the body, together with the physical response to a desire to 'fight or flee'.

And so we are jolted back to reality, disconcerted and puzzled that anxiety can occur when we are meant to be relaxed. In fact, this event was an indication of progress. After years of high tension, I was now capable of relaxation! Having thus survived panic within the meditation experience, I was then better equipped to go beyond it in my everyday life. Now a new, positive response was impressed upon my subconscious mind, further replacing the anxiety response.

More than the physical energy I had regained, I found I now began not only to 'know' but to *experience* the inner strength which Dr Meares promised; with that came increased emotional security. I began to feel renewed confidence in myself generally. Thereafter, steadily and surely my agoraphobia disappeared, along with all its negative complications. No longer did I feel afraid to do something or the need to fight whatever I had to do — I just calmly *did* it. I challenged myself to attempt things which would formerly have been impossible. But in doing those things I knew that I must not do them by force but 'with ease', so when faced with a shopping trip or a visit to school or a social event, I cultivated the habit of going forward easily.

Soon this habit began to replace my old ways, inviting even greater challenge. How far could I go in this manner? I was soon surprised and overjoyed to discover that I was able to drive my car to the city to attend the meditation sessions, park it some distance away and enjoy walking the rest of the way without apprehension.

So driving, even in heavy traffic, was no longer difficult. The red light was an opportunity for me to 'let go' rather than become tense against my former perception of this as an oppressive obstacle. Driving on a motorway now felt 'free' and expansive, where once I had felt controlled by such situations. I recall the first day I travelled freely to the city by public transport, triumphantly saying to Dr Meares upon my arrival: 'I feel that I've been dead for ages and am now reborn.'

It is important to reiterate that I had had my phobia for eight years. Suddenly, within less than eight weeks, with regular sessions with Ainslie Meares, the phobia had virtually left my life. Fear, and all its unpleasant symptoms — the nausea, giddiness, unreality, apprehension — had dramatically subsided and life was taking on a finer glow. For years I had been constantly afraid of panic. Now, panic attacks simply never occurred — nor have they recurred since.

And now, with reduced tension, the picture was clear to me. I came to understand the truth of agoraphobia, that this reaction is one of defence and a habit of avoidance, built upon the habit of being tense. Therefore I no longer felt so vulnerable and if occasionally little reminder symptoms dropped into my day, I was able to dispose of them calmly without further concern until eventually they simply never occurred. The vicious circle was broken — I had only now to replace old unwanted habits with my newfound attitude of ease.

More achievements followed. I remember my elation at shopping in supermarkets without fear. Instead of hastily collecting items forgotten from the weekly order, or sending the children, I now had the power to choose again. The shelves of garish products glittered seductively, now that I could calmly observe and buy. To think that one could know joy from buying the groceries! And yet the happy release from that constant apprehension was so great that on my first couple of visits to large stores I found myself having to suppress my desire to laugh aloud for joy.

With each triumph over fear, I gained extra confidence. Never again did I cancel arrangements because of fear. No longer did I need to keep my husband within constant view when we were out together. It was a great thrill to enter an auditorium and not feel anxious if the seats were in the middle of the row, or think about where the exit might be. Now that I could do it, I luxuriated in the idea of impulsively driving to another suburb to shop, or simply browse — an expression of ease in itself.

Evidenced by the decline of my bank balance, fitting rooms no longer held any dread; nor did department stores, queues or waiting rooms. Open areas such as tennis courts were no longer defeating — the pleasure of the game was more important; and the beach and the countryside were glorious places to be enjoyed once more. How unbelievable that so much of life could be spoiled through a habit developed from an incident which alerted fear within me.

I noticed too, that other little anxieties had disappeared. For example, throughout my life I had never been too keen on spiders. A spider in the room was quite disturbing for me and always meant finding someone to dispose of it. During my years of agoraphobia, a spider in the room would, to my anxious mind, assume gigantic proportions, comparable with one of the props from a Speilberg movie! As my overall tension level diminished, so did my image of spiders. If one appeared in my presence, now it was simply a spider and, if necessary, I could kindly dispose of it myself.

With new liberation the loneliness that I had felt within agoraphobia was now transformed to an appreciation of independence. Having learned to be still and to be alone with myself in this way, I became content with being alone in everyday life. Solitude became for me something to be treasured, where once to be alone would have caused me dread. From time to time I pondered the gift of solitude, aware that my endurance of agoraphobia and my overcoming of it was leading me beyond pain to greater growing discoveries and the assurance of my*self.*

Yet I also treasured the gift of company and the happy times spent together with family and friends. Without the burden of tension, my life was far more interesting, becoming busier and busier, and yet being so involved seemed quite easy.

The daily discipline of stillness and the order that flowed from that experience moved me towards other self-care routines. Regular exercise, especially a morning walk, became part of my day. It was easy to revise my diet, explore healthy alternatives and make recommended adjustments. I embraced the idea of journal writing and made time each morning for my thoughts to flow on the page. And I took up tennis again and later swimming, on a regular basis.

One of the most rewarding disciplines I then imposed upon myself was to go regularly to my husband's office. My involvement in even the most menial of tasks provided me with the opportunity to practise my newfound freedom in situations which had formerly generated fear. I practised the release of tension in long queues at the bank or visiting other establishments. I experienced the ridiculous joy of waiting my turn in a crowded post office!

Thus the anticipation of unpleasant symptoms lessened with every achievement. No longer did I find myself weighing the possibilities as to how I might fight my way through whatever situation I was facing — fear was fast becoming something of my past. Often the absence of fear caught me unawares and I would momentarily wonder whether I had left the house forgetting to bring with me something important. And the urge to look over my shoulder in search of my former unwelcome companion caused me some amusement from time to time.

Since energy and order now provided me with an increase in personal space, I soon yearned to pursue those other things which had been denied me for years. In the deepest part of my being, my soul, she who had been bruised and had 'slept' for a long time, gently woke and nudged me towards my need for spiritual nourishment. The time was right to satisfy some of my more personal, soul-satisfying needs. My first step in that direction led me on a special trip to a suburb some distance from home to find a particular shop which specialised in art materials; I had decided that creative expression would be a good start to fulfilling my wishes. I recall standing there in that shop, unfamiliar circumstances for me, and hardly daring to believe that it was me there, miles from home without fear. The feeling was euphoric.

But singing, my former passion, had been idle within me for too long. When the time was right, I tentatively sought a teacher. Although one-off trips to distant places were now readily carried out, I was not yet ready for a regular commitment to lessons too far from my general locality. I was fortunate to find a lady nearby, elderly, talented and somewhat eccentric, but with an exultant enthusiasm that welcomed me back to the world of music. I enjoyed about a year with her re-learning my skills sufficiently to move further afield after her health failed and she retired from teaching. Gradually I became accomplished again. And happily, my soul danced with delight, rejoicing while immersed once again in the mystery and grace of the perfected art of other musicians. I was re-building my life from the foundations to the top floor, the stable foundation being, of course, the meditative stillness from which I was increasingly gaining strength, confidence and joy.

In recalling these significant steps to freedom, I am glossing over the most important ones; the spontaneous car trips to take the children here or there; the hours spent driving and waiting at riding lessons, swimming lessons, dancing classes; the impulsive agreements to take an enthusiastic five-year-old to see fifty cartoons. Now I was able to participate fully in those many components of the modern mother's lifestyle where previously my participation had been truncated or carried out in the company of fear. As with so much in life, it was the little things that meant so much, now that they could be fully enjoyed.

So I progressed to freedom from agoraphobia — the fear of fear — even *forgetting* what it had felt like to live that way. Amazingly, all these changes commenced within a year or so of my first visit to Dr. Meares. After those first twice-weekly sessions, I attended weekly sessions with Dr Meares for some time, then every two weeks. Later I would visit monthly over some years, for maintenance and the reward of the deep meditation experienced in his presence. I had lived eight years in fear, at least five of which had been occupied in analysing myself to try to find the cause of that anxiety. Now I was free of this problem and the freedom had begun after only a matter of a few weeks.

I remember thanking Dr Meares for his help. His reply was: 'You really did it yourself, you know.' And he was right, for the fact remains that any achievement depends upon someone making a start. No matter who we are or whatever our ambition, unless we take the first step towards our goal, nothing will ever happen to alter or improve our position; and this is especially so where fear stands in our path. The whole process of dispelling fear is one of self-achievement. But one needs to be shown the way. As soon as I had the guidance, I could let go of the tension within me and replace it, with the strength of my own tranquillity.

Destiny had taken me by the hand and I was on the right path at last.

Eleven

REFLECTIONS, OBSERVATIONS AND GROWTH

This Quiet, all it hath a mind to do, doth.

Robert Browning

The click-click of my heels on the tiled floor was the only sound that echoed throughout the massive structure of grey stone. I had been walking to my car from a meditation session at Dr Meares' rooms and, moved by my having gained the wonder of tranquillity in an otherwise noisy and congested city, I impulsively detoured from the sunshine outside into the chill quiet of the cathedral. And here, in another setting of peace, I stopped to contemplate the disappearance of my past companion, fear, and to give thanks for the *ease of being* that had emerged from stillness, improving the quality of my life in a myriad of ways.

In musing over those earlier years, my thoughts drifted back to the first time I experienced panic and to all that had occurred in the months preceding it. A great deal of stress had come my way and I did cope with it, but I coped with it in a state of tension and therefore I did not cope well. It was little wonder, then, that my anxiety soared and that I experienced a memorable attack of panic — which scared the 'living daylights' out of me and led to agoraphobia.

The belief that we must fight stress is a common one. Obviously I had picked up this belief and at the onset of stress I certainly fought with all my might. New responsibilities, worries and concerns had entered my world, and one way or another had caused me restlessness and a sense of pressure. Rather than *listening* to those responses, I braced myself against them. I was very good at bracing myself. I had practised the response of bracing myself, steeling myself and fighting discomfort to the point that I had become a virtual master at it. I knew how to pretend to the world that all was well when in fact my inner self was hurting. How had this come about? Sitting that day in the stillness of the cathedral led me to wonder about my life's journey thus far. And so, with the practice of stillness ever supporting me — in fact, *guiding* me — I began a reflective search over my former years, exploring and defining those aspects of my life which had been obstacles in my path and may have contributed to my experience of agoraphobia. In this search I discovered the jewels of stillness, diamonds rough and smooth: the pain and the joy of getting to truly know myself.

My starting point lay within the element of tension itself. Former treatment offered for my phobia had been centred upon anxiety, taking the line of approach that my fear of leaving home was caused by significant issues from my early childhood — either a severe fright or an unresolved conflict. In reviewing this approach, none of these recollections means to imply criticism of the medical treatment I received at the onset of my phobia. For it is true that from alarming events and difficult conflicts much anxiety can be born. And, as I now began to see, like many others I was indeed carrying unresolved 'baggage'. The psychoanalytic form of treatment for anxiety can bring relevant past experiences to consciousness where they can be understood and dealt with and this can assist in alleviating emotional pain.

But at the time I was seeing the psychiatrist, my tension level was so high and my mask to the world (himself included) was so securely in place that it was impossible for deeper insight to open to me. Even *had* I gained that knowledge then, it would not have been the magical wand I needed to dispense with my phobia — of that I am certain. For the 'baggage' in itself was not so severe; it was my personal way of coping with the baggage, my fighting of it with tension, that was keeping me ensnared. Any former treatment I received had apparently not considered the governing influence of tension, the counterpart to anxiety.

Now, through stillness, I was able to see that agoraphobia was the way I had adopted to defend myself against something I feared. Stress had increased my anxiety (a response to a fear within myself, though as yet unidentified), producing the symptoms of which I was afraid, so to avoid these symptoms, and any danger those symptoms might bring, I fought with tension. I did not recognise that element of expression — for expression it is, since tension speaks its own language — until Dr Ainslie Meares spoke those words to me at my initial consultation with him: 'You are rather tense' . . .

I remember the instant he made that statement. Subdued by fear for the previous eight years, I had felt myself to be a lesser person, a weak person and a kind of failure in life. At Dr Meares' words, one part of me felt greatly relieved; for an excess of tension seemed much more acceptable than personal weakness as a reason for my phobia. But there was a flicker of doubt within the other part of me. It all seemed too simple. And yet, of course he was right. Through my newfound vision, it was obvious to me that my old automatic response to life — and thus agoraphobia — had come about in that way, tension in my body, but more importantly, tension within my mind. With agoraphobia now behind me, I began to explore my beginnings.

That little girl who had wandered joyfully in her next-door neighbour's garden was, I am certain, relatively tension free. There were protective rules and restraints upon my life, of course. But generally speaking, I was then a blithe spirit. Being the elder of two girls by almost four years, I had also the knowledge of a certain kind of freedom. No doubt the arrival of my sister interrupted this flow, but I have no memory of any animosity towards her. On the contrary, she was someone to share my life with. In those early years, we had no immediate cousins or young friends and neighbours, so we relied greatly upon each other for company and for intimate childish play. They were happy years. And yet at times life was unpredictable. For my mother was not a relaxed person.

As a child, I was sometimes troubled when my mother appeared to be 'harassed' (her word) — but I didn't realise then that she was *tense*. She was quite flamboyant and could be dramatic, speaking her worries aloud, usually about the fact that her blood pressure was too high. This concerned me and I somehow felt responsible for her well-being. But among her many gifts, my mother was fairly optimistic and had at her fingertips the ability to enjoy a sense of humour, fun and nonsense, accompanied by ready peals of laughter. So while on the one hand she demonstrated worry, on the other she brushed her worry aside and busied herself as usual. Never would the world at large have guessed her uneasy feelings. Now, in hindsight, I could see that she was quite tense, but concealed this under that mantle of busyness and good humour; only we at home sensed her intermittent dis-ease. In her capacity to cover her tracks, she taught me to do the same while raising certain queries in my child's mind. She also ignited that sense of doubt within my soul: was she really likely to become seriously ill? Was illness something that didn't occur so long as you laughed? How do you judge whether illness is serious or not?

The emotional lessons I learned from my father were of another stalwart kind. By nature he was more reserved than my mother, a very strong though sensitive and gentle man who pondered philosophical theories and read literature; a man who was internally frustrated by not having realised his vocational potential. His affliction of deafness, the onset of which occured in his twenties, I later recognised as immensely distressing and a powerful source of tension for him. Generally speaking, I think the suffering and the isolation of the deaf is not always comprehended by others as the onerous problem that it is. In particular — and this must have caused him great pain — spontaneous communication with his two little girls was practically impossible. The shared moment, the whispered word, the intimacy of family togetherness were largely lost between our father and us children. He withstood his loss in silence, bracing himself against the hurts in his world, and covertly teaching me to do the same. If some of my mother's characteristics contributed to a little insecurity within me, my father's presence compensated for that, and he betrayed no hint of his distress. But his tension was evidenced by the strain mirrored in his eyes.

Our maternal grandmother lived with us in my early years, an indomitable character who largely 'ruled the roost'. I don't believe she created problems for us children, but I do think her company contributed to tension between my parents and the wholeness of their relationship. Such issues were never openly discussed. Intuitively, though, I sensed their existence and knew that, at times, one had to tread carefully. These three figures were of course, the major influences in my early years. And then there was Nessa, whom I have earlier described. If I enjoyed many hours enchanted under the spell of her garden, she also enjoyed many hours enjoying the warm hospitality of our kitchen table. Together with my aunt who visited regularly, Nessa and other women friends of my mother's provided dominant adult company, a very secure daily life and an extended family experience which is not so commonly found today. Within this tender and pleasant environment, as recalled earlier in this book, fear could be easily forgotten. It was a deeply loving home, but with the truth of hindsight, the use of tension around me was, in subtle ways, established as a reality.

The practice of stillness, seedlike, produced memories of my starting school that were not so pleasant. Having had no experience in interacting with other children or the rough and tumble of the playground, Preparatory class and Grade 1 were something of a nightmare. I felt very lonely, different from the rest and quite shy. This was unusual for me, because at home I had the reputation of enjoying an audience as I 'held the floor' — singing songs and reciting nursery rhymes by heart from a very early age and receiving much attention for my efforts. Now, suddenly, at school such posturing was not permissible — nor, under the circumstances did I feel any inclination to perform in that way. My first lesson at school was an introduction to inhibition!

Here I believe, was where my own tension began to arise. As my parents did each in their way, I too began to pretend. It seemed important to *appear* to be learning easily, enjoying myself, making friends, feeling secure and comfortable; but I was definitely struggling and alerting my tension more and more to assist me in that struggle. My mother was generous in her attentiveness to this insecurity, but her presence, though comforting, also caused me great discomfort and metaphorically pulled me in two directions. This created another kind of tension — a conflict of interests: my need for security and my embarrassment at having that need satisfied. *The result of this was an intricate mix of confusion, embarrassment and shame very similar to the feelings that accompany and maintain the agoraphobic response.*

Unfortunately, teachers in those times were often intolerant of the whims of young children. I remembered only impatience or indifference from my teachers, never compassion. It seemed too that I could never please those teachers. In being 'good', I was often humiliated in the classroom by adults who ought to have known better. And then, if occasionally I ventured into the realm of naughtiness, I would be strongly reprimanded, punished and told that such behaviour was not like me at all. Confusion! I was a well-behaved child, but I wasn't a 'wimp' — and I wasn't stupid either. Although sensitive and often hurt by these adults, I could see right through them and their ways. But the young child cannot match the power of the adult; nor does the child have words to communicate such observations, and so in this it seemed I had to fight a lone and silent battle.

An inherent strength or stubbornness pushed me to prove myself beyond these no-win situations, tilting my tension level up a little more to do so. I pressed on with my school work and was successful. In the course of this success, I also cemented wonderful friendships with my peers and forgot the insecurity of my early days. But I know now that elevated tension was by then becoming a way of living for me and I had also learned some more negative beliefs: it was shameful to have personal needs; I must remain on guard; I was the sole defender of myself; and there were many people I could not trust — most obviously, those powerful adults outside the home.

Generally happy, but carrying these beliefs, I proceeded at school to the time for secondary education. This evolution coincided with a financial crisis for my father and to my dismay, my parents' concern for the future prevented me from making the transition to senior school with my peers. Concurrent with this, a particularly influential teacher had used her power to exclude me from sitting a scholarship examination which may well have changed the situation (and the course of my life).

Today, that turning point might categorise me as a victim of discrimination, but I lay no blame. People do the best they can with the abilities they have at the time and as it has all turned out, my life is better than I could ever have dreamed. This only proves to me that we all have a destiny to follow and that whatever occurs during one's life, occurs for good reason. As it happened, my story led me with only one companion from primary school, to enrolment elsewhere. Again, bravado rescued me — for I felt largely on my own again — but this time I was armed with new beliefs and of course, my established weapon of tension to deflect a smouldering anger at the injustice of this turn of events.

In spite of my initial disappointment, the schooldays that followed were very happy, productive and anxiety-free. But now, after the introduction of stillness into my life, a greater understanding of the pain surrounding that experience was revealed to me. I was able to see that this untimely separation — in my most formative years — from the achievements I had made at school and the secure relationships I had built there, hurt me intensely. Buried within the deepest part of myself, my psyche or soul, the idea grew that I was less worthy and less competent than the rest of my friends, to some extent a kind of failure. This idea fuelled the subtle shame I had already learned, and at that time I felt publicly humiliated and similarly judged by others.

Here was a critically negative experience to fight against, needing much more tension to drive me; I feel this was the point when I completely assimilated tension into my life, believing it to be normal and a useful way to live. Clearly, from early childhood through adolescence and beyond, stoic fighting from within was the attitude I had adopted to help me in my lone and silent journey through conflicts, questions, insecurities, doubts, injustices, losses, hurts and misgivings. And so I employed that same inclination to fight in an effort to preserve *the integrity of my own identity*. I was driven to prove myself a worthy person by concealing what I believed was shameful about me.

It is noteworthy that none of these difficulties in my life was unique to myself. The tapestry of most people's lives is woven from such matters, or worse. Certainly I was fortunate in that I had experienced no cruel assault or abuse from which to become anxious. However, these difficulties were influences in my young life to which I responded with aversion. And I had learned (as do many other people), to deal with difficulties in a way that was unhelpful and in a way that set me up for a later crisis. Also, I had accumulated more negative beliefs: that deep personal feelings were of no consequence, and that it was best to disregard my own needs and give attention to pleasing others.

As we live each day, our brain is constantly receiving information and responding accordingly at both a conscious and unconscious level. If our general level of tension has increased too much, the mind becomes over-stimulated, too alert. Then our anxiety also increases, bringing with it feelings of agitation, restlessness and an attitude of being keyed up, unable to relax.

This was certainly my developing reaction in the years that followed. With education completed, (tertiary at that time was not an option for me), my working life was happy, my family life was secure, I enjoyed happy, fun-filled friendships and a splendid social life, I was bright and cheerful and my creative interests were richly fulfilled. But inwardly, negativity simmered and tension kept me on guard, determined to prove my worth and ready to defend myself against potential humiliation of any kind.

And then the happiness of early married life was interrupted by the advent of my father's sudden death and a chain of further sad happenings. Under stress, physically and emotionally exhausted, and carrying many responsibilities at that time, my anxiety increased, sending me messages — or symptoms — of a need to care for myself. When I refused to listen to them, the symptoms culminated in panic, an attack which alarmed me greatly.

All people have the need to feel that their life is in control, otherwise feelings of insecurity arise. Within my reflections I came to realise that, over many years and with the use of tension, I had tried to keep a particular control over my life for the prime purpose of self-preservation. Within my own heart (or psyche or soul) I had formed certain positive and negative beliefs about myself.

In that appraisal of myself I had, in a way, split myself into two parts. One part I positively appreciated, valued and fought for. The other, the part I was ashamed of, was largely fashioned from my own vulnerability. When panic sought to overwhelm me, this seemed like the moment of truth. I viewed normal human vulnerability as unworthiness or personal weakness, representing failure which panic would fully expose. My negative beliefs told me that if this failure was exposed, I would be open to unfavourable judgment (and probably rejection) from other people. I *must* defend myself. And this meant *myself* in total. I must fight to preserve the part of me that I appreciated and wanted others to know — and I must also fight to prevent the other part from public exposure. The shame of some final reckoning and total humiliation, should that 'failed' part of me be fully exposed as the end result of a panic attack, loomed largely. Here then, was my conflict, the battle *within* myself that I had sought for in vain outside myself.

Blind to that truth all those years ago, with tension ever-ready, I had fought harder and harder, creating continuing symptoms from which I then craved refuge in avoidance as a means of self-defence. This was the agoraphobic reaction which plagued me, my defence against what I feared: panic. And although at that time I was only aware of my fear of panic itself, what panic really meant to me was the risk of loss of the wholesomeness of my identity — my integrity, my life, without shame. Such dread amounted to fear of the annihilation of myself in a manner worse than death. At least in death one is still identifiable — without shame.

In my defensive fighting, I had lost control of my life to the limiting life of fear. The true control of one's life does not happen this way. As I became more tranquil and my mind became clearer, I was able to see that there was no need to go to such lengths in self-preservation. In fact, I had been my own worst enemy. Now I was able to look back and know that I was probably not significantly judged by others. I expect I was quite well accepted and appreciated as a person, as much as any other. But carrying the belief that part of me was unworthy and trying desperately to prove this otherwise, I had developed a life attitude of inner defensiveness. And so I had lost true control until, from within stillness and learning to 'let go', clarity like a golden sword pierced the cloud of my anxiety. As I became at ease *within* myself, I became at ease *with* myself.

With new clarity of mind, I began to identify fear as poison to the soul. In fear I had disowned a part of my whole being and in so doing, I had judged myself very harshly. With this attitude and its accompanying tension, any of my personal limitations became, for me, unacceptable. I was unconsciously striving for perfection. But perfection is a pipedream; it does not belong to the reality in which we live. All human beings have their frailties, weaknesses, brokenness. These are part of our story and they represent our truth. It is only in acknowledging our limitations that we can fully accept ourselves as we are, and then set about the enduring task of changing and growing. I had to learn this.

For I had only been prepared to accept one part of myself, the part that (in my view) would show up all right under public scrutiny. By trying to keep control over hiding the rest of me, I was denying the truth of myself and therefore I was only half alive! Because, whenever the other unacceptable part looked like making an appearance, my anxiety would soar and I would run for cover. It was only when eventually I could embrace that 'other' part that my wholeness, despite the acknowledgment of limitation, manifested to me. This embrace was a transitional step on the way to my identification of a new aspect of that eternal quality, love. Where there is love fear simply cannot exist and so, through love drawn from the depth of stillness, I truly took control of my life.

In being so self-defensive, I had been rather hard on myself and later discovered that I had also been pretty hard on others. Serenity and a clearer mind then assisted me to begin to let go of old judgments. In doing so I began, tripping and stumbling even still today, the lifelong lesson of forgiveness, where the practice of love through greater tolerance, patience and compassion can lead to happiness and peace.

As I began to understand the source of my *real* fear (a fear *for* myself and therefore a fear within myself), I realised that in coming to this point I had travelled full circle — from the unsettling times in childhood where tension became my weapon, to the moment when that weapon failed me by leading me into panic. Yet still I had trusted it — after all, tension was as natural to me then as breathing. I had faithfully employed tension as my greatest defence. Yet now I saw that tension had been my greatest obstacle of all.

In more clearly recognising tension in my own life, I could now observe the powerful contrast between tension and tranquillity apparent in the behaviour of other people. Tension contributes to many discomforts, which we accommodate. At the very least, the prolonged clenching of our muscles in chronic tension will bring extremely painful results. Among other indications, physical tension can aggravate fatigue, cause us to feel dizzy and off balance, contribute to motion sickness. But tension also affects people at a mental level, increasing our irritability, damaging our productivity, depriving us of sound sleep and generally intensifying our anxiety level. I noted with interest the mannerisms of many as they 'let off steam' or covered their inner anxieties in various ways.

In spite of the discomfort it creates, tension, so I saw, was too readily accepted and, as I did, people were living with it, believing it to be normal and part of the pace of modern life. I learned that many who would never consider themselves anxious nevertheless had great difficulty enduring formal functions such as church services, meetings and theatres — the places where one is supposed to sit still and passively participate in whatever is going on. Such people apparently also felt overwhelmed by an acute desire to escape from these apparently restricting events in a similar manner to my own former anxieties. As increased ease came more naturally to me, it appeared that not only I but many had lost that natural gift, exhibiting instead edginess and wariness. Certainly it seemed that it was not difficult for people to maintain tension amid the noise, pace, expectation and challenges of daily life. Even joy could be seen to be expressed with tension, perhaps modelled inadvertently upon characters from some of the television sit-coms?

It seemed to me that tension was contagious. I had acquired the habit of tension from my own family and upon reflection, many of those with whom I worked or associated had also been quite tense. In the wider world, tension was now apparent to me in people's impatience and irritability, their overreaction to minor happenings, the whitened knuckles on the steering wheel, the aggressive or reckless driving witnessed on the road.

Tension, our major self-defence, apparently spoke of a very anxious world indeed, considering that wherever tension is present, so also must be fear. Tension apparently was communal and, as already observed earlier in Chapter 3, was an integral part of the anxiety we see today. Was it possible, then, that anxiety 'disorders' are so prevalent in our society today due to increased expectations and the broader scope of knowledge from which fears can arise and therefore generate tension? This possibility would not surprise.

But if tension was contagious, so also must be tranquillity. And so, as stillness gently moved me in a better direction, I came to learn that defending oneself, or fighting in this way, is hazardous. Ideally, acceptance and *management* of difficulties was the solution. If I had had the lifeskill of stillness years before, panic could never have occurred. If in those early weeks following that first panic attack I had been sent to Dr Meares for meditative stillness, I know I would never have endured those years with agoraphobia. I came to realise that agoraphobia is complicated by one's initial lack of understanding of the problem and the effect of various treatments which tend to prolong the state of fear. With fear intruding and with tension clouding any hope of objectivity, nothing is clear. Now I was able to stand back and see that agoraphobia is far more simple than people have been led to believe. It is the lack of understanding and the resulting lack of corrective action that allows agoraphobia to develop into an ongoing 'disorder', an insurmountable problem that seems to defy solution and cause a state of awe for patient and therapist alike.

In searching for ways to improve our health and well-being, magazines and newspapers present many ideas, though frequently with a focus upon 'illness' rather than 'wellness'. In improving my own anxiety and therefore my general health, I came to understand the importance of holistic health care, *especially* the need to care for our mind. We readily rest our body when we are physically tired, but our mind, which does most of the work, rarely gets a break. It is clear that just as eating provides energy for our body from the intake of food, sleeping revives us through rest and exercise increases our physical fitness, meditative practices can provide ease for our mind and spirit. And so, these days, the word 'relax' is heard more often. However, this can become merely a catch word. I now knew that real relaxation does not mean basking in the sunshine, playing sport or watching television. These are diversions and recreational activities which are also necessary. But experience had taught me that these alone will not bring calm to the troubled mind or reduce the level of tension and anxiety in the same way that meditative stillness will.

I find today that many people, like I once did, will say, when relaxation of any kind is suggested to them: 'I can't relax.' This tends to convince them of failure before they even try. A person may try once, and because he or she doesn't experience something new or discover an immediate solution to a problem, will give up, saying: 'It doesn't work.' But it *does* work! I have learned that every moment given to stillness is worthwhile. Like the squirrel that stores its food for the winter, we must be patient and store all those moments until one day the reward becomes obvious and we wonder how we ever lived without it.

People have asked me: 'What is so different about this way of meditation? We have tried this and that approach to meditation or relaxation and have not been helped significantly.' With most other methods of relaxation and meditation, some amount of mental effort is required: concentration, endurance, thought patterns, breathing or visualising techniques. What I learned from Dr Meares I now identify as *stillness meditation*; his approach involves only an experience of the stillness and calm of one's own being. During this experience, the mind is temporarily *free of anxiety*. Since anxiety (or fear) stimulates physical and mental tension and creates unpleasant symptoms, from the stillness experience within our deepest selves, gradually we learn a new, tranquil response.

It is from that experience of stillness that powerful change can occur, the healing, the ease and the growing, without our *trying* in any way at all. While we are concentrating, enduring, thinking and trying, even though in a relaxed manner, we will never experience *stillness* in the same way.

When the experience of stillness is repeated, little by little the 'over-alertness' described earlier relaxes, and a calm attitude of functioning flows on and into the rest of life. This effect, then, is cumulative, giving rise to a generalised tranquillity as opposed to generalised agitation — a complete reversal of the way by which anxiety and tension increase. In other words, through stillness, one's internal response to living shifts and changes for the better and from this one begins to understand life a little differently, as happened in my own case.

In encouraging others to find this ease within stillness, I recognise that people who are anxious may hesitate to attempt something which at first may seem new and even slightly mysterious. It may well be new but there is nothing mysterious about being still; it is a completely natural response. But until this response becomes familiar to us, stillness may seem to be a practice that is a little different from what we are used to. The fact that the practice of *stillness* is something different makes it something unusual; and there is always something to be gained from mystery. It was Einstein who wrote:

> The fairest thing we can experience is the mysterious. It is the fundamental emotion which stands at the cradle of true art and true science. He who knows it not and can no longer wonder, no longer feel amazement, is as good as dead, a snuffed-out candle.

So to try something different is to recognise that we have discovered something we hadn't owned before which may help us, along with other endeavours, to begin to unravel and understand the mystery of life itself.

People may object to relaxation or meditation, saying that it only brings temporary relief to stress and tension. This may be true of some techniques, which only bring about physical relaxation. Physical relaxation is only an *introduction* to a far deeper experience; for physical tension is only the visible weapon. Laying down of firearms is not sufficient to end a war! The practice of *stillness* is much more, and goes to the heart of the matter. While one searches in vain for the elusive panacea to bring peace, the simple and obvious have been missed: our personal ability to access the natural serenity within. And without fail, should we falter, the repeated experience of stillness will renew our sense of well-being every time.

People need to feel in control, because all people crave security. Whether we realise it or not, to some extent we all aim to keep ourselves safe, to maintain control over our self and our life, to 'save our own skin'. This is perfectly reasonable. And this craving involves much more than remaining safe from physical harm. Here is where hidden fears, from the smallest to the most powerful — and our means of defending ourself against these — come into being. Here also is where I personally had made another mistake. For eight years I had sought freedom from fear and a sense of security from a limited therapeutic position. To develop that sense of security, and therefore our self-composure, much more is required; we need to attend to the needs of body, mind *and* spirit.

The practice of stillness provided security for my physical body and within my mind and it led in time to that 'something' that had been noticeably missing: spiritual sanctuary. There are many ways to honour our spirit, some of which I had already commenced through art and music, the natural world and more. But I believe this chapter would be incomplete without my exploration of the element of faith with regard to the way we cope with stress or the anxieties we encounter.

The word 'faith' implies a belief in something while having no clear proof of its existence. The word faith, though it can be widely applied, is usually linked to a concept of the Divine. Some people whose faith in God is strong may place their problems in His hands, obtaining help, solace and meaning by doing so. Others may find comfort from a faith that has emerged from specific religious teaching or from developed concepts such as a Creative Source, Higher Power, Universal Energy. And others will find an equivalent faith and spiritual comfort by alternative means.

During my years of agoraphobia, my ability to access a satis-factory faith-consolation was erratic. Now something had changed and my understanding of faith began, with freshness, to stabilise and expand. I would not like to suggest that my own perception of faith must apply in the same way to others. But I do believe that it is important to address the needs of the spirit *in whichever way is appropriate to ourself.* In this part of the mystery of life, I feel it is necessary to be open-minded and listen to any possibility from which personal faith may grow or spiritual succour be obtained.

It seemed that in learning to 'let go' in stillness, and having begun to learn again the gift of trust, eventually I began to learn a new meaning of the word faith. Because of the practice of stillness in my life, in the first instance this lesson involved my trust and acceptance of simplicity and naturalness, where originally I was suspicious and leaned towards the need for substantiation through complex explanation or tactile matter.

Through this phase of personal growth, I learned how limited had been my former faith. I had always been a God-person, a believer, brought up in Catholicism. Following the teachings of my religion, in childhood I was devout, trusting implicity. In adolescence, life was too much fun and, though attentive to religious practice, I was somewhat distracted. As a young adult, though I still practised my religion, I practically forgot God, paying lip-service only to what I then considered to be my faith. Later, in fear I prayed, my pleadings scattered without substance like idle leaves in an autumn wind, hoping He would hear me and miraculously change everything for the better. Then much later, through stillness and therefore less desperate, in my thirst for meaning I was drawn to explore spirituality, life and death by way of valuable, diverse and comparative theories, religions and philosophies. These explorations opened my eyes a little more and I came to see that during my years of fear, real faith in a Divine Power had been effectively absent to me. Though I wanted God to fix the problem for me, I had, out of balance, put all my faith in something negative: the defensive use of tension.

As I more fully recognised the part I had played in my own suffering, I learned, with truer faith, that it was I (not God!) who was responsible for my situation. And the Christian message, the story which had been so much a part of my background, flew open with meaning.

Suffering had been what I had feared as I smothered a part of myself, my soul. And, like any polarity, suffering is part of a whole, its opposite I believe being love. Love is all-tolerant, forgiving, joyful and accepting — regardless. So suffering (which can always be linked to fear), when acknowledged, accepted and lived through, becomes love. As my life involuntarily changed through my faith in *stillness*, and I came to accept (and appreciate — or love) myself regardless, I also came to discover a renewed faith in my God and the greater satisfaction of my deeper spiritual longings. Faith of this kind, I think, brings a particular kind of security — where the Divine meets our innermost human needs, towering above the kind of faith that exists only in the presence of other people or material comforts. I began to see God, the Almighty, the Creator, the Giver and the Lover, anew. And so I began to see myself, my life and my role in life as part of that creation and gradually all of me, my pain and the peace that had now entered my life, began to feel far more integrated. New faith in my God grew stronger as new faith in myself grew stronger.

There is a link here, I think, to the practice of stillness itself. To experience a sense of integration I had had to accept the wholeness of myself, my lightness and darkness, strength and weakness, ease and difficulty. Within our humanity we have been given the means — body, mind and spirit — to overcome difficulties as they occur. In mastering these, the energy within us, particularly that of our mind, is challenged. This is our most creative force at work (or perhaps play!) moving us to desire something different, stirring our need to educate ourself to change, inspiring our determination to succeed and tasking us to take the necessary steps to do so. And within our mind we can also learn to accept, as with all contrasting matter, that beside the power of all that energy we also have the power to be still.

Meditation is one of the oldest and finest forms of prayer, yet in the main, the idea of meditation has been reserved for the cloisters, or we think it is only for Eastern mystics. Those who pray may do well to consider including times where the simple stillness of *being* occurs within the context of their meditations or formal prayer. It is good to combine all of these; and if we want our stillness to be a prayer, it is a prayer. Like Elijah of old, we can find God 'not in the earthquake or the wind or the lightning, but in a gentle whisper'.

Those who do not pray can be led towards stillness through other avenues. At times I wondered myself why I hadn't discovered stillness and my newfound peace in other places: in the quiet of a cathedral, or my garden, or on a secluded beach surrounded by the rhythm of life, or the wonder of rainforest or bushland where nature and our instinct for nurturing is very close. Of course it *is* there, in all those places, just as it was in the garden of my childhood. But we have to need it. We have to seek it. And we have to have guidance. Then we will know how to find that stillness and the inner peace that comes from it, freely available to us forever, in any situation.

In reflecting upon my story, I had to some extent re-travelled the journey. The road during those eight years had been rocky at times, but I had finally found freedom from domination by fear and thus my story of fear drew to a close. Looking back, at the time I very much resented my struggle with agoraphobia. Now I was able to appreciate it as a detour that happened for the best. The experience, for all its discomfort and for what appeared to be a waste of precious years, made me a stronger and wiser woman.

By overcoming this fear, I was not provided with lifelong immunity from stress, anxiety and tension. No-one can be so and remain alive! Living the journey taught me to value a balance of those elements as necessary motivators for all people, helping us strive towards fulfilment. However, I learned with great conviction that there is an easier way to do this.

Through *stillness meditation* I conquered fear. That was a triumph in itself, but it led to more. I had also gained a new way of living that brought personal transformation and enabled me to enjoy the fullness of existence far more deeply than I had ever thought possible. And the greatest and smoothest diamond of all, my self-containment.

Life itself is not necessarily difficult — it is what we make of it that matters.

Twelve

A BRIEF HISTORY AND OVERVIEW OF STILLNESS MEDITATION

Some run for shelter,
The tree holds firm
And sways with the storm,
The eagle is borne higher and higher.

Ainslie Meares

With the telling of this story, first published in 1983, Dr Ainslie Meares invited me to offer my services to others as an exponent and teacher of his concept of meditation. Three years later, unexpectedly, Dr Meares died; but not without leaving the legacy of his innovation — the natural management of stress and anxiety through his particular form of meditation. His was a pioneering concept which has contributed to a broader view of healing in Western society and of self-help by natural means.

Dr Meares' ideas, revolutionary in the Sixties and Seventies, alarmed many of his peers. His work was at times viewed with suspicion, sometimes with scorn, frequently with scepticism. In the days when *medication* ruled as the cure for all ills — and this had to be administered by the doctor — Ainslie Meares empowered people to help themselves through *meditation*. Those who accepted his teachings and were healed by them, rose to admire him, respecting his courage, respecting his wisdom. He wrote prolifically on the subject and his numerous papers and books were published and translated throughout the world. In the latter part of his life, his discoveries relating to the practice of intensive meditation and the remission of cancer largely paved the way for more liberal advances in health care adopted by progressive medical practitioners today.

Let me backtrack for a moment to consider where his new ideas began and to present an overview of this particular style of meditation. If I was searching for a solution to my phobia during the Sixties and Seventies, some twenty years earlier Dr Meares had begun his own search. Disillusioned with people's reliance upon sedatives and analgesics together with what he described as costly psychiatric treatment, Dr Meares sought a *natural, simple and effective way* to help his patients to find 'calm of mind and control of pain', a way of helping themselves towards a better quality of life. Dr Meares, already a distinguished psychiatrist, was also an expert in clinical hypnosis and one-time President of the International Society for Clinical and Experimental Hypnosis. In his new search, he travelled the world, seeking throughout 'twenty-one lands' an understanding of the skills and abilities used by people in Eastern cultures; yogis and mystics who, through control over their bodies, were reputed to be practically immune to pain. His fascinating experiences he later recorded in a small book *Strange Places, Simple Truths* (Souvenir Press, London: 1969).

Impressed after firsthand contact with Eastern mystics, Dr Meares was thus inspired to experiment with what he found — that the sensations of anxiety, tension and pain could be significantly reduced and personal ease maintained by consciously inducing a state of mental rest for a short period of time, once or twice each day. Coupled with his scientific background and his expertise in the use of hypnosis with his patients, he then adapted his principal findings to a simple method of self-help, requiring only a little patience and personal self-discipline. In his first book on this subject, *Relief Without Drugs*, he describes the technique he adapted from his discoveries as *relaxing mental exercises*. A later work from 1978, *The Wealth Within*, takes the reader a little further as his own ideas developed. In that work, Dr Meares coined the phrase *mental ataraxis*, meaning 'absence of disturbance in the mind', to distinguish his approach and describe what he shared with his patients.

In time, this exercise in mental rest became accepted as a form of *meditation.* His approach, nevertheless, was unique. Though influenced by Eastern ideas, Ainslie Meares' approach differs significantly from traditional or mystical systems of meditation. It does not involve philosophy or religious practice; nor is it intended in itself as a pathway to spiritual realisation or enlightenment. It is foremost a straightforward exercise in self-regulation to assist well-being by the reduction of tension, anxiety and pain. In its simplicity this exercise lends itself appropriately to modern Western society as a skill for self-help. It was to this refinement of Meares' ideas that I was introduced in 1974.

In his writing Dr Meares referred to his meditative style as 'the discipline of ease', a paradox in itself, illuminating in this instance the shades of effort and effortlessness required to make a whole experience. Like great or small, light or dark, black or white, good and bad — all matter and experience is of two opposites. In this case, the *effort* we require is that which disciplines us to take action to change, while the outcome of that effort is an experience of absolute *ease*, which will bring us relief. It's really that simple; we put something in and we receive something back. If we do this exercise each day, *spending a few minutes experiencing our own calm and stillness of being, in time the ease gained from the experience will flow naturally into daily life, bringing us the changes we seek.*

Ease is a normal human response — if apparently at times unattainable in our busy everyday life. And Dr Meares' form of meditation is typified as that — an effortless experience where the mind of the meditator is temporarily resting — in much the same natural manner that spontaneous reveries occur. The meditator learns to spend a short time each day *experiencing his or her own ease of being.* Here, he claimed, lay the healing and change necessary to relieve anxiety, tension and pain. In one paper published in the *Journal of the American Society of Psychosomatic Dentistry and Medicine* in 1978, Dr Meares distinguishes his form of meditation thus:

There is an absence of mental activity, an absence of sensory experience and an absence of emotion. It is a regression to a very simple mode of functioning. The consequence of this experience is an absence of anxiety, and what is more important, the subject remains with a low level of anxiety for some time after the meditation has ceased, so that there is an on-flow of a low level of anxiety into the patient's daily life.

It is said that when an idea occurs in one part of the world, through synchronism within the collective unconscious, ideas will spring up in other parts of the world by like-minded people. At the time Dr Meares was introducing his ideas to patients, others in other parts of the world were investigating similar approaches. Since then, much research has been carried out into the physical and psychological effects of meditative practice. This research includes the influences of ancient Eastern philosophies and Western spirituality throughout the ages, together with enquiries that extend as far as extrasensory perception, altered body states and the scientific observation of brain patterns. From this research, a new approach to medicine has evolved, described today as psychoneuroimmunology. This is the area of mind-body medicine where the mind and its related effect upon the function of the body are explored.

Today, further to Meares' ideas, numerous styles of relaxation and meditation are accepted in our society. Any and all of these can contribute great value to people's lives. Many of these meditative approaches, however, are related to culture, philosophy or religion and this background does not suit all people. Some techniques involve complicated rules or rituals which can be confusing or time consuming. Most involve some *mental effort*. Meditators are taught *the use of a mantra or to concentrate, visualise or breathe in a particular manner, to listen to music, to make their mind a blank, to focus upon prayer* and so on. For the purpose of *meditation per se*, such techniques can be necessary and important. However, to attain *mental rest*, according to Meares, it is contradictory to the experience of *ease* to involve any effort in the process. The compelling difference between his

innovative self-help skill for today's world and traditional meditation techniques, is *the simple regression to being still.*

In learning to *be still*, we may, of course, be led further to
follow other enriching meditations — as a different, separate
exercise; but I know, after twenty-five years' regular practice of
*being still, that to successfully reduce tension and anxiety, and
indeed as an adjunct to life enhancement, there is no need for
anything more.* And each week I see the effect of that stillness
benefiting those with whom I share it.

In those three intervening years between the commencement
of my consulting practice and Dr Meares' death, I was fortunate
to have many opportunities to discuss case studies with him. His
informal supervision of my work was enormously valuable to me
as I further absorbed his approach. In particular I paid attention
to his personal bearing as a demonstration of what he taught.
Though this too was occasionally misunderstood by others, his
demeanour totally exemplified what he wanted his patients to
learn. When I, in the midst of agoraphobia, first met Dr Meares,
my general response to life sprang from *agitation and fragility.*
My immediate impression of him and his *attitude* was one which
imparted a response to life based upon *calmness and strength.*
Obviously he practised what he preached.

From the first moment of our meeting, I knew there was something basic I had to change within myself. Dr Meares, as teacher,
exhibited his own ease to his patients, in his voice, movement
and general attitude. In this way, he taught what he wanted people
to learn in an immediate and subliminal fashion, demonstrating
his own ease and calmness of mind, sometimes before he even
knew their name. And so his patients were learning to assimilate
change even before commencing his meditation therapy. His
manner taught me the immense importance of *any*one's attitude
in life and even more importantly, the immense importance of
attitudinal example. We learn — and we teach — by example.

In this style of meditation there is no formal instruction. Once
again, the influence of example can be seen. The experience is
an *experience* and only that. But the experience is enhanced by

the environment and the presence of the teacher; so a prominent aspect of Meares' meditation is the communication of *ease* through touch. During the sessions Dr Meares conducted, his firm yet tranquil touch, especially on the shoulders, chest and forehead of the meditator, imparted an essential deepening of the meditation and the reassurance and support necessary for the letting go of tension.

Touch used in this way is a non-verbal message, more powerful than continued verbal instruction and devoid of any need for the meditator to keep his or her mind active by listening or concentrating. And, very helpfully, should the meditator become anxious while learning to let go, the presence of the teacher and his or her touch contributes immensely to restored confidence. But there is more than this. Since his use of verbal instruction was minimal, touch was Meares' most powerful form of communication, enabling the meditator to experience fully the state of mental stillness. His touch communicated and shared his own inner ease, a gift which when imparted to others powerfully deepened their meditation. Of course, in order to receive this gift, one had to trust.

It is important to explain that the essence of Meares' meditative approach is this: the experience is less about learning or being taught than it is about being assisted to *experience our own stillness*. So to benefit by this means we do not *try* or *strive* or *do* anything. We learn to allow ourselves to 'be' within an experience that transcends difficulty, discomfort, distraction or disturbance, sensing only the silence and stillness of our own inner tranquillity. It can be seen, then, that while one can benefit from the presence of a teacher, essentially the stillness comes from within ourselves. With this understanding, stillness may readily be achieved by following the idea and practising regularly at home.

Some people with faith only in fear express a fear of meditation, believing if they abandon themselves to meditative practice they risk the influence of evil or other negative preoccupations. Perhaps this could be a concern if one was meditating in association with cult-like involvement, or where other people can powerfully control or influence the meditator's mind. And, since

I am by nature a cautious person, had I glimpsed danger of any kind or found anything but peace, my involvement with *stillness meditation* would have ended before it had begun. But the simple experience of stillness bears no relationship to exotic practices. It only brings peace, and where there is peace there is safety. Even more importantly by way of definition, the experience of stillness could be likened to a daydream or reverie state which is a normal, natural and safe mental occurrence.

If in our normal waking state we occasionally drift into a daydream, we don't have to do anything to make that occur. Daydreams and their accompanying mental stillness just naturally happen, almost without our knowing and often we are jolted back to reality with a start. *Stillness meditation* is something like that — an experience of mental rest. Except that while daydreaming is a spontaneous, irrelevant happening, meditative stillness is a discipline, deserving of priority as a daily practice that will make life better.

When we avail ourselves of the experience of stillness as a regular discipline, first the body deeply relaxes, becoming heavy and still. Physical ease *always precedes* mental ease. The mind cannot come to a state of ease if the physical body remains tense. When the body is at ease, gradually our rational thought becomes suspended as our mind too, drifts at ease. Thoughts become disconnected and unimportant to us. In moments we may become aware of *un*awareness — and then of course we are aware again until that too, drifts away.

The general experience of stillness is not available to us until we leave it and return to our usual state of alertness. If we then pause to look back, we will recall quiescence and repose . . . just stillness . . . and from that, a sense of peace, inner strength, wholeness, capability and order will flow. We will feel refreshed and energised with new positive perceptions, rather than gloom or foreboding which may have been the case before our practice. In the wake of the experience, we feel a calm control over our life and little by little we become renewed. With such rewards there is little need to embellish its natural process.

Frequently, people examine the process too closely, as I did myself at first: *Am I doing it correctly? How do I regress more? Should I make my mind relax?* These enquiries are understandable, but they get in the way of the effect. I advise people to wait, to be a little patient and answers will involuntarily arrive — or no longer matter!

Another significant aspect of the experience of stillness is that it must be experienced in a physical posture of *minor discomfort*. Some systems of meditation or relaxation advocate a *comfortable* position for the body. Dr Meares emphasised the need for slight discomfort. By slight discomfort, he means being seated at ease in a symmetrical posture, where the spine is erect and the body is supported by the chair and the floor beneath one's feet. In other words, physically we maintain an upright posture, in repose and quite alert; but not cosy in an armchair, or slumped irregularly or lying on a bed. The purpose of the physical alertness reflects the discipline of ease and leads to a 'global' letting go: complete relaxation of the whole being-body, mind and spirit. It seems that *mental* ease cannot be attained *if physically, we are too comfortable.*

As we give in more and more to the meditative experience, without forcing ourselves in any way or trying to make it happen, the *mind learns* that it is safe and natural to be still. And as the mind becomes still, our physical sensations, discomforts, distractions and so on, gradually disappear. In the stillness, we are learning to go beyond pain, tension, anxiety and ill-feeling. Thus the stillness experience is somewhat like a rehearsal for our state of being in everyday life. If we are able to transcend discomfort or distraction while relaxing in stillness, then the onflow of that experience will enable us to transcend the discomforts which life may present to us.

It is important that we remember, after adopting *stillness meditation* into our lives, that life *will* present further discomforts. New challenges are always arising and in these we have a choice: to view them as challenges; or to view them as potentially stressful events. While the former view will always serve us better, either way, we need to be prepared. The lesson I think, is to know that we must always care for ourself. We, as individuals, are best able to do that; no-one else can do so as well as we can ourselves. So, when challenges or stressful situations occur, not only do we maintain our regular times of stillness, but we learn to recognise that sometimes we need to increase those practice times. When challenges push us to our limit, we must balance that pressure with longer periods of meditative stillness.

While agoraphobia was for me perhaps the greatest obstacle I have yet experienced, my life has still been endowed with many challenges. In seeking greater personal growth or in solving various problems that have come my way, I have explored my inner life and my past life, I have read widely and investigated many theories for well-being. I have attended conferences and seminars, listened to tapes and kept a journal. I have immersed myself in one of the loves of my life — music — and I have participated in role-play and visualisation. I have attended to my soul, developing my faith and my spiritual self. All these paths I have found immensely enriching in their own right. But I return again and again from visiting the complex to *simple stillness* to maintain my ease — and in fact, to more ably reap the rewards of any and all life experience. For no matter what we *do*, the doing will be greater enhanced when it is accompanied by the wonder and mystery of the power of *being*.

In the past sixteen years as a teacher of *stillness meditation*, I have been privileged to witness profound change in a great many people. Some of their stories you will read later in this book and you will see that these people too have found contentment through this simple meditative practice, as their symptoms have vanished. Among these have been many sufferers of agoraphobia, panic disorder and depression, and many others seeking help for general anxiety, improved health, spiritual development or a higher quality of life. I have learned much from my clients as they share their stories with me and I thank them all for their intimacy and their trust.

People tell me how their symptoms have left their lives, how their health has improved; that they now cope with life more effectively and achieve more with greater ease. They speak of better sleep, improved concentration and increased self-confidence. They share perceptual changes — how something is causing them worry and distress, but after stillness they can view the problem positively and with hope. They speak of their creativity flowing freely and the development of insight and intuition. They observe their life changing, renewing and improving in many, many ways. Perhaps my greatest joy in this work is to see people's fear subside, soothed away in stillness. It is vital now, to take you, the reader, on the *stillness meditation* journey, so that you too, may benefit. But before doing so, a final summary.

The Meares form of meditation is very easy. It is not constricted by detailed structure or by mental activity. It does not place undue emphasis upon esoteric or unconventional practices. It is not related to any religion, though the power of stillness resonates with spiritual development and leads to life enhancement. It is a completely safe practice, because stillness is a natural function of the mind. It is simplicity itself, and in fact the less this meditative practice is complicated by reading about it or questioning its detail, the more effective it will be. In desiring a life-skill for positive change, study of it alone is of little value. In the words of Dr Ainslie Meares, 'It is only the doing of it that counts.'

Thirteen

CAPTURING STILLNESS

In quietness and in confidence shall be your strength.

Isaiah 30:15

What I am about to describe is of a subjective nature. Therefore my description and the experience itself is open to many nuances and interpretations by the reader. In this chapter, I will take you through three varying descriptions of the approach to *stillness meditation* in the hope that from a choice of narrative you will more easily find an understanding of what you are about to learn. This is a guide to your own practice.

But before we commence, here are several observations surrounding the practice of meditation in general:

- Meditation is not merely a crutch, as is sometimes supposed, but a vehicle for strength and growth.
- The practice of meditation does not imply inactivity, 'opting out', or laziness. Rather, it is a personal investment, providing for richer and fuller lives.
- Meditation, while not a panacea for all illness, releases our restorative powers and regenerates our natural equilibrium or harmony of body, mind and spirit.
- During meditation certain changes take place within the body, among which the heart rate slows and blood pressure decreases. Breathing becomes almost imperceptible as the need for oxygen is less; cortisone production lessens with decreased anxiety, allowing the immune system to function more effectively.

- Meditation is more than relaxation, more than a technique for stress management.
- Meditation is the *antidote* to stress.
- Meditation provides the single most powerful means of achieving and maintaining a high standard of well-being.
- Meditation facilitates physical, emotional and spiritual well-being and contributes to personal growth and peace of mind.
- Meditation facilitates productivity through heightened energy and clarity of mind.
- Meditation provides health for the mind, as physical exercise provides health for the body.
- Meditation is a completely natural means of self-help.
- *Stillness meditation* is an experience of effortless being. Within stillness the mind experiences an absence of anxiety. This effect carries over into daily life. Therefore the repeated practice of *stillness meditation* brings general ease into life and an ongoing reduction of anxiety and tension.

In an earlier chapter, I discussed trust and how it is often missing in the life of the anxious person. In offering this guide to *stillness meditation*, I ask now for your trust. Please trust the concept of *stillness*, its simplicity and its power. Please begin to trust yourself, and me. This natural practice can change your life.

Here is my first approach to proceeding with your practice.

1. Physical posture

Adopting the correct physical posture is the first step and is necessary to the process of *stillness meditation*. It is not possible to relax the mind *if the body is too comfortable*. To find mental stillness, the body must be at ease, but mildly disciplined in *minor* discomfort.

To meditate effectively in this way, I find the most suitable posture is sitting erect in a straight-backed chair with the feet resting flat on the floor. The shape of the chair supports the weight of the body and allows one to give in with confidence to that support. Although sitting this way for a prolonged time may seem a little unusual at first, this symmetrical position is a natural posture and ensures the minimum of muscle strain. With practice, one can meditate very easily in this regular and balanced position for long periods. If the chair has armrests, you can rest on them, otherwise let your hands lie loosely in your lap. The head and neck are held erect — not tense, just evenly balanced. Let the shoulders drop and experience the weight of your body sinking into the chair, your feet on the floor, as you give in deeply. When seated correctly one is poised in calm control — relaxed yet disciplined, upright but at ease.

Any difficulty or discomfort in the body will pass with regular practice. The more we practise 'letting go' within the body, the more the mind learns to 'let go' in mental relaxation. Eventually, when the mind is still and the body is also free of discomfort, the varying discomforts of life will be transcended in a similar manner.

Try sitting like this now and experience the naturalness of it. Don't force it, just let it happen.

2. Physical letting go is the pathway to the meditative state

In your seated posture, the next step is to recognise any tension anywhere in the body. For the first few practices, begin from the feet and work up through the body, sensing the tension and letting it release. Please don't try or force, but simply sense the tension and let go, let go, let go, giving in all the while. Particular areas of tension are the stomach muscles, the shoulders, the neck, the mouth and the jaw — and especially the face, in particular the forehead. Recognise all the tension and let it go. Relaxation will occur for a time but will be patchy. Tension will return, but don't give up. Each time you practise, allow the tension, wherever it happens to be within your body, to ease away. Learn also to recognise physical tension at any time throughout the day — and let it go. After you have practised regularly in these ways for a while, you will realise that any need to physically let go of tension will be unnecessary; you will sit down to practise and physical ease will just naturally occur.

This 'letting go' should be quite effortless, without deliberate trying or striving, just letting it happen. If we try to *make* ourselves relax, the effort involved in doing so is counterproductive to what we seek.

3. Trains of thought

The mind takes longer to become *easy* than does the body. Newcomers to meditation often find it helpful to have a few words or phrases with which to get started. These are not rigid thought patterns on which to concentrate, but simply ideas or trains of thought that encourage people to give in and experience the effortlessness and ease of *being*. Such ideas are particularly helpful to highly anxious people who are afraid to relax deeply. These words or phrases within our own mind as we relax (or spoken by another by way of instruction) should continue only for a few minutes, since the whole idea of this form of meditation is never to concentrate, visualise or focus our attention upon anything. Remember, we aim to experience only *our own inner stillness*. As you practise, use words in your mind (self-talk) if you need to, just to commence and until the mind eventually loses interest in pursuing them. The inner words or thoughts used should be positive but without stimulus, encouraging your mind to be infused only with **a sense of your own ease**. For example, one might allow the following words to surround the experience: 'effortlessness', 'easy and natural', 'a good feeling', 'drifting deeply', 'letting go', 'more and more', 'really wonderful'.

In your posture, let your eyes close now; sense the release of physical tension and allow your mind to accept some of those trains of thought. Don't try in any way, just experience the ease of it all. Continue this for a minute or so — just taste the *being*.

4. Stillness of mind

Now, ever so gradually, those ideas will fade, become rhythmic, blurred to our conscious mind. Thoughts lose their logical or critical content and recede into an ebb and flow where they are barely distinguishable. Sometimes on the journey to stillness of mind, certain images, colour patterns or dream-like experiences may occur. These distractions are of no concern and will pass as we learn to let the mind relax more and more. Noises, discomfort and other distractions fade into the background to assume unimportance. The whole self is very still, and we remain in that meditative state, knowing only the ease of ourselves for as little or as long as we wish . . .

When ready, we simply slowly open our eyes, rest for a short while and then, refreshed, resume our day's work. And that's it: *stillness meditation*, the art of doing absolutely nothing — while remaining in calm and absolute control.

The four steps outlined above to help you proceed are really one effortless experience. The process of meditation is not a series of steps to be mastered, so don't become involved in trying to perfect your posture, physical relaxation, trains of thought and stillness as four separate exercises. Each factor is important, but *stillness meditation* is not divisible in this way. Remember that it is rather like a daydream state; simply give yourself wholly to it in favourable circumstances and in time, stillness will occur quite naturally.

Here is another way to approach practice. While *stillness meditation* is really the experience of *doing nothing*, we reach that experience of *be-ing* by accepting an element of *do-ing*, summarised in the following five steps:

Desire

Commitment

Environment

Posture

Practice

Desire

As we move towards participation in anything, the first requirement is *desire*. To *desire* is to wish for something. Within our heart we wish perhaps for *relaxation, peace of mind, improved health, freedom from fear or general well-being*. Or maybe for *a life focus, better relationships or spiritual growth*. Whatever our wish, it is prompted by a desire for something to *change*, for something to be *different*. Desire, then, is a motivating force — an action, the *do-ing* of something. It moves us closer to our goal. And so our *desire* for stillness is the first step in attaining this as part of our life experience.

There is a practical advantage in *desiring stillness meditation*. From a matter-of-fact position, this practice of stillness is surely the least complicated, the most portable and the most easily and naturally accomplished. We don't need to be in a particularly special place or wear special clothing. We don't need to have a tape player at hand. We don't have to remember individual words, nor do we have to spend energy in creating or maintaining visual images. We don't have to *depend* upon anything — once we have learned and integrated the exercise into our daily life, we don't even have to have a teacher.

And we don't have to bring anything to the experience of stillness — but our heartfelt desire for it — and *commitment*.

Commitment

Successful participation in anything requires *commitment*. Commitment to anything we pursue will *always bring positive results*.

When we commit ourselves to our *desire*, we access the tool that really inflames our enthusiasm and brings the reward of achievement. And while *stillness meditation* is not about *achieving* as in 'doing', nevertheless it is a life experience which will not occur without our commitment to its taking place. Commitment stands at the threshold of all hope, promise and purpose. Through commitment we state responsibility for ourself and our desire for change — from which will spring the satisfaction we long for.

Stillness meditation is a *beautiful experience*, therefore it is deserving of a beautiful *environment.*

Environment

Since beauty is always in the eye of the beholder, there is no universal environmental requirement for the meditative practice. We simply create the opportunity of a space in which to meditate that brings joy to our heart.

As beginners, we will most likely seek our stillness in a restful room, perhaps where the sun comes in through the glass on a winter's day. Or we may wish to meditate in an environment that accents our special treasures — family photographs, a classic sculpture, a sacred icon, books, a favourite armchair, seashells, flowers, crystals or candles — *our personal things of beauty.*

A beautiful environment may be a secluded place in the garden where the stillness is discovered amidst fresh air, a gentle breeze and our silent awareness of the movements, scents and sounds of nature. Or by water, the flow of which can enhance tranquillity.

For beginners, quietness is important to the meditative environment. So is soft light and freedom from the distraction of such things as the telephone or the fax machine. Later, when we have become more proficient meditators, it is possible to find stillness within the hustle and bustle of modern life — in fact, in any environment at all.

Posture

In the meanwhile, we learn correct meditative *posture.* The purpose of *stillness meditation* is to *relax the mind.* We can only experience that under the right circumstances. Therefore the *ease* of our body is a prelude to the *ease* of our mind and occurs as follows:

We sit symmetrically in an armchair, not *too* comfortably, just in minor discomfort as explained earlier and so that we remain poised and alert. In this posture we have a sense of *control* which, paradoxically (in a kind of effortless self-discipline of our entire being) leads to the giving in of total relaxation. Our body is erect, balanced. Our feet are flat on the floor, our arms resting in our lap, or on the arms of the chair. We are completely balanced, poised and at ease. Quiet effortlessly.

Practice

In this posture of ease, when we are ready, we *let* our eyes close. We make no effort. We *let* our eyes close, and, *giving in*, we let our *practice* take place. Remember, to practise stillness is to *just be* . . . We are not going to *make* ourself relax in any way. To try to do so would completely contradict the experience. For *stillness meditation* is an experience of *not trying*.

Poised and at ease, we hardly notice our physical body — but as a beginner, learning to practise this simple practice, it may be helpful to observe tension anywhere throughout our being, and *gently let it go*. To 'let go' may be challenging at first — especially if we are particularly tense. (Tension, of course, is an habitual and negative way of keeping control. In fact, tension, rather than availing us of control, propels us *out of control*.) So, to experience *ease*, we learn to let the tension go.

The face, in particular, is a reflection of our inner tension. In practice, we allow a smoothing out of the muscles of our face — noting the tongue, the jaw, around the eyes and especially our forehead, and we let it all go, *just being e a s y* . . . Poised and at ease, we sense the ease in our face, radiating throughout our head and flowing down and down to the very centre of our being. In *stillness* . . .

Our WHOLE being, easy and natural, gradually becomes a unified being of stillness. We sense it — and we give a little more, letting ourself BE more and more completely. There is no effort. No technique. No need to try in any way, or do anything. As we

sit in this way, we know only stillness. *And 'the mind learns'*
something new, different, calm and still. *And so we remain, for
a time embraced in a state of whole relaxation, body, mind and
spirit at peace, and at one.*

After a little time like this, when we are ready, we allow our eyes
to open gently as we return to the present. Then we rest quietly
before resuming our daily activities. A short transitional rest is
important. Remember physical changes will have occurred as our
body slowed down. The body now requires time to readjust.

Here is a third descriptive passage, taking you in another way,
into the *stillness* experience.

You sit in an upright position, disciplined but at ease, just
slightly uncomfortably.
Your feet are flat on the floor,
Your hands are resting loosely in your lap
You allow your eyes to close
You allow your shoulders to drop a little
You sense what it's like to let the tension go a little,
This is a taste of what is to come.

You may feel some resistance to letting go
You may feel slightly afraid.
Let go a little more
Observe your entire body.
Observe its resistance
Perhaps you notice yourself gripping inwardly,
or you may notice the gripping of tension in your shoulders,
throat, face or jaw.
Allow all this gripping to ease away, gently, little by little.
It will grip, you let go
It will grip again . . . you let go again.
Observe other parts of your body:
Where are you gripping?

Notice how the gripping occurs again and again, quite
habitually and spontaneously.
Remind yourself that this has been your 'normal' response to
life for some time.
Remind yourself that you can let this go,
It will take time and repetition —
But you *can* let go

Observe your face, especially your face,
The face expresses the tension within.
Observe your whole being and the way you return to old
habits . . .
holding on, steeling yourself, fighting something as yet
unidentified . . .
This response is within you, but it's not your natural response
— it's a defence you've learned.
What we now seek is *naturalness*
the way we once were, the way we really *are*,
In this moment, let go a little more throughout your whole
physical being.

If I were with you, I would be speaking gently,
And now I would let my hands rest on your shoulders,
Gently communicating the ease of your whole being.
Suppose you could sense my touch here and now and
experience this encouragement,
My touch is light, expressing everything I want to tell you:
that it's safe to let go; that you can do it; that, in letting go,
inner stillness will come to you and you will be restored to
peace and strength.

You sense that touch on your forehead, smoothing away the
stress of many days, months or years.
Let go into that touch and sense its message.
At this moment you are like a child who is distressed, now
being comforted and reassured,

It's safe to languish in this reassurance,
It's safe to let go.

You sense the touch fall gently away, taking with it all your
strain.
You are distantly aware of quiet words of reassurance
The words become more and more distant, less frequent,
until they too, disappear and there is stillness.
In the stillness you may feel afraid again,
Let the fear fall away;
Move beyond its illusion,
The reality is within you, your own strength, naturalness
and truth.

You stay a while in this stillness,
It's a good feeling.
You let go into it more and more and more completely,
You glimpse something wonderful, a temporary journey into
something new.
Your conscious mind may register this newness with alarm,
may try to warn you of risk or danger,
may pull you up with a start.

There is nothing to fear,
Just old habits, testing you,
You let go again and allow the stillness in once more.
Your body is at ease,
Your mind is at ease,
Beyond distraction or disturbance to the silence and stillness
of *being*.

Just being. Naturalness.
Effortlessness.
And you stay with this awhile,
Just letting . . . not trying, just letting yourself . . . simply be.

Yes, there may be thoughts,
There may be itches or distracting sounds from outside,
But you let yourself go beyond these.

And you sense the peace,
Trust yourself and allow it to come to you,

in stillness . . .

And, having remained in that safe place for a time, when you're ready, gently allow your eyes to open and rest quietly.

Now that you have these specific guidelines to practise with, there are probably some questions or other considerations to address. I believe the following will cover most of these.

What do I feel when meditating?

At a much later date and after regular daily practice has been established, a profound sense of ease and well-being is felt. During meditation, the mind will never be completely 'blank' for long periods of time — only for intermittent periods. Rather, the mind is quite alert — but very still. Physically one feels very little, apart from an inner knowledge of being untroubled, within an all-pervading comfort, certainty and the security of peace. It is not really possible to specify how one feels, since the meditation experience is unique to each. When your meditation session has ended, in retrospect you will know that stillness was captured and a state of rest was sustained.

Where and when should I meditate and for how long?

Once the practice is established, one may meditate at any time and in any place, at will. Most people meditate best in a familiar place and usually somewhere private. But to meditate out of doors is a beautiful thing to do. Experiment as the quality of your meditation improves. It is wise to set a pattern for practice from the start and it should, as a minimum, be practised for ten to twenty minutes twice a day. One can meditate for longer periods and can, if necessary, get by on a little less. It's a good idea to meditate first thing in the morning before the day is in full swing and again in the evening, preferably not too late at night.

Many business people and other professionals find that fifteen minutes' practice in the middle of their working day brings welcome and beneficial respite. So don't become tied to time. The most important thing is to meditate *some* time.

Some people are distracted during meditation by a concern that they will go on for too long and be late for work and so on. If this is a worry, use a timer for a while, but soon you will find the body-clock giving a satisfactory reminder that it is time to end the session. Above all, meditation should be treated as *the most important event of each day.*

How soon will I see results?

In my experience, you should see significant benefits within a couple of months of regular practice. The achievement of deep stillness takes time, so remain constant in your application of it. Likewise, full freedom from specific problems can take up to two years of regular sessions and practice. However! From the onset of your dedication to this meditative state, *changes will begin to take place.* So the sooner you commence, the sooner you will feel relief.

In the case of severe anxiety conditions such as agoraphobia, remember that these have become habitual responses which may have existed for a long time. Therefore there is much undoing and re-learning before confidence is fully restored. But as long as you are practising stillness, you will begin to feel better just the same.

For these conditions, I suggest practice sessions lasting one hour, several times a week, over and above regular practice times. The longer the session, the greater the quality and therapeutic value. When practised in this way, stillness is more powerful and the results will be hastened. Remember too, that as individuals we will respond to this individually. Eventually the results will be apparent. After all, what is a couple of years of gradual improvement compared with five, eight, twelve or more years of anxiety?

There is a parallel to the recommendation of increased practice time for higher anxiety levels within Dr Meares' work with cancer patients. When he observed that deep and prolonged stillness in meditation may have a positive influence in arresting the progress of certain life-threatening illnesses, he emphasised that people using meditation under those circumstances must devote much longer periods of time to its practice each day, at least in the critical stages of illness. It makes sense that the higher the anxiety, the more times of stillness will be needed until things improve.

What should I do to avoid interruptions to my practice?

The best way to ensure twenty minutes' peace is to warn those around you that this is your time and you do not wish to be disturbed. This is perfectly reasonable. Learn to ignore the telephone for that time and only cease your meditation if there is no alternative. It's a good idea to slot your practice time into your day where the likelihood of disturbance is minimal.

How can I overcome a tendency to fall asleep during meditation?

Some people tend to become drowsy during their session. This often occurs during an evening session after a day's activity and is generated by normal fatigue. Those who become drowsy, I find, are people who can *physically* relax very easily. While sleep is not the aim of the meditative experience, this state is not that of normal sleep and the meditator still gains, regardless. When I first began practising as a teacher, I held classes in a church hall. The only available chairs were quite hard and uncomfortable. Yet some people fell asleep! I discussed this with Dr Meares at the time, and he was impressed that these sleepy people were relaxing deeply enough to go beyond the discomfort of those chairs. The positive changes to their well-being soon proved that their drowsy state was not sleep, but very deep mental rest. In experiencing *stillness meditation,* ideally the mind is clear, calm and still. Once again, this will come with practice and the passing of time.

However, some people become annoyed by the drowsy state. The best way to prevent its occurrence is by increasing the discomfort a little more; increased alertness can be maintained by keeping the posture more erect, using an even harder chair or stool, keeping cooler or temporarily making the mental decision to aim to stay awake. Meditation is best practised early in the day, anyway, when one is fresh; so if you are simply too tired, abandon meditation at that time; go to bed and truly sleep instead.

What do you think of alternative or advanced postures?

I don't think they are particularly necessary. However, as you become more confident and proficient in meditation, you may experiment with a variety of postures. But it is unwise to flit from one to another too frequently at first. Lying flat on the floor can be useful if you are extremely tense, or if through illness you are unable to withstand sitting for any length of time. Lying flat is a very 'giving' posture, particularly with the palms of the hands open. But lying flat (even on a hard surface) can sometimes become too physically comfortable and therefore not conducive to relaxation of the mind in the meditative state.

Kneeling is challenging and takes practice — it is not for beginners. Sitting on the floor cross-legged suits some very well, and is a versatile posture for use in spontaneous situations, such as out of doors. One can also try using a high-backed armchair and rest the head on the back of the chair. This is an alternative that is good for beginners, but at times it can cause muscle strain or conversely can be too comfortable. As pointed out earlier, never hope to achieve mental rest while lying on a bed or curled up in a cosy armchair. True meditation cannot take place under those circumstances, because the physical comfort of such situations prevents mental relaxation.

Why is one session really deep and at other times nothing seems to happen at all?

Learning to meditate is like learning any new art or skill and one must expect fluctuations in progress. Yes, one session may be excellent and the next apparently not so good. That is normal and will eventually stabilise.

Perseverance is necessary

Some people can move into the meditative state quite readily and see results quickly. Our gifts differ, and what comes naturally to one may not do so for another. But all who persevere with meditation will benefit, of that there is little doubt.

As mentioned earlier, within a month or so of frequent meditation sessions with Dr Meares, I was aware of a significant improvement to my state of fear. But it still took me a good twelve months of regular sessions and regular practice to be really free of agoraphobia. For some it may take less time, for others much longer. As we are individuals, so we will individually progress — providing we persevere.

The less restriction the better

As beginners, the less restricted we are in any way the better we can relax. When you approach your meditation session, it's advisable to remove heavy glasses or jewellery and to loosen any tight clothing. Undo your belt and slip off your shoes. When learning this skill, the freer we are, the better. Later, when the meditative state is readily achieved, freedom from restricting garments is less important, providing, in fact, a discomfort to learn to relax beyond.

Stillness flowing into everyday life

I am sure you now understand that the objective of the practice of stillness is that of a better life. The exercise in itself is a special encounter, but it doesn't end there. The stillness then flows on into all we are and all we do. You can enhance this occurrence by bringing stillness and ease to your awareness from time to time throughout the day; by deliberately releasing tension whenever you feel it, and by carrying the tranquillity of the meditative state into your every response. In this way, we truly live with ease.

General considerations

As stated before, achieving a state of stillness will not usually occur readily at first. In fact, this may not happen for quite a long time. The exercise in itself is easy. But in my experience it can take up to two years of regular practice to reach deep and fulfilling *stillness meditation* — and then the rest of one's life to maintain it! But be consoled: as stated above, the power of the experience will have a positive effect on your life right from the time you begin.

At first, there will be many distractions in the form of aches and pains and a stiff neck, or back or muscles in general. There may be boredom, irritation or despair. Itches will become evident for no apparent reason and the desire to cough or to sneeze may tempt you. There will also be tension and there may even be mild panic or other unwelcome sensations. But please stay with it. Your body is learning something new; your *mind* is learning something new. It may take some weeks of regular practice before one can even feel relaxed in any way at all. So when you feel frustrated, don't be too concerned; the next day's practice will be different — and probably more successful.

Through daily meditation, in due course you will begin to feel at least physically relaxed and may start to enjoy the time. There may be small signs of general ease in daily activity, where before perhaps, life was almost always difficult. As physical relaxation develops, the mind begins to relax as well. At first, stillness of mind is elusive. Remember that in everyday life the mind is never still; even in sleep it is busy caring for your body and expressing your innermost self through dreams. So we cannot expect the mind to come to a state of ease immediately.

When meditation is first attempted, the mind produces lots of wonderful ideas to keep it occupied. Never before has thought been seen to be so active! Our worries surface; we remember what we should have remembered before; a song repeats and repeats itself like an old recording, stuck in the groove; the traffic in the street outside seems incredibly loud and we wish someone would do something about the racket those birds are making. People frequently become despondent, judging their progress harshly: 'My mind will never be still.'

Please be reassured. This is a gentle discipline, so we need to employ a little *practice, patience and perseverance.* In time, the activity of the mind *will* diminish. Intermittently, moments of calm will occur. At another time, or perhaps on another day, more calm descends and thoughts are less intrusive, until eventually in exquisite stillness, nothing disturbs us at all. And yet you will always be in control, because it is always possible to cease the session immediately, whenever you wish to.

Practice is for ever

It was my habit, long after I had overcome agoraphobia, to continue to attend sessions with Dr Meares occasionally, simply for the extra pleasure and benefit they afforded. *Stillness meditation* is a procedure to be first established and then well maintained. Where it is not possible to attend classes with a teacher or benefit from the help of another person, the practice of stillness must be regular to ensure ongoing benefits. It is unwise to find success by this means and then become so casual that old habits of tension arise and anxiety builds once more.

It is not uncommon for people to stop practising stillness once their symptoms disappear. People believe they no longer need it, as life becomes easier and more inviting. But predictably, problems will arise and without the benefit of ongoing stillness, symptoms of stress, tension and anxiety will manifest once more. Stillness in each day is a lifetime commitment for those who wish to live well; but a very pleasant one.

And finally . . .

Our practice of stillness provides a special opportunity, a time of quintessential rest for the whole being. Yet this is also a growing, living art and therefore each meditative experience is as unique as the meditator. It is a beautiful experience. Do it, and enjoy it. And within it will come a certain knowledge that all is well.

Fourteen

CONQUERING FEAR

The world is too much with us; late and soon,
Getting and spending, we lay waste our powers:
Little we see in Nature that is ours;
We have given our hearts away, a sordid boon!

Wordsworth

I have told my story and discussed at length the symptoms and the experience of living with agoraphobia. But agoraphobia is only one manifestation of anxiety and tension — albeit a severe one. At grass roots, any phobia, obsessional reaction or anxiety disorder originates in our personal level of anxiety and tension. Please understand that the practice of *stillness meditation* is effective for any anxiety condition — or destructive emotional obstacle. The integration of that practice can change your life, no matter what symptoms you may be experiencing.

In addressing the effectiveness of *stillness meditation* and in guiding you towards your own daily practice, I have given you what I regard as the golden key to the door of freedom from fear. I would now like to share some additional ideas and practical suggestions which may also be supportive to the reader in over-coming fear in general. For once the door has been unlocked, to discover what lies beyond the threshold one must take practical steps forward. But before we proceed, please remember that no matter how your anxiety manifests itself, it is unlikely to lessen or leave you until you have satisfactorily reduced your tension level and begun to respond to your life calmly as one does when practising stillness. You must attend to this first.

Having said that (and in various ways I will no doubt repeat it again and again), remember too, that there are differing degrees of the anxiety reaction — from minor inconveniences to full-blown phobias which leave many virtually helpless; and of course there are many stages in between. Although the general pattern of symptoms is always the same, people *cope* differently, according to their own temperament and life experience. So while in two individuals, anxiety may be equally severe, one may develop a restricting phobia and the other may have learned to live with anxiety in a completely different manner. Therefore whatever suggestions follow can be of help to anyone who is interested enough to explore these pages.

Only you can do it

If we wish to improve our life, only we ourselves can make that happen. We can learn from others and be assisted in our progress, but the first step to change and the will to succeed in what we desire is each person's responsibility. We must also have the ambition to become independent again. If you are too well supported, it is easy not to try. Anxiety 'disorders' are well recognised in the community today, and this relieves some of the embarrassment one may have associated with one's predicament. However, it would be inadvisable to adopt the attitude: 'Lots of people have this kind of fear, so I don't really have to change; and I'm used to it anyway.' This is definitely not aiming high enough. You are worth far more than that.

Blind acceptance is not of much help either. Acceptance of the problem for what it is will be the right attitude — but not without understanding — and never to the point of resignation, simply accommodating fear. And keep perseverance at a premium. Even the friend I described whose leg was broken did not feel safe without her crutches for some months after the plaster was removed. Many lives have been dominated by fear for much longer than a limb in plaster, so allow time for positive change to stabilise.

Discard the label

Acceptance of the existence of anxiety in life is realistic. But to accept a specific label for oneself according to that anxiety is practically to accept an indictment of personal limitation. Today, people are categorised as having anxiety disorder, social phobia, agoraphobia or obsessive compulsive disorder; such categorisation may be diagnostically useful to the clinician. But I find that these labels are rarely helpful to individuals. If you have been given such a label, heed it for purposes of understanding and then let it go, detach yourself from it. Labelling, to a sensitive, anxious person, fuels their susceptibility to negative suggestion and therefore increases their anxiety. You don't need to complicate your fear with other issues.

Incidentally, this subject matter points out the necessity for anxious people to take steps to positively develop their self-image rather than reinforce existing insecurities. Ignore the label and carry with you instead the affirming thought that you are a beautiful human being — who is sometimes insecure.

It is easier to overcome a problem when we understand it more fully

Most people who fall victim to fear do so because anxiety and their own natural defence against it has not been properly explained to them. I hope my story of agoraphobia has made this a little clearer. Lack of understanding or incorrect understanding increases people's vulnerability, hence they feel more readily threatened. The fearfilled person defends him/herself by increasing tension and avoiding whatever is feared. Avoidance becomes habitual and, just as in agoraphobia, the body becomes trained to react whenever a similar situation is presented. Each recurring occasion brings about more defence and therefore more tension; so the victim becomes trapped on that not-so-merry-go-round described throughout this book. In understanding this pattern you will be empowered calmly to take control of your situation.

Know and believe that you are not alone in fear

It is very natural for human beings to feel afraid. It is comforting to know that all people experience fear of some kind at some time in their lives. As you continue your journey, observe others in theirs, and with compassion observe their vulnerabilities; theirs will not necessarily be the same as yours, but they will exist just the same. Be encouraged by what you see and consider sharing your story with a trusted friend. The stories within this text are a demonstration of people's courage in their pain. You, too, have an abundance of courage with which to achieve a happier and easier life.

Know and believe that the symptoms you dread will not hurt you

Assuming that you have no illness to cause similar symptoms (and you will have been reassured of that by your doctor), accept those symptoms for what they are and you will dread them less. No matter how long those unpleasant feelings have peppered your life, or how greatly they alarm you, you have been deceived by a flimsy illusion: fear feeding on fear. That is all.

Tension is the reason for compelling fear

In seeking to conquer your fear you will have explored many different forms of treatment. I hope these have brought you comfort and help. But if fear is remaining as master of your life, you are still carrying a high level of tension in your body and in your mind. Watch yourself and you will certainly discover that your usual way of living involves holding yourself tightly, bracing yourself to face the day, fighting from within to maintain control. From having read this book, you should now know that the opposite reaction — the way of tranquillity — is the way to harmony, health and happiness. Here are two examples that substantiate my argument. The anxious person usually seeks relief from symptoms or panic in the following ways: *swallowing a tranquilliser or retreating from the situation.*

In the first instance, symptoms will be temporarily averted because of the lowering of tension due to the effect of the drug. But as soon as this effect has worn off, the cycle repeats itself and you are back to where you were. In this case, you either become dependent upon medication or continue to feel insecure — neither of which is a satisfactory solution. In the second example, the act of retreating from the situation to safety brings a flood of relief. It's not the fact that you have reached your car or arrived home that stops panic, but the letting go of tension that accompanies the relief you feel at reaching safety. Unfortunately, until tranquillity is personally integrated, this tension release will only be temporary. Therefore it is of paramount importance to become a naturally relaxed person. Then, and only then, will you become the master and fear the servant.

Learn to breathe correctly

Long before I experienced agoraphobia, I had learned diaphragmatic breathing as a student of singing. In the midst of my mounting tension and anxiety, somewhere, somehow, my breathing technique got lost. Re-learning this technique came readily to me once I regained my confidence, and it was some years before I realised that a vast majority of people have never been exposed to the concept of correct breath control. It is very important for *anyone* to breathe correctly and I particularly recommend this to anyone who is anxious.

One of the major reasons we first panic is the unfortunate experience of hyperventilation, which occurs from fast, shallow chest breathing. When you can manage your breath well, you reduce the possibility of panic while at the same time caring for the well-being of your body. Correct breathing is natural breathing. Find a baby, observe him or her breathing as they sleep and copy what they do. You too, breathed naturally at that age. If you can't change your breathing without more assistance, seek a reliable source from whom you can learn and integrate diaphragmatic breathing.

Move through panic, not away from it

A panic attack always follows the same pattern, featuring some or all of the following sensations: the stab of fear and pounding heart, giddiness or unsteadiness, sweating palms, nausea, breath-lessness, hyperventilation, visual disturbances, weakness or faint-ness, palpitations, 'pins and needles' or numbness in the extremities of the body, feelings of unreality, confusion, a sense of being overwhelmed by something unidentifiable and a general feeling of terror, with the urge to escape the situation.

Calmness and tranquillity prevent panic from occurring; there-fore the practice of stillness will provide you with the antidote to anxiety. It is not possible to be *anxious and calm at the same time.* However, should you feel this state of tension rising, you must let go into it and allow it to pass. Remember, fighting it or running from it in terror involves an increase in tension which will in turn increase anxiety, prolong the attack and eventuate in full-blown panic. Every time you take that action, you reinforce an existing habit. Every time you act in the opposite way you reinforce a new, tranquil response. This will enable you to truly face your fear.

Habits, when recognised, can successfully be overcome

To the phobic or obsessive person, this point may seem to be an impossibility. This is not necessarily so. At some stage of life, tension has been learned as a 'normal' coping mechanism and it has become an automatic response — a habit. Now you can make a decision to try another approach — relaxation — and make that a habit. Tension brings no happiness; the opposite can bring much happiness. Phobic or obsessive reactions are habits in themselves, where people automatically practise avoidance or compulsions to allay their anxiety. These are defence strategies, based upon past experience. The past is over; stay in the present. In this way, you can cease being burdened by two negative habits working against you.

The following example, familiar to the agoraphobic, will explain what I want to say. Occasionally, when all excuses have failed, the agoraphobic person may be in a situation where an engagement or appointment must be faced. He or she is absolutely cornered, and short of breaking a leg in the next fifteen minutes (a choice many might prefer!), will be on the way to the dreaded place. Once there, he or she will feel some relief and a release of tension, reassured that having got this far with no harm yet (although on the alert for it) he or she may survive the occasion.

As anticipation of the event is always more fearful than the event itself, the sufferer may even begin to relax a little more — but only temporarily. Ultimately, habitual tension will creep back and anxiety will rise, bringing with it potential discomfort, symptoms of panic. Note that when relaxed a little the fear temporarily abates until the familiar attitude of tension intervenes. What now has to be learned is the reverse, making *relaxation* the familiar (or normal) attitude. Very simply, the bad habit has to be broken.

Let go of habitual worry

Constant worry, another expression of anxiety, gets us nowhere. We all face from time to time matters that cause us concern. Regardless of the worry that may preoccupy us, problems resolve themselves eventually and usually our worrying had no influence upon that resolution. Worry complicates issues when our energies would be better spent in seeking positive proactive solutions and developing the power of optimism.

Like tension and other negative coping strategies, worry becomes habitual. Worry is a response learned from somewhere in life and the worrier, through his or her negative thinking, can then contaminate others. Among other things, people who are fearful are often also inclined to worry unnecessarily about the 'why' of their condition. Gaining self-awareness through an understanding of our beginnings and our life path is a valuable growth process; searching for the specific cause of one's anxiety can become a fruitless and introspective preoccupation which often increases anxiety further. If you faithfully address the matter of tension in your life, worries will diminish.

Laugh and have fun!

It has long been said that laughter is the best medicine. To live without laughter, nonsense and fun now and then is to take life far too seriously. I have a special friend with whom I share laughter and fun. I treasure her friendship and look forward immensely to the times when we get together. Her ability to find humour even within very testing situations, (and she has known many of these), is her special gift and perhaps her greatest strength.

Make sure you invite laughter into your life by seeking friends who can laugh and have fun, by watching films or reading books that make you smile, by looking for opportunities to see the bright side or the funny side of incidents within your day. And find occasions that call you and those around you to rejoice and celebrate. Bring fun into your life and fear will be replaced with elation as your spirit soars.

Waste no more time

Since the breaking of old habits largely constitutes the overcoming of your fear, do not delay any longer; begin now. Observe the tension in your physical being as you read this. You will notice it in many places — particularly in the muscles of the face, forehead and jaw. You do not need to be so tense. Practise letting it go. Let go like this continually as part of your life. It must become habitual to let go of tension, just as in the past it has become habitual to hold on to it. Constant awareness of this will assist you to break that vicious circle of which I keep reminding you. Practise letting go at home, in the car, as you're walking or working — anywhere. Release your tendency to brace yourself or fight from within; go with it all instead. When anxiety symptoms appear, go with them — and let them go. Do the same with thoughts that plague you; attend to them and they will hover, dismiss them and they won't recur. Here are a few examples to keep in mind.

A woman who has suffered from agoraphobia for some years told me that her main pastime is gardening. She loves her garden.

However, she prefers to work at the back of her home, as whenever she spends time in the front garden her neighbour stops to chat. I quote her: 'I feel so trapped. It's not so bad if I'm near the fence, because if those anxious feelings begin I can hold on the fence for support. But I dread having to talk to her without something to hold on to.'

In this story the woman is without fear until she feels trapped by her neighbour's presence. Her symptoms are telling her how little control she has in her relationship with her neighbour. However, that is not the point of this anecdote. She anticipates the scenario and is already prepared, tense. As her symptoms begin to rise, she is then afraid that she will panic and make a fool of herself — so she instinctively increases her tension to fight this possibility, making the likelihood of it happening far more probable. In trying to defend herself from embarrassment, this person has developed the constant *habit* of tension — and increasing tension. She must learn to go with, not against, the symptoms at (or before) their onset and then she will be free to enjoy the company of her neighbour without apprehension and fear.

From my own experience, I recollect a turmoil of anticipation of fear due to a particular dinner engagement. Some people who live with what is known as social phobia are daunted at the prospect of having to attend such functions. I was not afraid of attending the function itself, but I was always afraid that panic might occur in such a situation, and of what the end result would be. On that occasion when we were seated and as the hostess served me, I felt overcome by a sense of weakness and began to feel panicky. Because I had no wish to offend my hostess, I remember thinking as I picked up my cutlery: 'I must at least make a start.' This I did, eventually enjoying the entire evening. Had I known then what I learned later, I believe it was 'making a start' which relieved the tension.

If faced with that today, I would first physically relax, that is, let go of all apparent tension within my body. Then calmly make a start on whatever situation I was facing, and then, in the same calm and easy manner, go through with it. While all this positive action is taking place, tension is released and panic will not strike.

Someone else told me of an occasion when, after much worry and build-up of fear of leaving the house, she eventually drove to a meeting. By this time she was late and the meeting had already begun. The symptoms of fear rose up as she approached the door and the infamous invisible brick wall came up before her. All she could do was retreat to her car in panic and drive home again, thoroughly mortified. Had she been aware of her tension level and had the courage to let the tension go as she walked to that door, I doubt if the wall of fear would have occurred. She would instead have gone calmly through the door to the meeting, and her symptoms of fear would have abated and no longer troubled her.

The aim, as in each of these cases, is always to let go and move beyond the symptoms to achieve one's goal. This is the pattern which, when repeated and repeated, breaks the habit, breaks the vicious circle and gradually restores confidence. It is with this *life attitude* and by these means that all exaggerated and recurring symptoms of fear will be eliminated from your life. Keep experimenting. With anything that daunts you, let go. With every triumph over tension, no matter how small, your confidence will increase until suddenly you are fulfilling your life in ways you didn't dream possible.

A lesson

You have successfully reduced your anxiety and symptoms have left you. You are happily moving on with your life and bang! There it is again! Do not be surprised if occasionally symptoms seem to appear again. Remember, it is normal to experience anxiety, especially in times of stress. These symptoms are your way of expressing anxiety, therefore they are of value to you. Others may express their anxiety in physical illness and their illness will move them to take a holiday, get more rest, resign from their job, etc. Now is the time to ask yourself: what is the message that *my* expression of anxiety is giving me? Am I too tired? Is my relationship not compatible? Do I need a holiday? *Have I abandoned my practice of stillness?*

Any or all of these factors plus a thousand more can be reason for the temporary reappearance of symptoms. These are merely little echoes of an old melody, a part of your life that has made you who you are today. Please do not be alarmed. Should symptoms reappear, they do not mean that you are slipping back to where you were. You never *can* do that; you are a different person in a different place now, richer and wiser for it all — and you have the skills to prevent that happening. What you can learn from this, though, is that self-care is of vital importance for all your life, especially the care you give yourself in meditative rest. What you can also learn is that anxiety is a messenger, serving a purpose. Heed its message and know that anxiety can never hold you in awe again.

Ten positive ideas to read and re-read

1. Each day set aside time to practise *stillness meditation* as I have described. Do not try to fit it in to unsuitable times or rush the exercise. It is impossible to achieve any kind of ease if you know the vegetables are going to boil dry, or that you should have left for work five minutes ago. Remember, recognising physical tension and developing the habit of letting it go is the pathway to mental rest. And it is the regular and deliberate introduction of times of stillness that brings about a depth of inner calm to change your attitude to living.

2. Cultivate an attitude of ease in your everyday life. This will stem from the practice of *stillness meditation*, but in overcoming your fear you need to bear it in mind until it is the way you *live*.

3. Have the courage to say to yourself when you feel anxiety or panic symptoms arising: 'I am tense. If I let the tension go, the feeling will pass. If I hold on to the tension, the

feeling will increase and persist. The more I practise letting go, the less I will experience symptoms — and the less afraid I will be.' If you adopt this attitude, you can feel the tension and fear drain away.

4. Let go into your fear. To force and fight against it is to induce tension, and that is what you are trying to stop. No matter what situation you are facing, think: 'I will do this and I will do it calmly and easily, letting go of tension all the while.' There is a vast difference between forcing yourself to do something and simply doing something with a sense of ease. Keep in mind that you are easing your anxiety, not trying to control it.

5. Stay in the present moment! Every time you begin to recall former situations where you were afraid, let those memories go. People paralyse themselves even more into avoidance by recalling all the other times they have felt afraid or failed to accomplish something. Those memories keep fear alive and well. Keep your focus upon success *now*, challenging yourself gently to move on. With every success, no matter how small, there is a pleasant memory to dwell upon, making the next time easier still. And remember — others around you are scared too!

6. Keep going. Every time you rush home again in fear rather than relaxing, letting go and calmly making the distance, you feel you have failed again. A sense of failure destroys confidence; but with every triumph, confidence will grow. Believe me, no matter how apprehensive you may feel, never retreat — go forward easily and apprehension will pass like magic.

7. Learn to cultivate a positive attitude throughout your whole life. For happiness, positive thinking should be the automatic response. Negativity and the pessimism it produces are powerful, but, once a positive attitude becomes automatic, optimism will dominate. Take every opportunity to make the positive work for you. If confronted with a long queue, rather than considering its disadvantages,

remind yourself that this is an opportunity to relax and release tension. When stationary at a red traffic light, rather than continuing to grip the steering wheel, use the time to relax your whole body. When disappointment occurs, rather than viewing it as a catastrophe, look for the advantage it may bring in other ways. *Read books on positive attitudes!*

8. As soon as you feel remotely ready to meet a challenge, go for it! But approach it with that same attitude of calm and ease. Creative interests and absorbing hobbies, particularly when enjoyed among other people, are invaluable as distractions to place unreasonable anxiety where it belongs — in the background. You might have an ambition to begin a new career, or to commence a course of study you once dreamed of. Meet the challenge, and as you go from strength to strength, your life will become fuller and fear will be long forgotten.

9. Never give up; the worst is over. Even if you have lived with high anxiety for a long time and a future without it seems beyond contemplation, you will soon prove it otherwise.

10. Remember! It is the constant awareness of the tension within us that is the green light to freedom.

Fifteen

CONQUERING AGORAPHOBIA IN PARTICULAR

Keep off your thoughts from things that are past and done;
For thinking of the past wakes regret and pain.
Keep off your thoughts from thinking what will happen;
To think of the future fills one with dismay.

From a Chinese Poem: Po Chü-I, AD 826

Over the years, I have learned that the agoraphobic person has many questions he or she needs suitably answered. Most likely my own story has filled in many blanks and I will discuss in the following pages further symptoms. In seeking ways to help yourself, I will also offer some additional ideas for your consideration, addressing matters that may be contributing to your agoraphobia. But first, here are, in my opinion, the three major rules:

1. Take responsibility for changing your situation.
2. Learn and practise *stillness meditation.*
3. Face your fear through regular challenge.

Since these steps require substantial action on your part, the question may then be asked: 'If it is so necessary to make this much effort to overcome my fear, how can sitting still in meditation help me?'

Here is the contradiction, for once we accept that change is our own responsibility and begin to practise stillness, the calming occurs without our trying or making any effort at all and fear becomes easy to face. Metaphorically, as long as we chase the butterfly in the garden it will continue to elude us — but if we sit quietly and wait it is likely to land on our shoulder.

Of course, none of the following ideas will necessarily be appealing to or suitable for all people. Nor will they necessarily have an effect. However, they have contributed to my own success story and many others have found inspiration or motivation from them. You may find suggestions here which individually, or in combination, may be helpful at times when progress seems to halt or waver. In any case, these suggestions are all based upon positive action and practicality: it is always beneficial to do *something* towards change. Doing something — anything — will almost always dispel anxiety, whereas avoidance will reinforce it. For while the discovered 'ease of being' will open the door to freedom, we still must proceed to what lies beyond.

If you are severely handicapped by agoraphobia, you may not want to try these ideas at all. I know how great your fear and resistance can be. I understand how little confidence you possess and how greatly you rely upon others. But remember that no matter how severe your anxiety, or how many years you have been affected by this condition, you can still attempt to regain at least a partially 'normal' life. The process has to be gradual, because you are un-learning a learned reaction. Be positive and believe that you will succeed, for when we doubt, we falter. Progress may be very slow at first but that is the best way, slow and sure; for each person will overcome fear at his or her own pace and in his or her own time. *Most importantly, you must learn to become very relaxed.* Study the meditation instructions in Chapter 13 and put them into practice. They *will* reduce your anxiety. Then you will find each day easier to face.

I recall one woman in particular who had been housebound with her 'full-blown' phobia for some thirty or more years. She was very anxious, dependent upon a great deal of medication and very nervous about attempting meditative stillness. A relative accompanied her each time she attended, and after a number of sessions she relaxed a little. Soon she was coping far better than before. She even *looked* less afraid. She found she could remain at home alone and could now go to certain places and enjoy occasions, in the company of her relative, that she hadn't faced for a long time.

Before I proceed, I want to say again that *without being calm and easy in ourselves* no alternatives are likely to prove completely or permanently effective in banishing agoraphobia. That is my firm belief. The mental stillness experienced in meditation is the means by which ease is attained naturally, while reducing the level of tension and anxiety at the same time, and I quote from The Wealth Within by Dr Meares:

> In the case of a severe fever, we need rest. In the case of a fracture, it is a matter of immobilising the fragments of bone in their correct position. In the case of anxiety, it is a matter of allowing the mind to come to a state of quiet and stillness.

So meditation is a must, a calming and enriching way of life. Then, when we are calmer, we can make a start on other things, letting go of tension all the time and slowly confidence will be restored. In a manner similar to the development of physical fitness, the more we do the more we can do. We accumulate coping ability as we accumulate physical strength, extending ourselves more and more in a relaxed manner until the goal is achieved.

Firstly, here are some specific symptoms — aspects of anxiety that can accompany agoraphobia which may need to be reviewed at this point:

- The symptoms of anxiety usually prompt people to fear that there really is some 'other illness' causing them. Once you have sought adequate medical advice for reassurance, unless you are dissatisfied with the service you receive, don't run from doctor to doctor searching for new opinions.
- I have touched on the effect of obsessive thoughts or actions in the previous chapter. These are related to tension

and are a coping, or defence strategy. Thus these annoying symptoms can also become part of the agoraphobic person's life. Like anything related to tension, they will pass when you become wholly relaxed, but you can help them on their way by coming face to face with them. Take time regularly after each meditation session to contemplate why these obsessions are necessary. What purpose are they serving for you? Ask yourself what would be the worst thing that could happen should you dare to oppose your obsession. Question their presence in your life.

By doing this, you will come to understand when and why the obsession began, probably many years ago. From quiet contemplation you will more readily see that this response is no longer a necessity in your life. With the gaining of insight, try while very relaxed to face the obsession and break it. Even to attempt this will be a very small step at first. But with continued application, these symptoms can successfully be put behind you.

- Monday mornings often greet the agoraphobia sufferer with intense anxiety. Some people find that their fear diminishes noticeably when they are out of their routine and in the safe company of others at home. Weekends are wonderful! But when the coming week dawns, everyone else goes off for the day and the victim of agoraphobia is left to his or her own resources, feeling immensely troubled once more. Or the reverse can occur — routine suits some more than others, and at weekends these individuals fall apart. These reactions will vanish once *stillness meditation* takes over from anxiety.

- Depression is another common accompaniment to agoraphobia — and understandably, too. If the depression is severe, you need medical help and possibly medication for a time. But like other symptoms, it too will pass as stillness reduces the overall anxiety level. In some instances, as recovery occurs agoraphobia will pass but depression will replace it. This seems to indicate that a significant emotional issue is emerging and often expert counselling or therapy is needed — in tandem with meditative practice — to seek and resolve the problem.

- Lack of concentration is a frequent symptom of high anxiety and is commonly present with agoraphobia. Occasionally there is also a fear or resistance to reading books concerning the symptoms discussed here. These tendencies make it difficult to absorb helpful material — but they won't stop you meditating!

- I have discussed susceptibility to negative suggestion briefly among the suggestions section of the previous chapter. Further to that, it is imperative that agoraphobia sufferers watch your 'self-talk' for habitual negative suggestions. A collection of positive statements should be amassed to counteract negative self-talk. They must, however, always be statements of one's own. In other words, they must reflect your own want or need, and not simply be the repetition of an idea produced by someone else. Spend time when very relaxed quietly discovering what you need to do to counteract negativity in your life. In doing this, you will come to know yourself much better, and find eventually that for the most part you are producing your own pain.

- When people are extremely tense and anxious they are usually highly sensitive to noise, light, congested department stores or traffic. They are also highly sensitive to physical reactions (especially when related to the heartbeat), to temperature and to the reactions of other people. The anxious, potentially agoraphobic, person will jump at the clink of a spoon. Domestic machines will seem to vibrate beyond tolerance. With this level of tension dominating life, people feel the heating system is set too high, or they will ask themselves: 'Why is she looking at me like that?'

Among other symptoms, at this level of tension people can also experience severe headaches, difficulty in swallowing, breathing problems and the fear of choking. Insomnia, fatigue, doubts as to one's sanity and an inability to cope with life can also be present. Like the others, these symptoms will disappear when anxiety and tension are reduced.

In the last chapter, we looked at ways to overcome fear in general. All those suggestions apply to agoraphobia. These additional considerations presented now will expand upon what has already been said and perhaps be helpful to your general well-being.

Medication

If *medication* has been prescribed, it is wise to take it as directed until *meditation* begins to take effect and the need for a tranquilliser is no longer apparent. It is not sensible to remain dependent upon drugs indefinitely. When taken this way, these chemicals can produce symptoms like those of anxiety, and of course drug dependence can lead to the possibility of addiction and its unrelenting consequences. However, neither is it sensible to disregard the advice of your doctor. And in times of great stress it is quite appropriate to make use of medication — but only now and then and in the short term. For medication is never a cure, only a crutch; the problem with a crutch is that the more one uses it, the more one needs it. The wise person will aim higher than that.

One must also remember that because anxiety and tension are in themselves a natural response, they will, unless otherwise reduced, always override the medication; this means that the amount of medication taken is continually being increased to counteract symptoms — another good argument for the natural reduction of anxiety and tension. If you have relied upon medication for some time and you wish to discontinue it, do not attempt to reduce it without medical supervision or without the support of organisations dealing specifically with this process.

'Recreational' drugs

In the same way that prescribed medication can create anxiety symptoms, many people have developed agoraphobia following an experience of panic while smoking marijuana or using other powerful drugs. Be warned and avoid this destructive influence on your body *and* your mind.

Diet

Diet is important to everyone. Excesses of caffeine, alcohol or cigarettes are understood to increase anxiety. Too much sugar or junk food is known to be detrimental to good health. All the literature on health today emphasises the need for the right foods and the right vitamin supplements and so on.

Many health professionals today agree that certain foods can cause a sensitivity reaction in some people. Such a reaction is a form of stress in itself and *may* aggravate the anxiety condition. Whenever the body experiences stress of any kind, there is an instinctive fighting response which manifests in tension. This can be experienced by some in generalised feelings of physical tension, or as a more direct physical response such as an awareness of the heartbeat, shortness of breath and an overall sensation of being 'hyped up'.

Symptoms such as persistently recurring headaches, digestive disturbances, insomnia and many more have been documented by complementary health practitioners today. These are relatively new ideas and many orthodox medical doctors are inclined to discount them. But in looking at the problems of stress, anxiety, tension, panic and agoraphobia, we are looking at individuals who have reached their current position through accumulated stress and tension over a long period of time. Therefore it is important, in decreasing this accumulation of stress, to consider the multi-factorial aspects of the problem and reduce as many stress factors as possible by appropriate means to bring full recovery. In this respect, it may be necessary for some people to be tested for food sensitivities and, as a consequence of the result, to change their diet accordingly.

This is not to say that food sensitivity or intolerance alone causes panic or agoraphobia. Nor will diet alone affect the general anxiety and tension level. However, if there is a food problem which a change of diet can eliminate, then there is one less form of stress for the body to deal with, one less potential source of tension, one less set of symptoms to fuel anxiety and therefore, one less negative factor to contribute to the whole anxiety pattern. Seek advice from your family doctor, a dietitian or from a natural health practitioner.

Hormonal activity

Women, who are said to be the major sufferers of agoraphobia, often identify greater restriction by way of anxiety in the days preceding menstruation. Hormonal changes and premenstrual tension are widely recognised today as a form of stress for the body to contend with. It is understandable, therefore, that tension and anxiety will be higher at these times. PMT, together with the influence of fatigue, from time to time can be contributing factors to the agoraphobic condition. It is wise at such times to take extra care of your body.

The benefits of physical exercise

Physical exercise is an excellent way to dissipate tension and anxiety, and of course is beneficial in other ways. Seek exercise that suits you and determine to pursue it. Don't fall into the trap of allowing agoraphobia to prevent you from doing this. If you are really determined, you will find the ability to 'get there' — talk your support person into joining you in this! Walking is the easiest, least expensive and most natural of all. Take courage, start with small distances and build upon this gradually. Swimming is excellent. Yoga is ideal, where you can also learn to breathe correctly and complement the use of *stillness meditation.* Massage, though not a form of exercise, is a luxury which can ease tense muscles. And if all else fails try running on the spot!

Together with the fear of being away from home, some agora-phobia sufferers fear physical damage through exertion. Actually, your awareness of your heart and other physical discomforts are more likely to be your body protesting from *lack* of exertion. Seek your doctor's advice and with his or her blessing — though it may take time to build up fitness — do make a start on this. The practice of stillness after exercising is a lovely thing to do and as your body gains stamina, so will your mind gain ease.

Developing your spirituality

For fullness of life, it is important for all people to develop their spiritual self. Spirituality means different things to different people. Those with faith in God will relate their lives to His power, love and mercy. Others will find consolation in the natural world. Take time to reflect upon your commitment to spiritual growth and to sense where your needs and beliefs are centred. If religious practice is part of your life, draw deeply upon its gifts. Read and search widely all great spiritual, mystical, philosophical and literary writings for inspiration and action. In seeking meaning, understanding, self-control, greater tolerance and compassion, the inspiration you may have overlooked in your own scripture may be discovered elsewhere and so your faith will be strengthened and your life enriched. Psalm 46:9, 'Be still and know that I am God', is comforting. Likewise: 'I will always be with you; *I will never* abandon you. Be determined and confident' (Joshua 1:5-6).

From among the sayings of the Buddha, here is something to consider:

> Why do I remain thus in constant fear and apprehension? Let me bend down to my will that panic, fear and horror, just as I am, and just as it has come to be. So as I was walking to and fro that panic, fear and horror came upon me. Then I neither stood still nor sat nor lay down, but just walking up and down I bent to my will that panic, fear and horror.

These extracts may help to draw you closer to the comforting and consoling words to be discovered from many sources of wisdom and peace.

Join a support group

Support groups can be helpful. If possible, be part of one. Humorists joke about support groups for agoraphobics, because for obvious reasons there is rarely anyone in attendance! But rest assured that when you are there you are with others with the same fear. This increases confidence and builds courage. Even the fact that you can *sometimes* attend support group gatherings will aid your freedom from fear.

Sharing the problem in these groups and the strength gained from knowing one is not alone in fear mean that support groups for agoraphobia sufferers are valuable. Loneliness is lessened, people become open and wholehearted and bonds of friendship and contact are formed. Whether agoraphobia improves as a direct result of support group contact alone is doubtful, but at least it is a little easier to bear. And the elusive element of 'togetherness' in such groups can also provide some compensation for much of the closeness lost through dependence and isolation. However, support groups should aim to be constructive, not just another means of dwelling upon the problem.

In recent years, agoraphobia clinics have become established in most cities. These can prove beneficial, particularly from the point of view of reassurance, taking positive action about the problem and providing ongoing support.

Sharing your fear

Much earlier I discussed the advantages (or disadvantages) of sharing your fear with friends. As you gain confidence by sharing your difficulty in a group, you may feel ready to seek encouragement from others. Anyone you trust can be your source of encouragement; but someone who inspires you will have a greater effect. Discuss your difficulty with a trusted friend or professional counsellor. Surprisingly, wisdom can often be found right at hand, not necessarily from professionals but often from those with a wealth of life experience.

Driving

If you enjoy driving a car but have resisted doing so for some time, build your confidence again by asking your support person to drive his or her car ahead so that you travel in tandem. In this way you won't lose sight of your support, but you *are* driving alone. This is best tackled first on short, familiar trips and gradually extended to more exciting places.

Steps towards personal fulfilment

Lack of personal fulfilment is a major contributing factor to agoraphobia. By this I mean the development of 'personal identity' through achievement in the work we do in the market place or at home. Many who are agoraphobic have not found satisfaction in their work, nor do they balance that lack of fulfilment with satisfying activities in their leisure time. It is important to seek what one needs in life to feel fulfilled and to take steps towards achieving that. At first those steps may be tentative, but they are of great significance, nevertheless. We don't *have* to live a life of compromise. We are meant to seek happiness. Set your goal and gradually move towards it. Agoraphobia will retreat as you go forward.

Creative activity

Creative arts are highly therapeutic and may lead in time to greater fulfilment. Any of the many forms of music may be one of the best art forms in this instance, because music provides companionship even when one is alone. Music is beneficial too because it is very disciplined, and discipline (with ease!) leads to order in one's life. Gradually set about finding a way to involve yourself in your preferred field of creative activity. Some teachers will come to your own home, an excellent way to begin this part of your journey.

Helping others

As soon as is possible, take steps to do something for someone else. Join a fund-raising committee. Volunteer to keep someone company or give of your talents to help others. As you become to a certain extent a support person to another, you will find that your own fear is likely to recede. When we give out, in due course we receive. Do not, however, see it as your obligation to live at the beck and call of others — a situation which may provoke anxiety via the covert negative emotions of guilt, resentment and anger.

Finding self-awareness

Many sufferers of agoraphobia lack self-awareness, self-esteem, self-confidence, self-assertion, self-acceptance, self-love. Educate yourself further by reading relevant books and, where possible, attend courses and seminars to help you understand yourself, your reactions and your interaction with others. But a million books and seminars will be useless unless you put into practice at least a little of what is learned from them.

In seeking self-awareness, a good way to do this is to buy an exercise book and keep a journal to confide in. If one writes down what is on one's mind — about any issue, large or small — thoughts become clearer. Sadly, because of modern technological communication, the days are gone when we would pour out our heart in a long, handwritten letter. But we can keep a journal, just for our own use, and thus retrieve some of our own *feelings*. Rarely, we will discover, are we feeling what *we think* we are feeling. From the written word, insight into ourselves is often revealed. It is particularly important that this work be done by hand, thus involving the creative side of the brain. Painting or drawing as a means of self-expression are also highly recommended.

Setting goals

As you set about recovering from agoraphobia, don't attempt to follow a structured regimen. This can be overwhelming. Instead, keep things simple and natural. It is useful, however, to set yourself realistic daily goals and attempt some achievement each day — again, always when relaxed and with a positive belief in your ability to succeed. If agoraphobia is not too restricting and you already cope with many things without too many limitations, it is not so difficult to widen your goal horizons. If agoraphobia is very restricting, try to achieve *any* positive advance (even within the home) that is beyond your usual scope of activity. Positive actions are cumulative. And they make you feel good too! Eventually the day will come when the front gate will not be so threatening. Indeed, the world itself will open to receive you.

Keep it simple

Simple things are usually the best. You have very likely tried many remedies for agoraphobia and most have probably not helped very much. Some theories are very intense, some are complicated and others are less orthodox — such as the person who was recommended to smash her kitchen crockery to vent her feelings and then sit down and patiently restore it all with glue. As a strategy for alleviating agoraphobia this was unlikely to be effective!

Because of the influence of modern medicine and technology, we generally believe that the best in life must be either expensive or complicated. That is not necessarily so. Simplicity is part of our naturalness, so it must be good. Believe this, and adopt the meditative stillness I have validated.

As already indicated elsewhere, some people make fast progress to recovery and notice very quickly the difference that stillness makes to their lives. Others take much longer. Be patient and persevering. There are usually a great many ups and downs, and commonly much turbulence, before liberation is complete and a 'normal' life is resumed. (Please note that meditative practice should be applied with particular diligence if under extra stress, or when one feels temporarily overwhelmed.)

Do not be tempted to think that you have to be in any way exceptional to reap the rewards of *stillness meditation*. A great many people have successfully benefited from this form of meditation and doubtless for many different reasons. If I did not believe others could also find relief, I would not have dedicated so much of my life to promoting it. Trust the stillness and heed my support of it. But more than anything else, try it, for it is only by *do-ing* it that its benefits can be known.

Earlier, I noted that symptoms can recur and that there is always a lesson for us in this. As life becomes more inviting, anxiety may be present at times. To prevent this happening, one would have to reject everyday events and opportunities and take no responsibility for one's life or potential. In other words, one would have to remain a child. But that is to opt out. It is also boring, for we exist in order to grow. Our very existence is imperfect too, and the fact that anxiety is present sometimes only indicates a stepping stone to further fulfilment. With the practice of stillness, we can move firmly from that stepping stone to the next stage of development. *And while ever we rest our mind, anxiety can never overwhelm us as it has done in the past.* One flows with it all and 'it' passes, a ripple on the water.

So if at times you seem to go backwards a little, remember that this is only temporary, like a crack in a healing wound. When things go wrong, keep an optimistic attitude, knowing that for some reason it was meant to happen this way. Good always comes from bad, in time. When you wake each morning, give thanks for this day with the promise it holds. Recall regularly, with interest and affection, all the events and those people who have touched your life, knowing that each has made their contribution to you, forming you to be the person you are now. Look forward to all that is still to come. And each evening, as you drift into sleep, gently bring to mind at least one good moment from the day that's just passed. That keeps hope alive.

Sixteen

AND OTHERS SAY . . .

*Success nourished them; they seemed to be able
and so they were able.*

Virgil

The anecdotes of others who have made their way successfully through anxiety could be likened to lamps burning in the darkness to light the path and lessen the journey.

Storytelling is an important form of sharing that can reassure, guide and assist as we grapple with the inevitability of our personal passages. Here is a potpourri of others' stories, the contributions of a selection of the people who have travelled with me since the first publication of this book. While some are more self-revealing and more complete than others, each story is a microcosm of individual lives and reflects memories, thoughts, ideals and triumphs. Above all, each tells of calamity being transformed primarily by *stillness* into personal growth and change.

Douglas

Here is a recollection from which the reader may be inspired by the richness of a life, its vulnerability and strength and its limitations and liberations. Fear or anxiety can especially be seen here as a path to travel, not as an end in itself.

Douglas, an Englishman, was born in 1926 to a military family. In his early life, the family moved around the UK following his father's career, which also included a two-year stint in Malta. His father was discharged from the army for health reasons and Douglas has early memories of hard times during the Great

Depression. He also recalls his secure home life and immense love for both his parents (with a special admiration for his father), his painful shyness as a child, causing an utter aversion to school attendance and the avoidance of social interaction with his peers. An early rise in tension occurred at his mother's reprimands when he didn't 'join in'. Discovering the countryside and a life's desire to live close to nature became powerfully implanted within him as a source of joy. Some disruption to his peace occurred, however, after the birth of his younger sister, when his mother's new requirements of him created a barrier in the closeness of their relationship.

An incident at school where Douglas was blamed and punished on behalf of others taught him 'not the difference between right and wrong but the significance of justice'. Then followed his failure to pass an examination for Grammar School and the opportunity to attend Technical College to study engineering — but no opportunity to study art, a passion in early life and a gift only finally achieved in more recent years.

With the outbreak of the Second World War, 'life took a different direction'. His father was called back to service, and though Douglas was miserable and ill from missing his presence at home, he pushed himself to 'get a Saturday job and begin to study aviation'. Seeking an escape from college (which reproduced a way of life still greatly disliked), he began finding excitement and respite from visiting airfields and bombed villages nearby. This led to a search within the services for a future and to Army Apprentice School. Though the thought of war both 'excited and saddened me', Douglas found happiness and success along this path. He was recommended for officer training, volunteered for India and was commissioned into his father's regiment.

The practically non-existent social life in India was of no consequence to Douglas, but he found it increasingly hard to cope with the purpose of being in India at all. A sense of monotony, of being 'shut up' without variety, and the British approach to the Indian Raj created feelings of conflict — he was there to fight for a cause, but 'my inner feelings were for Indians to be allowed their own destiny'. He described his feelings at the time as 'full of anxiety'.

'For a change of routine I decided to give the Officers' Mess a miss for a time. The rebel was being born!' These actions led to his hospitalisation, and because no illness could be found, he was written down as wrongly employed. Back at his Unit, he waited until his turn for leave arrived and he was sent home to England on his twenty-first birthday. Douglas then left the army with the idea of finding a new life in Australia. On the brink of departure, his father died, leaving Douglas grieving and with the task of settling his mother and sister in England.

Three major events then occurred: the Korean war was on the horizon, Douglas met and married his future wife and he was given his Commission back, but instead of being sent into defence he was posted to West Africa. Health conditions were very bad there, and his young wife was unable to sustain the environment. Douglas endured his posting for eighteen months separated from her, exhausted and strained to his limit. The Africa experience was for him exactly like the India experience but at a greater level of intensity. 'I loved the army, but not the system by which it operated. My sympathy was with the African people and my inner tension grew as I literally conducted a private war against that system'. Douglas claims he would not have survived there at all had he not taken steps to tackle the issues that upset him. But in doing so he became ill, suffering a 'nervous breakdown' which led to his return to England. Away from that tension, 'I recovered within days of this notable event, back at work in a tremendous job in a delightful country area.' This was the start of a phase of 'fabulous working years', promotion to the rank of Major and various postings leading to settlement in Australia.

Participation in the Vietnam war was upsetting, not the war in itself so much as the disappointing military standards and 'I concentrated on looking after my soldiers and at providing an attitude that would help them find laughter to ease their situation.' Once again, the inner struggle at this situation clearly caused an excess of tension, with accompanying anxiety being his personal expression of the frustration and anger he was feeling. 'I arrived home in Australia a very angry man, making myself unbearable to all and suffering recurring outbreaks of flu coupled with tremendous fatigue. I began to find it impossible to socialise and anticipatory anxiety at these events found its expression in hot spells and severe headaches.'

Douglas finally left the army in 1976 after studying for an alternative career in Art and Building Construction. A fine artist, Douglas threw himself into painting and exhibiting his work and was very successful. But he began to suffer severe depression. 'Once again my feelings were at war.' The separation from his world of many years equated with 'loss of family and I struggled with civilian thinking and therefore, expectation'. Here again was a situation of powerful conflict, no doubt fuelling tension for him. 'On the one hand, though I detested many facets of it, I was missing the Army a great deal, while on the other, I was now free to do as I liked yet somehow didn't know how to handle this.' He was referred to a psychiatrist who recommended medication. 'I knew this was not the answer. I started to drink alcohol, never heavily but daily, and the dependent habit developed.'

Seeking peace of mind and believing that to be the answer also to overcoming 'my lesser habits', Douglas attended intensive meditation in Melbourne with Dr Ainslie Meares. 'The result was absolutely beyond my greatest expectations. Something about Meares transported people beyond their pain. My return to good health and happiness was gradual, but decisive.' This lasted five years but began to fade when,

> . . . like so many other things in my daily routine I let my practice of meditation slip away and I just lost control of my life. I attended counselling for six years and tried hypnosis. I learned a lot about myself and how to handle situations, but I still worried. The effect of counselling was so temporary. Anxiety and depression plagued me and I lived with this, largely because of support from my understanding family.

Travel was also a source of relief and an opportunity to put his art to work. Douglas was unsettled, dividing his time between conducting a community workshop which he had initiated, his own artistic skills and his ongoing interest in aviation.

Four years ago, he experienced health problems involving his heart: fibrillation, spasms and a heartbeat of up to 130. This deterioration in health led to . . .

> my first serious panic attack. I felt disorientated and very frightened, especially at the experience of chest pain and visual disturbances. The diagnosis was asthma, arterial fibrillation and suspected blood clots. The treatment made me feel like an invalid — several different forms of medication, an asthma pump, routine hospital visits for extensive testing and various visits to specialists. I began to stay at home more and more — quite agoraphobic — and feeling extremely anxious and aimless. I was unable to clear my head of thoughts. I was greatly afraid of an asthma or heart attack or perhaps a stroke.

A retrospective of events reveals that the amount of stress Douglas experienced as a result of leaving the army was great indeed. 'I had no idea of just how different my life would be.' The earlier conflicting feelings he experienced within his profession and the persistent conflict between his desire to be free of the army and his difficulty in fitting into civilian life accelerated his fighting with tension and therefore an increase in anxiety. It is also apparent to him now that his life has been determined by movement and a belief that two or three years at most in any one posting is sufficient. Moving on, for Douglas, is energizing. But on leaving the army, this movement had to cease and so for Douglas there was no escape, no prospect of re-energization, possibly no prospect of hope — so a prevailing depression occurred.

At this point, Douglas approached me seeking 'peace of mind and with an aim to rejoin the human race'. He had known immense success from *stillness meditation* some years previously. Would it work for him again?

> This has been a sort of miracle really. I maintain daily meditation practice for up to an hour. After five months experiencing this form

of meditation with you and practising at home, my heartbeat has returned to normal, that is, it now beats at 75 as opposed to 125. My doctor is amazed at my progress. I'm as healthy as any time, my mental approach is geared to my age and I am enjoying this 'rebirth'. And quality of life has returned to me. It seems incredible that to get to my first visit to you I had to battle with all the circumstances of driving that caused me nervousness. But now I drive around better than ever without a thought for worry. I'm at peace with the world and with things around me. That really sums it up. Even the things I don't like about my life. I'm at peace with them. My sense of humour has returned. I had lost a zest for life and all the things I couldn't do without extreme anxiety I'm doing now with delight. The *stillness* entices me to go the way I want — not the way of the world. I'm not religious but I am very, very spiritual. I know God sits on my shoulder, guides me at crossroads. Things always work out for the best.

By way of a message to others who are encumbered by tension, anxiety and depression, in summary Douglas says:

It is necessary to gain and retain complete control over your well-being, your mind and thoughts — and your physical health as well. And, be stubbornly truthful to yourself. It is not true to think you can't do certain things like drive the car freely, go to shopping malls, use public transport and attend social gatherings. The truth is, with adequate help and guidance, you can!

Jennifer

Jennifer's anxiety manifested in recurring panic attacks and she described symptoms which included claustrophobia, breathless-ness, the fear of going crazy or dying in the midst of panic and a sense of being unable fully to trust herself. On a scale of 1–10, Jennifer estimated her anxiety level at 7 or 8. After two months' experience of *stillness*, this level dropped to 4 or 5.

I have now been able to sense a life without panic attacks which is fantastic! I have a stronger sense of inner calm and feel more equipped to control anxiety. I am enjoying life more and gradually releasing my fear of panic attacks.

Two months later, we reviewed the situation again, finding her anxiety to be down to 3 or 4.

Jennifer is thirty-four, is married and a theatre performer. When we spoke at length, she readily admitted to having been brought up with an attitude of tension within the family.

> Alcohol was used as a way of coping for my parents, but in fact this dynamic only fed the existing tension and led to violent behaviour.
>
> At around the age of sixteen or seventeen, I became aware of what I perceived as a potential flaw in my nature. It was said within the family that I had my father's tempestuous nature. I saw this as a profound criticism of my personality and therefore I felt like I needed to hold myself back, as if holding in an angry monster. If I let myself be myself, this monster might run loose. From then on, I really felt quite on the back foot — unsure of myself and with my confidence rocked. I was so very afraid of myself, because I felt I could possibly hurt people. This was very shameful, so I began concealing that part of me from the rest of the world. Being nice became very important to me.
>
> As time went on, I discovered a very strong desire, like a force beyond myself really, to pursue theatre as a profession. The study of drama is so revealing — you really do face yourself and that began to stimulate my existing shame and fear. Perhaps my desire to make theatre my life was pushing me to seek and accept that other part of myself, because it was during this time that I became overwhelmed by panic. I was a student at drama school in Paris and although this was exciting, coping and studying in a foreign country presented many stressful issues to raise my tension level. Simultaneously, I gave up smoking marijuana. Giving up smoking meant giving up a way of managing my tensions. The change in physical environment and being cut off from people I knew helped trigger my crisis.
>
> I was pretty desperate at that time really. Panic made me terribly afraid and I used to picture myself going out of control, being ugly, screaming, having a fit, frothing at the mouth and being seen to be a monster! It was very important that I keep that part of myself hidden. At that time, I began a personal journal and with support from a friend and a lot of reading, I spent a lot of time in self-analysis. This was very informative and I learned a great deal about myself, but the panic and the fear of panic remained constant.
>
> Now I'm calmer. It's become easier and easier to become still and safe. Negative thoughts and anxieties have lost their grip on

me. I have a general sense of being more centred. I feel something natural that's within me is gradually being uncovered. I haven't had a panic attack since commencing *stillness meditation*, whereas panic had been a regular part of my life. I especially notice how calm I am in various situations that I know once would have caused me anxiety. Also there are fewer swings in my tension level and those powerful images surrounding panic have passed.

I have also become more reflective, and I realise that reflectiveness is really very important. From this you can see a lot more about yourself and your life. I'm now finding that the things I need and want in life are coming to me, whereas before becoming experienced in stillness I was putting in a lot of effort to achieve. It all seems easier now. Even the tortures of life. My father has a serious illness and is slowly dying. In my grieving for him I had felt quite overwhelmed — as if I was somehow losing myself. Now somehow from the stillness I'm being helped to make some kind of sense of the journey of life and death.

I'm not so attached to things, not so caught up by the rollercoaster ride of latching on to issues and making them problems. Therefore I'm more able to observe these things and deal with them in a more positive way. And I have a little more courage to be myself. Because now I can see the link between my panic attacks and my fear of letting that shameful part of myself be seen. My fear really was that if I let that part of me out it would wreak havoc. Now I'm more accepting of that colour within my personality. I have also come to the major decision that I want to have a baby. I used to have a fear of getting lost again if I had a child. Now I feel stronger — more complete.

I'm realising that in stillness there is an opportunity to shift your belief systems and that the stillness gives you the calmness to do those things that we all think are so terrifying. The stillness takes great care of you and will not harm you. Out of this I can feel myself changing but on my own terms, my own sense of what is good or unhealthy for me. It is totally a worthwhile path to follow . . . my life becomes better and better. I would not have been able to see, believe or trust such things six months ago.

Alley

At the onset of anxiety, Alley was nineteen and a second-year student at university. She had become overwhelmed by panic attacks resulting in agoraphobia, and 'felt very much alone with no idea of what was happening to me'. In recounting her typical symptoms, she reported 'feeling out of control with lots of irrational fears and stress waves'. Several significant events of a demanding nature had occurred in the preceding weeks and these had included the death of her grandfather.

> I remember during the summer break, one very hot night I became dehydrated and experienced delirium. I felt absolutely awful — scared! That seemed to be the crisis point and from then on, I was very unsure of myself — anxious all the time, afraid to be left alone, avoiding situations, terrified of driving my car and of leaving the familiarity of home. I was very dependent upon people close to me.

When we first met, Alley spoke of 'my mask of confidence but I'm frail inside. What people think of me is very important.' That was two years ago. Today, she says:

> I've thought about my story in terms of the advice I'd give to others — let go of tension and change your mind! During my anxiety and agoraphobia *I was lost*. In a way I was partly lost before the anxiety. Now that I've come out of it I can look back over the experience and see my breakthroughs. I can also recognise that with a response of long-term tension it doesn't take much to push you to breaking point.
>
> The first thing of importance I learned was patience. This was reinforced very strongly a couple of weeks after I began *stillness meditation*. I began that with the belief that my awful feelings would just go away and I would be back to 'normal', that is, back to where I was before the anxiety overwhelmed me. But soon I realised that the releasing effect of stillness was a gradual process. Then I learned the second important lesson: my anxiety wasn't coming from one single place or thing or even the way I was thinking about it, but it was a combination of matters tied together by my attempts to cover up a part of myself.
>
> When we *[she and I]* started looking at my life I gained awareness that the anxious feelings were coming from notable moments from the past and that trying to overcome the anxiety as if it was just a current thing wasn't going to help much at all. What

was going on currently were our clues to figure out the whole picture and those clues were somehow broken down as I released my tension level in the stillness of meditation.

The stillness was also like a place to work from and this was my third lesson: from the practice of stillness I could become free from anxiety and I could also change. I'm different now. There's more of me than there was before. Even before agoraphobia, I felt small, closed, withdrawn. My external appearance was normal, I'm sure. Others wouldn't have seen what was inside me. But my core, my kernel felt shrivelled, dark and closed. Now I feel bigger, as if my core is now touching my body. I feel closer to whole.

Alley's unacceptable part, the part of herself of which she was ashamed, was her childhood fear of staying away from home. Needless to say this fear had come from somewhere and she had invested great energy and, of course, tension, into concealing that part of herself. In early childhood she had experienced anxiety and tension at 'not being trusted'. By this she means that as a very little girl she felt excluded from knowledge or information with regard to a life-threatening illness suffered by her mother.

I felt uncertain, bewildered, confused all the time. I wasn't a protected child but the *not being told* period of my life left me fearful and doubtful. So I wouldn't trust myself either. And this self-doubt led to my not being comfortable staying away from home. I saw this as very shameful and my sense of shame increased because, as time went on I realised that, while this behaviour could be acceptable from a little child, now I was an adult and still limited by my reservation. This was a huge inner pressure for me. I would become so tense about it that I would become physically sick. And I was tending towards losing control of my life because the issue kept coming up. Then, with all that tension, after several stressful incidents I was absolutely swamped by panic and then agoraphobia.

It was really strange for me to become so reclusive because I had always been fairly outgoing and quite confident. I was a sensitive child, but confident, with a very strong, loving and supportive family. So I always had a good general self-esteem. In fact I believe it's when you have a good self-esteem that you want to hide what you haven't yet accepted about yourself. At that time the whole 'me' wasn't truly living. I was acting in a way —

overcompensating for my limitation, and then feeling ashamed of the overcompensation as well!

I had always pushed myself and this had worked for the most part. But of course I was pushing with tension which had only an exterior effect. It's not healthy to fight the immediate fear — you have to challenge the real thing. This fighting attitude didn't give me anything of value — all it did was build my anxiety to the maximum. So I see now that it's pivotal to reduce the tension and to change what we believe about ourselves — that we don't have to fight and that limitations are an OK part of you too. Then you can change.

The first part of my change lay in learning to let go. This came through the meditative stillness. The next part of my change was to recognise where my shameful belief had come from and to accept that childhood fear as something I was now free to challenge in an adult manner. I continue to practise my stillness without fail each day, and over the past months as I relaxed mentally and learned to let go of tension more and more, the challenges I faced were much easier. I know now that letting go leads to wholeness in contrast to disintegration. When we're disintegrated we become smaller and smaller. But when we're more whole we can choose the bits we want in life and they become part of the expanding whole.

I've made great progress in the past two years. Being home alone is normal now, driving is easy and 'wild' social events, having fun, overnight stays, holidays with friends, uni camps and interstate flights have become part of a very full life.

As well as her personal achievements during this time, Alley's distinctions at university are evidence of a very capable young woman.

Also, I can now discern the things that hurt me or the things I don't want in life and make positive choices. Even death . . . of those close to you which are so out of your control. *[Alley's life was touched substantially in this way during her recovery from agoraphobia.]* . . . you can choose how you deal with it, either with fear or with calm acceptance.

I've learned that having information is important to me. Even today if I sense people are keeping things from me it can be a sticking point. But today I don't succumb to this issue like I used to. I am free to act upon it. I now have the experience and the skills to, yes, be affected by life — but not break down, just bounce back. And I have a very strong sense of a future that holds a lot of positive living — *a great future!*

Mardi

Since the age of seventeen Mardi had suffered depression, obsessional behaviour and agoraphobia. She had travelled the usual paths, seeking help. Hers is a success story of great courage and an excellent example of the need for perseverance, especially in the practice of *stillness,* for at times she felt she was making no progress at all. When asked what was different about her life she laughed and replied enthusiastically,

> I've *got* a life — that's what's different! I remember the first time I came here. I was so anxious. I hadn't driven on a freeway for years and I thought I'd be an absolute mess during and after the session. But as soon as we talked together I knew this was the answer, this was what I had been searching for.
>
> There were times when things were really difficult — when I doubted meditative stillness and I was tempted to give up. But deep down I knew life had to be better. I just wanted to have some form of life, anything, to be able to live semi-normally. I used to be tense, anxious and withdrawn and very aggressive really. That's all in balance now. When I began to meditate regularly the aggression changed to determination.

Mardi's first big step to freedom came when she was able to drive to the beach.

> That occasion really stays in my mind. Going to the beach is something you do as a kid . . . when you haven't had that for a long time you want to get it back. So that trip was very important to me.
>
> I used to see agoraphobia and all those awful feelings as a kind of punishment. I know now that it wasn't something I did that caused me anxiety. I've learned to be more tolerant in life and I've learned that I am a good person after all. There have been dreadful dips along the way but I have always come out of them — as long as I maintain my stillness.

Mardi knew she had overcome agoraphobia when she was able to move out of the family home, buying her own together with her partner. Soon after, she made the commitment of buying a business, successfully establishing herself in her own right in a field at which she excels.

> They were positive things to do, though 'scary' at the time. Making a big commitment is cause for anxiety for me, but I'm more able to deal with this aspect of myself. When I was anxious and agoraphobic I was child-like really. Now I feel strength, as if I'm an adult doing adult things and being seen and treated by others as an adult. My partner is very supportive and is proud of my achievements. He has always encouraged me to move forward and not to give up.
>
> I feel sorry for those people who do give up and succumb to anxiety as a part of their life. I can understand why they do — it seems easier. I can look back and recall a lot of panic and fear and pain and a lot of tears and confusion along the way. But because of that I've got my life back. I think now that the only thing to be afraid of out there is one's own vulnerability. I see myself today as a strong, calm, happy person — so different from the person you first met! And I'm not stopping here either. There's a lot more of life available and I'm going for that too.

John

John, a scientist, recorded his major symptoms at the time of his commencing *stillness meditation* as anxiety and compulsive thoughts. He rated his anxiety level at about 5 on a scale of 1 to 10; after seven weekly sessions this dropped to 2–3. He wrote the following:

> There is certainly more ease in my work and social life. I am more productive and more focused. Also, just recently, I have noticed a quite discernible change in the way other people relate to me. I find this amazing as I don't believe I have been behaving differently. Also the compulsive thoughts are greatly lessened and it seems that, slowly but surely, a more natural sense of security is coming to me.

Lorraine

A forty-two-year-old mother of two young children, Lorraine expressed symptoms of anxiety, stress, tension, panic attacks, agoraphobia and depression. These had been part of her life for the past nine years. She was taking regular medication and stated that one of her goals was to terminate this. Lorraine rated her anxiety level at more than 6; after eight weekly sessions she had successfully phased out the medication. She stated a greater sense of calm in the face of adversity together with greater clarity of mind: 'My unfounded fears are becoming less frequent and I am more relaxed generally.'

Lorraine also found herself communicating better with others and therefore making new friends. After sixteen weekly sessions, Lorraine estimated her anxiety level to have decreased to 2.

'After years of being unable to relax, I now truly can do so. I seem to know myself better as issues become clearer, and most importantly, I seem to be able now to harness the calmness at will.'

When we last spoke together, Lorraine had commenced a course of study and was considering the possibility of part-time work.

Margaret

Margaret persisted with regular sessions in *stillness meditation* for well over two years, attending weekly, and for a generous length of time twice weekly. She had been suffering stress and anxiety for some time due to certain sadnessness in her life. She then developed quite severe depression, triggered by the loss of sight in one eye, the result of several operations and faulty surgery. Margaret's anxiety was accompanied by a 'constantly churning stomach'. She was taking several types of medication for her condition and was very keen to overcome her need for these. Even more significantly, Margaret's greatest wish was to regain her joy in living. She had tried another form of meditation and had not experienced any change to her well-being before taking the step towards stillness of mind.

When asked the question 'What meaning does the practice of stillness give to your life?', her answer related to her greatest wish:

> It's given my life new meaning. I enjoy each day again. I had lost interest in my garden and my home — and in doing anything much — and now I've regained all that. I love my garden and together with the time I put in to developing and maintaining that, I go each day to help at the library (a community organisation). . . helping people who are less fortunate than I am. The practice of stillness has just given me this desire that there's so much in life to do — and I didn't have that feeling before.
>
> The most important thing is that now I am calm when I go to bed. For a long time I couldn't sleep and was taking sleeping tablets, which weren't helping me much at all. Now I don't take anything to sleep. I can just go to bed and I'm asleep in a few minutes and I sleep the whole night. It's all through *stillness meditation* that I'm able to live a normal life again.

Margaret no longer takes medication of any kind.

> It took me all of two and a half years of regular sessions to get to this stage — until I just came to a point of tremendous change, when I really achieved what I believed would never occur. Now when I'm facing anxiety or in stressful situations I cope calmly. My problems and my life concerns are still there — but I approach them with serenity.

The remarkable point of this story is that Margaret is a beautiful and lively lady who has almost reached her eightieth birthday. That years could not prevent her from faithfully persevering with so radical a form of therapy is commendable indeed. She above all must surely be most deserving of the granting of her wishes!

Sharon

Agoraphobia had taken over Sharon's life at a time when her marriage was failing, reducing her to a state of disintegration and despair for at least seven years. A mother of (then) two teenage daughters, Sharon related this story of recovery.

I am a logical thinker, and I was trying to solve my problems in that manner. It was all very stressful and I fell apart. On bad days I could not leave the house at all. On good days I would manage to do things — always locally — with the help of Valium and with great difficulty. My reaction to agoraphobia followed the usual pattern: no spontaneity, no confidence, no pre-arrangement of events, no enjoyment and no independence. I couldn't participate properly in life with my family and, in short, I was a real pain.

I saw a psychiatrist for four years without any improvement to my condition. I went to a programme for agoraphobia sufferers, but it was totally drug-oriented and I didn't want that at all. A friend who was a psychologist helped in a supportive way, supplying me with literature and ideas, and from that assistance I decided to try a self-help group. Through that group I discovered behaviour therapy. That was very traumatic for me, but later it proved to have been useful. I was also introduced to the drug Xanax, but I was not interested in relying upon permanent medication. I settled for a mild tranquilliser that I could take, only when needed, as a crutch — something that would at least help me to do those things that were absolutely necessary, such as attending to the needs of my children.

My marriage had really ended by then, and my husband had left. So *I had* to look to the future of myself and my children and try to take some control of my life. At that time I realised that the behaviour therapy had helped, despite the trauma it caused, because at least it had familiarised me again with places I would never have gone to alone. That got me off the ground.

From reading your book, I discovered *stillness meditation*, and as you know, I began meditation sessions with you. Soon I terminated the behaviour therapy and gradually the tablets. I joined a women's study group which helped me understand a lot more about myself, and I was also attending your meditation sessions weekly and meditating regularly at home. It was becoming easier to leave the house alone.

After some months, I was able to make the decision to re-enrol at University to complete my Diploma of Education. The mere thought of a campus was quite overwhelming but, being a fiercely determined person, I told myself that I would try enrolment day and if I got through that, then maybe I could face the first lecture! Enrolment day brought a great deal of apprehension but nothing 'terrible' happened so I ventured further. Success built on success. I got to the lectures and achieved excellent results. During that time I was offered a part-time teaching job, and accepted it. With my duties as mother and housekeeper, plus studying and the part-time work, I often felt great exhaustion. So I took pains to compensate for the fatigue with lots of rest and lots of meditation in between. My confidence gradually built more and more.

I feel now I am a person who has regained a lost part of myself. I am now more like the person I was fifteen years ago and am unrecognisable as the agoraphobic I was for seven years. I have boundless energy and enjoy everything I do — sometimes I experience a sense of wonderment at it all.

The Chinese characters for 'crisis' can be interpreted as *change* and *opportunity*. That really impresses me. When crises occur they are usually associated with illness, depression, anxiety or marital problems. To experience agoraphobia means you have been given an opportunity to learn and to change. And it's absolutely true that there is no gain in life without pain. I believe overcoming fear is a combined process of *reducing the tension and anxiety and getting to know yourself.* The rest falls into place. Now I understand my strengths as well as my weaknesses. And I have also come to see and accept those parts of me that I don't like. The total experience has also given me more of an insight into others too, and into my expectations of others. I've come to realise that together with the parts I do like in myself and others, what I don't like adds to the richness of the whole.

It's OK now if I don't live up to old expectations. No-one has to be perfect. In the course of recovery, I happened to meet a young woman who had lost the use of her legs and was confined to a wheelchair. She amazed me by sharing the thought that if her greatest wish could be granted and somehow she could have her legs back, she would refuse. She was adamant that in losing her legs she had gained a hundredfold in strength, tolerance and self-knowledge. And that's how I feel about my experience of agoraphobia. During my years of fear, I used to have frustrating dreams that I was in the city, or driving here or there and I'd wake up thinking, 'Hey, I shouldn't be in those places.' Now it's as if my dreams have become the reality and what my actual dreams contain is just peace and togetherness.

Sharon successfully completed that part of her study and the last time we met she was working three days a week as an administrator in a support organisation. In her work she was recruiting and training staff members, and driving anywhere and everywhere to interviews. She was also teaching two days a week at a tertiary level and furthering her own qualifications in relevant fields. With agoraphobia long forgotten and having spent a month in Europe on a holiday, Sharon now felt free to travel wherever her dreams might take her.

Susie

Susie was stricken with panic when she was seventeen and was severely inhibited by agoraphobia for over seven years. She was unable to leave the house unaccompanied, or to remain at home alone. To her extreme credit, she had never swallowed a tablet in her search for freedom. Her persistence and her determination to succeed in the face of what some would regard as insurmountable obstacles along the way was quite remarkable.

> I think the most important step you take towards getting better is when you realise that the only person who can really help you is you; and that you've really got to learn to trust yourself, rely on yourself and not fear yourself. I suppose once you've learned those things then you have to believe them, and that's the hard part — the part I haven't quite mastered yet.
>
> I used to believe that the anxiety I felt was mostly involuntary, but I realise now that my frame of mind, my attitude to life and the thoughts I make happen are the things that trigger or cancel out the anxiety. I guess in a way that's how the meditation works. It helps your mind become calm and enables you to make the choice — to stay calm, as you do in stillness, or give in to your old patterns and gather up all the ingredients to pave the way for a good old panic session.
>
> It [stillness] is also important because it's yours. You own it and control whether you do it or not. It's a kind of gift you give yourself, even though at times the prospect of doing it can feel like a chore. But it's the times when it doesn't feel like a chore or a duty that are good. It's a back-up, a support too. If I don't do it I feel more vulnerable. When I've done it, I'm calmer and I feel as though I have the edge over things.
>
> All these strange sensations really do inhabit everyone's lives at some stage (to a lesser extent perhaps), but they are all normal ways of expressing, feeling or dealing with anxiety. People really

are very complex and, also, very ignorant of the way they function or malfunction.

Because those feelings seem to occur in your head (or your heart) you can believe you can't escape from them. Often I wished I could take a holiday from myself, hang my head up in the wardrobe and take off without it. The people who mean most to me rate very highly in my heart and I react quite easily to the ups and downs they trigger. But that's me and I'll always care too much, worry too much — but I think that's OK, as long as I can accept it and carry on regardless.

There are too many books around that tell you how to become more loving, forgiving, happier, wealthier, successful, and so on. These books give people in crisis false expectations of themselves and the future. Dr Meares, however, was different. I get a lot out of his writing because he points people towards themselves; no ideals, just the desire to be at ease with yourself, and that's the most important thing people must learn. It's OK not to be perfect, but it's not OK to always feel ill at ease with yourself. That's what Dr Meares was meaning.

It's good to draw on experiences you've had in your own life for comfort. When I'm not really feeling like approaching a challenge but nevertheless know I have to take the plunge, I remember back to when I was little. I was a very late swimmer and didn't learn until I was twelve or thirteen years old. When I finally got up enough courage to bob under the water and then let go of the edge, I realised there was nothing to it, and the biggest problem was the fear I had of actually *letting go* of the edge. Once I did that, there was nothing to worry about at all!

How simple to let go — when we know how! It took two and a half years of regular attendance at meditation sessions and a great deal of encouragement and support along the way for that young butterfly to emerge from her chrysalis. From her first faltering steps to the corner shop, she blossomed to enjoy full-time employment in a field suitable to her creative talent. Later she completed her degree, qualified as a teacher and fulfilled that vocational part of her life before marrying and moving interstate.

Elizabeth

The progress made by this woman, a primary teacher, in a relatively short period of time was quite remarkable. Elizabeth had been agoraphobic for over twenty years and was completely housebound when her husband first accompanied her to consult me. She commenced regular attendance at meditation sessions and persevered well with her regular practice at home.

> Not only had I endured the effects of agoraphobia for all those years but I eventually developed a fear of being anywhere alone, even in my own home. My mind was forever in a state of panic, and this made life extremely difficult.
>
> I tried various treatments including eight weeks in hospital, private psychologists and an organised programme for anxious people. Each of those forms of treatment contributed something in helping me understand my difficulty. Despite each, I remained in a stable, but fearful, state. I began to realise that the problem was within myself. I was the only one who could help me! At about that time I read your book and after eighteen months of meditation I am now able to stay at home alone and enjoy the peace and quiet that solitude offers. I feel quite comfortable in crowded places and shopping centres again. My greatest triumph is my return to part-time work in my former profession and I find the practice of stillness helps me greatly in this.
>
> I still have some hurdles to overcome. My next goal is to learn to drive again so that I can work on venturing further while unaccompanied. This is not easy to pursue at present, since there is no public transport in our area.
>
> I now have every confidence that with patience and determination — and regular practice of stillness — I will succeed in fully overcoming fear and find freedom, serenity and independence.

The last time I saw Elizabeth I was struck by her ease and the composure glowing in her face, as opposed to the haunting, straining tension and anxiety that had been so apparent on our first meeting.

Kris

This young woman developed agoraphobia following attacks of giddiness and blurred vision each morning, noticing these symptoms first while driving to work. Thinking her eyes were at fault, she consulted an optometrist.

My sight was said to be perfect, but the problems remained. I visited my general practitioner and was prescribed medication for a sinus condition. This treatment made no difference. The giddy feelings and visual disturbances increased. I began to avoid leaving the house and didn't want to drive the car, because these activities seemed related to the unpleasant way I was feeling. I became very depressed . . . weepy all the time. I believe the depression was a result of being at home so much and not knowing or understanding what was causing it all.

My general practitioner was lovely. I can't speak highly enough of him. He was helpful, tolerant and sympathetic. He was a kindly, elderly gentleman who went out of his way to assist me while trying to solve the problem. He often made home visits because I was unable to go to him. And later, when I had progressed a little, he would let me know exactly when to be at his surgery to spare me the dreaded waiting that phobic people find so difficult. At this time this doctor prescribed anti-depressants and minor tranquillisers — and I really needed them. There is a place for this kind of medication, at least for that time when it's virtually impossible to cope without it.

The medication enabled me to achieve such trivial things as going outside to my letter box. I was determined to win this battle, and in time I could walk to the corner, a few houses away. I tried driving and could only manage a trip around the block (certainly no traffic lights!). But I continued to persevere anyway. My sister was marvellous. She has experienced similar symptoms throughout her life — though not agoraphobia — and she would accompany me in my experimental outings. Often I came out of a shopping centre in tears.

A lot of time passed and I was really not progressing. So (against my doctor's advice) I decided to consult a psychiatrist. This man seemed very highly regarded and I felt confident that I was doing the best thing. It surprised me though, that his rooms were on the top floor of a tall building! Only my sense of humour got me through those visits. My sister was with me. She dislikes enclosed places, so by the time we had left the elevator we were both crying and sweating and shaking. Then we would observe other patients arriving in a similar state!

The psychiatrist prescribed drugs to reduce my anxiety and at the same time took me off all other medication. I had suffered from high blood pressure long before any of these anxiety problems emerged, and for years I had taken tablets to control that. Now I was to take nothing but the tablets prescribed by the psychiatrist. I persevered with them and I really believed that one day I would wake up calm and peaceful and completely free of anxiety and all the awful symptoms that had become part of my life. Unfortunately, the opposite occurred. Without the necessary medication, unknown to me my blood pressure soared. And my anxiety, rather than disappearing, was increasing rapidly until depression returned once more. I was visiting the psychiatrist weekly. He kept telling me that it would take time to improve . . . while increasing the dosage. But my anxiety was becoming worse. I was sleepless, my heart was thumping dreadfully all the time and I became worried that there was something seriously wrong with me.

The crunch came one day when I began having blackouts, so I decided to go to a hospital, and by the time I arrived I was unable to walk properly. In the casualty section that day, my blood pressure was 240/140 and the staff on duty could hardly believe I was still alive! When I showed them the medication I was on, and they later had it analysed, it turned out that all those tablets I had taken in good faith were only placebos. I was terribly ill — and I have never forgiven the psychiatrist his treatment. In all, I had lost twelve months of potential progress and I was now back to square one: blood pressure tablets, anti-depressants, Valium. After my blood pressure stabilised, I sought avenues for counselling and therapy. Unfortunately these made no difference to my symptoms. However, through one psychologist I came to realise that if I wanted to get out of this mess, it was up to me to make it happen.

Then I read your book and wrote to you for information about learning meditation. I had previously thought that such 'pastimes' were ridiculous, but I was prepared now to try anything. It took months of sessions before I even 'got the hang' of what was meant by *stillness*. I feel sure that for this reason many people give meditation away before they achieve anything. But I persevered, with a positive desire to recover from the situation I was locked into.

My husband, and later my sister, used to drive me to the sessions. Little by little, things began to improve. I was able to cut down the medication and my GP was very pleased to see the change in my progress. I was too fearful to drive, but started to ride a bike and found this a very useful way of getting out a little. After a time I took on a small job, door-to-door selling, not for the income but to make progress and gain confidence. I joined the local gym and would run down for a quick aerobic class and then run home again, about three times a week. Soon I began to enjoy these times. One day, surprisingly, I was offered a part-time job there, teaching aerobics. I took the job, and although at times this commitment wasn't easy for me, the rewards were great. So after some months of work I decided to enrol for a two-year teacher training course in the fitness industry. When filling out the enrolment form I had no idea how I could travel that distance to the college on a regular basis to complete the course — but I wanted to do it, and I did.

My life was becoming busier. Now I was running classes, studying, finding freedom in general life, and meditating. I passed my first year and things were definitely looking better. I went on to second year, completed my first aid course and decided to buy my own car. At the end of that year I qualified as an aerobics and gym instructor, so I applied for a position in a large fitness organisation. After six months there, I was so confident that I was promoted to gym manager! I have now been working in that role for two years. I take no medication, not even for blood pressure — there is no need to.

My greatest interest now is running, and my greatest achievements have been in running marathons. I have raced among 40,000 people and finished in the top third. Physical activity is what I most enjoy.

I have no regrets about having experienced agoraphobia. It has given me a greater tolerance and sensitivity to the needs of others. I have learned that each of us is on our own and life is what you make it. There were probably things in my childhood that contributed to my phobia, but I don't think that is the important issue. The best people to help sufferers of anxiety are those who have experienced something of the kind themselves. It's almost impossible to understand the feelings and symptoms if you've not known them yourself. And I have always told others about my former problem. I have never been ashamed of it in itself and I think this attitude helps in overcoming it.

Sometimes I feel anxious — I'm sure everyone does at times — but this anxiety is nothing at all compared with those phobic years.

I'm really interested in this problem and some day I would like to help other sufferers.

My mind had never been quiet for a moment until I learned to meditate. I would like to see stillness taught in schools. It's very difficult to break all those bad habits of tension when you've been repeating them for years. Life would be far simpler if people were introduced to meditation in childhood as part of the day's routine. The experience of stillness opened the door for me and now I have completely changed my direction. I love my career and I am very happy.

The last time I saw Kris she had three ambitions: to start her own business in the fitness industry, to continue with further study and to win a veteran marathon — after her fortieth birthday!

George

An architect in private practice, George made the following comments after attending several sessions in *stillness meditation.*

I haven't felt panicky since I started here four weeks ago. I'm practising every day at home and this change in my life is fantastic! I just 'shut myself down' and all's well. I haven't enjoyed life so much for years.

Gloria

A client of many years who still calls in for an occasional time of stillness, Gloria defined her changes in the following narrative. When we first met, anxiety and severe depression were paralysing her life.

My life has been lived in two distinct phases — thirty-five years before *stillness meditation* and fifteen years after. The effect of daily stillness in my life has been profound. Not in an earth-moving, bell-ringing sort of way, but in an inner strength sort of way. From my early childhood, through my school years into adulthood, marriage and the birth of my children, I lived with a very high level of anxiety. There were many life experiences along the way to contribute to that but this is only known to me in hindsight and the wisdom of my 'new' life.

This new life too, has thrown many, many challenges my way. Serious health problems for myself and my husband, the demands of teenage children and a myriad of problems too numerous to mention. But my new life gives me a new thread which runs through me at all levels — spiritual, emotional, intellectual and physical. Now I am strong. I know myself and I am in touch with my inner voice. There is a peaceful equanimity in my life and fear has taken a back seat. I have a happy and rewarding family and fulfilling employment at a breast cancer clinic.

I have discovered a small talent for writing poetry which joyfully expresses my view of the world — a contrast indeed to years in my 'old' life where I never truly saw the world around me. And I play golf at weekends along with other hobbies. My 'new' life is full to the brim, almost overflowing with an ease I had not known before. There is joy and laughter, sadness and tears in this life . . . but it is my life, my season in the sun.

Isabelle

Isabelle, a senior teacher and faculty head, was on sick leave when we first met. Three months later she wrote this to me:

> I realise that I have lived in a nervous, anxious state for most of my life, always having quite unrealistic expectations of myself. I have managed my life by working harder and harder, keeping my mind and body always tense and busy. Although the years have provided many moments of happiness, I can certainly see now that I have made life very hard for myself.
>
> After the death of both of my parents and a close friend, my nervous tension and general anxiety increased greatly and resulted in some dreadful feelings. I began to experience panic attacks. I felt agitated for much of the time, constantly tired and unable to eat or sleep properly. I experienced periods of rapid heart rate and overwhelming fear. I was terrified and could not understand what was happening to me. My doctor was very sympathetic, encouraging the use of tranquillisers. He offered no alternatives and said if I did not take medication to reduce the symptoms, I would need to be hospitalised. I believed that there had to be another solution. Somehow I knew that I was responsible for my condition and therefore I had to be responsible for helping myself.
>
> Then I remembered that my brother had found relief from his anxiety in *stillness meditation*. After committing myself to

classes and home practice I could barely believe how quickly I began to improve. All those symptoms started to disappear. My doctor could not believe how quickly and how much my health improved.

After three months I have learned and experienced so much. I can relax, I can enjoy moments of stillness. I live my life more calmly. I approach problems more objectively. I appreciate everything in my world in a different way. I know that regular practice of stillness will be part of every day to come and I look forward to continuing along the positive and peaceful road I have found. I certainly have not stopped there — but I know that this skill has changed my life and given me confidence to free myself from the past and move to the future, living my life more fully and experiencing ongoing tranquillity. That my tension and anxiety were lowered so quickly and easily is still puzzling at times — *so simple, yet so effective.*

In closing this chapter, Sandra chose to express the changes wrought by *stillness meditation* in her special artistic way:

Sandra

Meditation distils the murky waters of my emotion, thoughts
    and anxiety.
By just sitting in the stillness . . . clarity comes
and its presence is felt on all levels and beyond time.
The stillness, the calm, the silence
naturally bring peace
like a fresh breeze soothing and awakening my soul.
I feel connected to myself,
not fragmented, but whole.

I can feel and be, just naturally
without rational analysis or judgment
and this is so liberating . . . I feel much healing in this 'just
    being'
without the 'thinking' our culture is so obsessed with.
It's an art, a way of knowing and being
far deeper than words or thoughts could ever take me.

It really is a matter of just sitting down and slipping into my
    inner world
. . . ceasing the doing
. . . letting go of the thinking
. . . going beyond my familiar zone
. . . and into my Being
and then the magic begins . . .

What happens while I'm there I can't say
because it is silent there
and Sacred too.
Enough to say it feels like the very core of life
the very place of Being
where healing happens
where life is built
where paths are corrected and set straight.

It is a Sacred space
Not one I necessarily 'go' to,
But one which is already there
A calm within my centre.
I just 'be' in the stillness and allow
the outer layers of thought, action, worry and tension to peel
    away
Little by little, layer by layer.
Until . . . I am with myself
Unguarded, uncluttered, enencumbered
Simply Me.
It feels comfortable, easy
The essence of wellness, inner peace, harmony.

And yet, it reaches far deeper and way beyond just Me.
It feels mysteriously connected to all of Life,
A oneness shared by all.

I am Home
I will reach my fullness.

Seventeen

TO THOSE WHO LEND THEIR SUPPORT

But the waiting time, my brothers,
Is the hardest time of all.

Sarah Doudney

One of the most generous acts offered to another is the act of selfless support given by spouses, partners, families and friends of the person with agoraphobia. To give out in this way requires either absolute dedication to the person concerned or absolute duty in the face of this constraining influence. There are few ready rewards for supporters. And the mystery accompanying this dis-ease, its apparent fickleness and its accumulating frustrations can put great strain on any relationship. Yet there is usually someone in the life of the anxious agoraphobic who can be there for those who need them, a fact that could be said to be astonishing given the apparent absence of care at times visible within our world. Those who continue to support and assist the anxious, agoraphobic person prove the truth that love appears in many guises and as always, will triumph regardless.

The thoughts in this small chapter are especially for those of you who lend your steadfast support to the person who needs you — a tribute to your dedication. If you, the support person, have read this book for the benefit of your wife, husband, partner or friend, I thank you. I hope my own story, my experience in this field and the contributions of others have helped clarify any aspects of the problem which you did not fully understand. You need to be clear about this problem as much for your own sake as that of the anxious person. For he or she, in suffering the symptoms of fear, has been affected by these to the extent that fear dominates their own life, and incidentally, the lives of those around them.

In your support you are indirectly being asked to give much. At the top of the list of giving there is a need for your presence and for that presence to be consistent and reliable. There is a need for your untiring patience when so often you reach exasperation point. You are required to impart, time and again, many forms of comfort and reassurance, day or night. You are required to be encouraging, when at times you feel you are wasting your breath. You must be helpful when for most of the time you feel quite help*less*. Great flexibility is required of you as plans may change without warning. Your faithfulness is required, demonstrating your love, compassion and commitment to the other person. And in all this you are required to remain calm and strong yourself. To meet the expectations of qualities such as these may at times seem impossible. And yet, in your support, you achieve this. And that is an admirable presentation of love.

The symptoms of anxiety are overwhelming in their grip. They are a genuine experience for the person you care about and they override reason. Fear, maintained by tension, perpetuates the consistent symptoms of physical illness which lead to insecurity and avoidance. But, as can be seen within my story, this situation can be corrected when the sufferer reduces tension, moves forward calmly and develops self-awareness. Until this renewal takes place, your potent assistance will continue to be needed.

Apart from the ongoing need for your physical presence, your reassurance is of enormous aid to the anxious person. He or she needs to know that you will continue to care, despite the intrusion of anxiety. The person who experiences acute anxiety, panic attacks or agoraphobia is generally not an ordinarily fearful or weak person. Although there may be some exceptions to this, you probably know already their characteristic tenacity and the capacity this person possesses in his or her personal strength, giftedness and capability. Your re-confirmation of these qualities will help increase lacking confidence. Added to this, helping the anxious person let go of any limiting diagnostic label associated with their difficulty can be another form of positive reassurance: he or she *is not an agoraphobic* but is a valuable human being — who is experiencing a form of vulnerability.

If your partner's anxiety has amplified to the level of agoraphobia and their life and yours have been turned upside down for many years, it may seem that in some ways I am oversimplifying the problem. But as he or she begins to take calm control and unwarranted fear diminishes, the essence of the battle will become crystal clear and its simplicity will be recognised. In the meantime, however, the constraints this situation puts upon your relationship cannot be rectified until the tension and anxiety levels have lowered, so a little more patience on your part is required.

The unpredictable nature of anxiety can create tensions of another kind within relationships or within the home. In the case of the agoraphobic, when safely within the household or in some other friendly environment, he or she no longer seems to react with need. A certain self-reliance and freedom in this comfortable space seems to take over. But in a matter of minutes, just when you imagined you could readily pursue something of importance within your own life, should a threatening circumstance arise, capricious fear will be aroused and the agoraphobic will need your assistance yet again. So your own life is, in many ways, just as precarious as the life of the anxious person. It is therefore helpful and important that you keep your own anxiety and tension levels to a minimum.

Tension, as I have said before, is contagious. If you too can learn and practise tranquillity, especially through meditative stillness, this can only be of benefit to all concerned. In participating this way and extending your support to embrace the possibility of making changes in your own life, you are offering a superior form of encouragement. To ensure positive progress and a return to composure for the person you support it is also very important that you enthusiastically encourage him or her in their own reduction of anxiety. It is crucial to their change that they obtain mental rest, if possible from the regular practice of stillness as explained in this book. And you can also bring your support to any of the additional suggestions for overcoming fear as outlined in Chapters 14 and 15 of this book.

To those who are tempted to be impatient with the sufferer or to make accusations of hypochondria or of their being neurotic, please try to understand their predicament. All people have 'neurotic' idiosyncrasies. It may be helpful for you to recall your own experiences of alarm or worry concerning your well-being. By putting yourself in the position of the other, you may be more able to recognise, at least to some degree, their discomfort.

Perhaps you are afraid of spiders, or maybe you cannot tolerate heights and you have tailored your own defences to meet these situations. Your partner or friend is also trying to defend him/herself from a specific fear, something larger than life which seems constantly to threaten. And as well as the apparently spontaneous symptoms, he or she is being pulled in two emotional directions — the way of reason and the way of emotional fear. This conflict in itself escalates confusion, together with more anxiety and tension.

The anxiety sufferer, as earlier discussed, experiences guilt within this condition. He or she is all too aware of the negative influence of anxiety upon the family or the relationship. In much the same way as an illness will affect normal living, certain concessions may have to be made and certain limits may have to be accepted for a time. But you — and the rest of the family — though you may be foregoing some privileges, are surely not being unduly deprived. In the meantime everyone will manage and eventually order will be restored. Within these circumstances, you, the support person, may be best able to appease unnecessary guilt and demonstrate your continuing acceptance of your partner and the existing problem, whilst still encouraging change.

You are no doubt the anxious person's sole confidant. You are honoured with his or her absolute trust. And he or she is extremely dependent upon you and your trust. Therefore, at the present time, you are almost a sustaining power to this person. It is really important that you cultivate maximum communication between you, so that you both know where you stand. Express your own frustrations, listen to those of the other person and learn to truly share feelings. You may consider seeking professional counsel as a partnership to assist in these areas. In communicating well, you both may discover areas of your life together where practical changes could bring relief which may also relieve part of the power of anxiety. And you may also discover needs of your own which your partner, though anxious, may be happy to assist with. Or there may be other factors surrounding your relationship to which the supported person can positively contribute by way of compensation for all you do in his or her support.

In your enthusiasm, please refrain from shallow advice such as 'pull yourself together' or 'get yourself a job'. Anxiety, panic and agoraphobia will not disappear simply through logical inter-vention or external distractions as some people suggest. Anxiety sufferers can sustain catastrophes such as the illness and death of a child yet still remain agoraphobic. However, the aim for fulfilment in life and the continual striving to be free from fear are in themselves powerful motivators to be approved of at all times.

It is possible that once the currently restricting fear is no longer preventing your partner or friend from accomplishing the task of living, you may begin to feel threat, disappointment or even anxiety. Life has been secure the way you have known it. Suddenly it is different. The one you love is no longer depending upon your presence, but is experiencing facets of life that you have no part of. You may really have preferred things the way they were. This is when it is imperative to talk, communicate and know each other. This is the time to acknowledge that life is comprised of spiralling growth experiences which peak and plummet, but when fully lived, lead ultimately to the good of all. Those who shield themselves from the fullness of life with all its highs and lows, and those who never learn, adapt, adjust or change can be the less for this. As one grows, so the other will be affected and have also the opportunity to grow. So when your partner finds freedom, please try not to resent this fresh independence. Some adjustments *may* have to be made between you, for once freedom is regained, there will be no holding this person back as they return to living in a manner which the rest of us take so easily for granted.

To those beyond the intimacy of the support person, those outside the family circle, I would note that the majority of people who develop anxiety conditions are not looking for attention or pity; nor do people in fear wish to be patronised. What is needed is reassurance, guidance and, above all, a clear understanding by themselves and others of the nature of their dis-ease.

The anxiety sufferer rarely experiences panic after the first attack. It is the fear of *possible* panic that causes dread, avoidance and eventual agoraphobia. But people in this situation may become agitated by their fear when alone or in a public place. Although most will fight the feelings and cope without assistance, sometimes someone in distress may seek help from a member of the public.

One woman recalled an incident where she became panicky while in a large department store. She knew very well that her discomfort was that of anxiety — the symptoms of fear — and her only desire was to escape from the store, away from the crowded and restricting situation. Those who came to her aid were, of course, concerned that her discomfort was something of a more serious medical nature and insisted upon taking her to the store physician. He was not immediately available and so her feelings of impending panic were increased as she was expected to wait for the doctor. All she wanted was to flee to home and safety. The managerial staff in this instance had a duty which they performed admirably. But unfortunately their care was not of very much help to the misery of the ongoing fear of the woman concerned.

The lesson to be learned from this story touches back to the rudiments of overcoming anxiety: rest, reassurance, reassessment and subsequent renewal. When these are engaged, panic is prevented and so the problem of distress of this nature is unlikely to arise. But the public should know that when a distressed person expresses a wish to 'get out of' a situation, it is more likely that he or she is feeling panic — the effects of fear and tension — than the effects of some major illness.

Probably the best advice to anyone who might encounter a person who is temporarily incapacitated by fear, is to take *his or her* advice and add to it their own serene reassurance that all will be well. If the distress passes when the person is calmly escorted to a place where he or she feels comfortable, then those who have come to give aid can be sure that they have taken the right approach by helping in this way.

The person who is fighting feelings of fear needs to hear 'Don't worry, I understand. The way you feel is caused by fear and fear is real and common to all human beings at some time in life. Relax, let go . . . be calm and the fear will leave you.'

When we move to reassure a distressed child, we use gentle touch and gentle words. Really, it is the same for all of us . . .

IN CONCLUSION

Not everything that counts can be counted.
Not everything that can be counted counts.
Albert Einstein

My intention upon telling my story was to put agoraphobia to rest forever and get on with other things in life. I have been able to fulfil the latter part of that ambition, but I have not been able to put agoraphobia to rest, for, as well as conquering that fear, it has also been my destiny to help others with that problem. And so I became 'the wounded healer', gaining insight through self-searching, gaining knowledge through training and gaining greater understanding while working with my own clients. Having witnessed at first hand the similarity between my own anxiety journey and the anxiety journeys of others, I have observed that all are basically of the same pattern. The problem builds like this:

- anxiety, at some level, is a universal emotion
- anxiety is an expression of fear
- tension becomes accepted in early life as a defence against fear/anxiety
- tension and anxiety feed each other in a negative coping circle
- the onset of stress increases both tension and anxiety
- stress, pressure and exhaustion escalate anxiety to the point of panic
- panic is very alarming and highlights natural vulnerability
- in seeking to avoid panic, a habit of circumstantial avoidance develops

- agoraphobia is the result of avoidance and is a defence against the fear of fear
- the problem develops from fear and simple self-defence.

If the problem is consistent and develops as a natural progression of defence, then it follows that the healing will be consistent and natural also — providing one knows what to do and does what has to be done to allow the healing happen.

From this personal theory or hypothesis, I offer a fundamental solution to the apparently complex problem of anxiety, panic and agoraphobia based upon:

- mental rest
- support from another source
- facing fear in tranquil action
- the pursuit of self-awareness to gain greater understanding.

These can be summarised in four basic words as mentioned elsewhere: *rest, reassurance, reassessment and renewal.* The foundation of this solution lies in the use of mental *rest* to reduce tension, and this depth of rest can be effectively gained through *stillness meditation* as described.

Then, for the agoraphobic to face fear, he or she needs *reassurance* from trusted people while learning to understand that what is feared is not an external object.

What is feared are the *symptoms* of fear, symptoms which occur primarily because of too much tension within the body and the mind. Because tension keeps the symptoms recurring, the phobic reaction of avoidance also recurs. When we cease the habit of fighting with tension and become calm, we reverse that pattern. The symptoms disappear, there is no longer any need to practise avoidance. We can then *reassess* the situation, applying strategies of our own and approaching everything before us with *ease*, and so the phobia too, is conquered. As with any activity, the more you do, the more you *can* do — and in agoraphobia, that is truly facing your fear.

Having come that far, life can be continued as normal. Then, if people so choose, they are free to explore their circumstances more deeply, looking to a *renewal* of their life by gaining greater self-awareness and the opportunity to change and develop further through new understanding.

A simple and natural approach is commonsense. *Stillness meditation*, far from being one of the many novel ideas promoted by 'new age' enthusiasts, is founded upon reputable medical expertise and empathic commonsense. It is a practical skill which simply makes life easier — and leads to the accomplishment of facing one's fear with success. Perhaps such a practical approach was what my local doctor intended to convey all those years ago.

There may also have been a grain of wisdom in my mother's desire to disregard my fear. Had both those people been able to take their suggestions a step further, and communicate to me that to ignore those symptoms *could have meant learning a new response and therefore let the symptoms go*, they would have done me a great service. For though anxiety may be more prevalent in the world of today, it has surely been experienced by people for all time. Sophisticated modern treatments can sometimes get in the way of simple matters which can then become complicated and prolonged.

In helping others regain their confidence, I view anxiety quite positively, as part of a philosophical search for peace and 'wholeness', rather than a 'disorder' of a pathological or psychological nature. *Pathology* generally refers to that area of medicine that is concerned with the nature and treatment of disease. *Psychology* is the scientific study of human (and animal) behaviour. *Philosophy* leans towards an understanding of human beliefs and concepts. It is my belief that agoraphobia has become over-complicated through an inclination by professionals either to: (1) pathologise the condition, that is, treat it as one would treat an illness, and by means of medication; or (2) psychologise the problem, that is, try to help the person find the origin of his or her anxiety or change their behaviour.

'Pathologising' the Condition

In the first instance, treatment has very little positive effect upon the phobia because, although the symptoms of agoraphobia cause the sufferer to feel ill, he or she is not suffering from an organic disease. The medication given therefore does not negate the problem, but only treats its symptoms. The result of medication is always temporary; therefore, in the case of the agoraphobic, he or she is in constant need of medication to fend off these recurring symptoms. At the same time, the actual problem — elevated tension — is being neglected.

I have found that the majority of people who consult me today for their anxiety, panic and agoraphobic problems have been automatically prescribed medication which has been taken consistently over many years. Even today, many general practitioners and psychiatrists still rely too much upon tranquillising medication in treating their patients' symptoms. This is despite all that is evident about problems of addiction, together with findings that in fact the medication itself eventually causes the very symptoms the patient is trying to be free of. In some circumstances, medication is necessary and helpful in the short term, but it is never a 'cure' or a real solution. For, unless otherwise aware, the individual will continue to fight with ever-increasing tension and so create the need for ever-increasing medication.

In recent years, medical researchers have initiated ideas that biological and neurophysiological factors, and biochemical and hormonal influences, may contribute to or cause anxiety disorders. Once more, medication is proffered as the answer. As one who can claim to have experienced the extreme low of the agoraphobic reaction and a complete reversal of this, I fail to see what point there is in looking for scientific evidence of this kind.

This pointlessness is further highlighted when one takes into account that the 'cures' offered do not constitute any form of enrichment for the patient. Is it better to become dependent upon tablets that may temporarily alleviate the symptoms, but result in dulling the fine senses of the patient? Is it preferable to go on relying on medication while simultaneously remaining in a state of static fear and further dependency? All living things are subject to variations in chemical and hormonal levels and we certainly inherit what we are from generations before us. But does this matter? At the very least, life itself is progressive. If it were so simple that all problems could be solved by taking scientific action, then humanity would indeed have discovered the secret of perfection.

In our imperfect world, however, science can give us one solution which in turn very often creates the need for another. This can be readily seen in people such as those who tell me, 'He says I'll be on tablets for the rest of my life'; 'There's no cure for this, they say it's in your genes'; 'Nothing can be done for agoraphobia — the doctor says I'll have it for ever'. The professionals who so readily accept agoraphobia as a permanent problem which can only be addressed by medication are unwittingly denying people the right to individual development. This attitude reflects limited thinking, to say the least, and the so-called healers who deal out advice such as this do nothing more than perpetuate people's dependency and rob their patients of hope.

'Psychologising' the Problem

It seems that the second type of treatment, which examines and acts upon causal or behavioural factors, is of little real use to the agoraphobic. For effectiveness, most psychotherapeutic approaches rely upon open discussion and the gift of personal insight. The typical agoraphobic shields him/herself from this kind of openness in their perennial passion for pretending that everything is all right (as I did myself), demonstrating this by being pleasant, co-operative and obliging, regardless of how they are really feeling. Hence, tension remains extremely high. And because tension blocks insight, there is little hope of the client finding freedom along this therapeutic avenue *unless the tension is effectively lowered.*

Some professionals favour psychoanalysis, as I have recorded within my story. In the psychoanalytic approach to treatment, childhood interactions and the role of the unconscious mind are explored. This can lead to too much introspection and often encourages blame. As can be seen within my reflections, it is relevant to problems to understand our beginnings and to recognise their influence. However, if the search for a solution does not progress beyond the past, the person remains frozen there and a great deal of unproductive resentment and anger may simmer. Rather than dealing positively with these feelings, the person may hold others responsible for his or her present predicament — and this is unjust. The first rule of self-care is responsibility for the self. One may not be responsible for all that has already happened, but one is, and must continue to be, responsible for all that is now and is still to come.

Both these approaches also require the use of logic in order to succeed. While agoraphobia is not an organic disease, neither does it exist at a logical, intellectual level within the person's mind. Rather, agoraphobia is an emotional defence against the unpleasant feelings associated with an attack of panic. Such a powerful inner defence cannot be overcome by logical intervention. And while psychotherapeutic and psychoanalytic approaches are extremely helpful in gaining self-knowledge, alone they rarely alleviate the agoraphobic problem. For even when the origin of the anxiety is consciously known (and this may take a very long time to be revealed), unless the excess tension is lowered the symptoms and the phobia will continue. While tension remains, the person will continue to fight.

In looking at the prospect of rationally changing one's behaviour, much the same applies. My friend could not help me to overcome my fear in a logical or rational way in his attempt at behavioural therapy. It is well nigh impossible to address by logic the defences that dwell powerfully and instinctively in our emotional being. Logic drives us to continue to fight. And the more we fight, the more we have to fear! So the behavioural approach to treatment I have found to be merely palliative, bringing only some temporary relief. People may, with a great deal of effort and will-power, learn to force themselves beyond fear.

But is it right to push people to their limits, to force someone, albeit kindly, through a fearful situation, creating immense strain in the process? In these circumstances, it is certain that in time this effort will all be too much, as a great deal more tension will have been required to meet the goal. This, of course, is counter-productive and once more that person will be left despondent, frustrated and disappointed in what will appear to be a never-ending, unsolvable problem. Moreover, from forced action, nothing will have been learned to enrich the spirit or beg the opportunity to grow.

Most popular for anxiety disorders among many therapists today is Cognitive Behavioural Therapy (CBT). This approach to treatment comprises breathing techniques, relaxation, the per-ceptual understanding of the anxiety-producing situation and the changing of negative thoughts surrounding that situation through positive re-conditioning. This form of treatment certainly has attributes. However, I have reservations about its supposed success rate. Many people travel that path, yet still experience panic attacks and are still affected by their phobia, accepting these as part of a 'disorder' they have now learned to live with. Any treatment of a rational or behavioural kind may see people respond and notice improvement for a time. But in my exp-erience, until the internal response, or attitude to life, has altered and personal beliefs have changed from living defensively with tension to living calmly with ease, inevitably their fear will return.

It seems that anxiety, and the 'disorders' it produces, is in fact serving an important purpose, signalling an opportunity for people to listen to their deepest needs. Therefore, anxiety ought to be regarded as a way to positive growth, whereas generally speaking anxiety is regarded negatively by most (professionals and patients alike) as something to be avoided at all costs. When tension is effectively reduced, and the road of life has opened again, agoraphobia and similar conditions can be seen as an expression of physical, emotional and spiritual need. Thus I believe they involve *philosophical* issues to be understood and acted upon. Those who suffer anxiety, panic and agoraphobia are almost always of a sensitive temperament, possessing a precious inner life. And yet it is apparent that many anxious people have barely recognised, let alone truly accepted or investigated, their more ethereal side, which holds their deeper needs and longings. They, perhaps more than others, have need to explore this. Once the mind is relaxed, the inward search may begin.

When I first published my story fifteen years ago, I defined agoraphobia as 'the fear of fear' and this is how we generally hear it explained today. While I still hold firmly to that belief, I would now expand my definition with the following: *agoraphobia is the fear of losing control for fear of taking control.* Here again is a case of opposites. On the occasion of my first panic attack, the dominant threat I felt was that of being removed from the scene with no control over the situation, being unable to properly communicate and somehow *losing the integrity of myself, my identity* — shades of my early life! This is the common agoraphobic reaction. Any threat to one's self is the ultimate human danger and amounts to loss of control.

The agoraphobic desperately fears losing control, and at an inner level this is a fear he or she has created while attempting to maintain a preferred image, striving to feel fully accepted in the world. The onset of panic threatens to expose all — in the dread of a crumbling façade and the risk of likely judgment, criticism or public shame. But the agoraphobic also desperately fears *taking control* — for to do so would involve letting go of the defences he or she fights with to prevent loss of control. Taking *true* control does not involve fighting. It involves *letting go* — of tension *and* of the belief that there is something we must defend ourselves from. In agoraphobia, letting go of one's defences is what is feared and avoided — not merely out of fear of an attack of panic, but out of fear of our whole undoing. So there is a double-edge to agoraphobia: *the fear of losing control, for fear of taking control.* Paradoxically, it's *in* the letting go that we successfully move through both edges of fear, with the result that we can then take calm control of our life.

All things in life have a practical value, phobias no less. The purpose or usefulness of agoraphobia as a defence lies, I believe, within the definition above. To understand *why* we are not taking true control we must look closely at *panic*, the emotional experience that the agoraphobic spends his or her life trying to avoid.

Panic is defined as the sudden overwhelming onset of intense apprehension, fear or terror, often associated with a feeling of impending doom — the feeling of loss of control. If we think about panic as it is commonly recognised, we can see that people feel panic-stricken when faced with a chaotic situation or one over which they have no personal control. For example, people may experience mass panic in a crowded place if told the building is on fire. The fire is beyond the control of each person present, yet each fears for his or her own safety. A sense of urgency and helplessness then occurs and as nothing *can* be done, the fight or flight reaction escalates and becomes *panic* where people irrationally fight or attempt to flee from the threatening location. Their lives are virtually in someone else's hands; the theatre manager, the ushers, the security guard, the fire brigade, necessary medical help and so on — none of whom is within a person's individual control.

Yet each instinctively must attempt to take control. As discussed earlier, a level of control is necessary or life would be constantly chaotic. But in situations of great threat or public danger, usually there is no way one *can* take control and panic is the only emotional release or action available. Under these circumstances, people may experience the same or similar feelings as those experienced by the victim of the apparently spontaneous panic attack associated with agoraphobia. For the agoraphobic, though, there is no fire or any other visible threat to escape from. For some reason, unclear at the time, he or she is also trying *to take control* of a particular situation. In a bid to fight, or to defend themselves, tension has increased. As nothing in life happens without purpose, there *must* be a purpose in these panicky feelings — even though it seems that nothing dangerous is imminent.

For the potential agoraphobic, the purpose of panic is this: danger is lurking wherever he or she is in *an emotionally vulnerable situation.* By this I mean a situation that threatens to expose one's major vulnerability and therefore the integrity of the self. This is a fundamentally philosophical issue. Through the need to save face by pretending all is well, by stoically fighting to keep false control and by striving to prove oneself beyond imagined shame, doubt, unworthiness or failure, the tension level has risen too high (in much the same way as I have described in my own case). Panic is the response when one experiences a feeling that there is no escape, there is nowhere left to go — except to a place that is unconditionally safe, home!

Those who become anxious and succumb to agoraphobia, I find, are expressing by means of panic what they cannot yet recognise in themselves. Nor can they express in any other way what is taking place within. How understandable, then, that people who experience panic begin to fight more and more, literally for their lives.

Let me take you, the agoraphobic reader, back for a moment to your first panic attack. You had been living with tension for some time. Recent stress had been high. You were notably exhausted. You were under pressure and you had responsibilities to cope with. In dealing with everything, you had become even more tense. You were out of the house, probably unaccompanied, and you felt ill and disoriented. Those feelings caused fear and anxiety to push your panic button; as panic rose within you, a sense of impending disaster overwhelmed. You felt you were about to lose control of your reason — or that perhaps you might be facing sudden death, or at least uncontrollable collapse of some kind.

What you dreaded in that instant was the exposure of your human vulnerability, a fragile part of yourself amounting to immense insecurity — and therefore the risk of your own public undoing. This is why at those times symptoms such as *feeling lost, diminished, out of balance, de-personalised and fragmented* occur. (Interestingly, when feeling safe, people are usually feeling *whole* and *in control,* and at those times they are symptom-free.)

Unconsciously, the agoraphobia sufferer has reached a point where, out of self-defence, this person has no more control over certain aspects of life than the members of the theatre audience have over a fire — *so panic occurs as the instinctive defence of tension increases*. It is easy, then, to begin to restrict oneself more and more in avoidance of panic, thus setting up the agoraphobic syndrome.

Prior to this occurrence, within your learned attitude to life you had found personal security through increased tension and 'toughing it out'. Unknown to you, this defence had been a contributing factor to your panic attack. Now, to avoid panic occurring again and in an attempt to retain dignity and integrity, in further self-defence, you have become even more tense, steeling yourself to fend off more rising anxiety.

The description of my early married life at the beginning of this book fits very accurately the experiences of many who come to me today as a client. Typically this person is female, often aged between twenty and forty, perhaps married and often the mother of young children. She will have a high sense of responsibility to others. She will be strong, though sensitive, creative and talented, often exhibiting the frustration of giftedness thwarted by lack of self-fulfilment. She will not be able to recognise her true feelings, being instead very aware of her *reactions* to her feelings in the form of anxiety and helplessness. Quite likely she will be physically and mentally exhausted. And she will have experienced significant stress, leading to anxiety, panic and perhaps agoraphobia. At some earlier time, she began her fight with tension, practising self-defence rather than self-reliance. In this she preserves a certain image for the world, and in her self-doubt, negates the wholeness (or integrity) of herself to the extent that she depends upon objects, or others, to provide her with a sense of her own existence. Her greatest dilemma lies in her inability to accept herself as wholly as she accepts others. As yet she doesn't recognise that whatever she is fighting against within herself is generally a belief of her own making based upon her own judgment. It should be noted that what we accept and believe as truths sometimes need questioning.

So while much has been achieved with regard to women's rights in society, it can be seen that many women do not understand the true meaning of the word 'liberation'. And what of liberation for the men who fall into the category of anxiety sufferers? While total human freedom is an impossibility, to aim for true liberation is to have the ability to accept the truth of what we are with the desire and the means to change or improve what we are not, *free from the defences that create limited living.*

Sometimes agoraphobia is associated with low self-esteem. This may be so for some, but most anxious people I meet seem to follow a similar pattern to my own. I had reasonable self-esteem. That was what I was fighting to keep. But I was also fighting to control my vulnerable side — so that the false beliefs upon which I judged myself so harshly would not escape and let me down completely. When I should have been working positively to fulfil my life — and even more importantly, correct the *real* inadequacies within myself — I was instead wasting energy, fighting negatively against something within myself that didn't truly exist.

When agoraphobic, I remained stuck in a self-imposed restriction where I avoided the symptoms of fear while maintaining tension, in the hope that by this means I could control my life. My example of trying to dispel fear by having a new hair-cut was a small attempt to take control; my experiment backfired because, at the time, I had no understanding of why I took that action. Therefore, once home again I immediately reverted to my ingrained style of living, the old learned habit — fighting my cause with tension. In other words, I was fighting a personal battle for self-preservation. Once again, control over one's life cannot be gained by fighting. As soon as I ceased my fight, I had won the battle. In stillness, true control came later, with the dissolving of tension and the disappearance of fear. Then self-acceptance was awakened, the acceptance of my wholeness — the good and the less good within me — offering the possibility of fruitful change.

Caring for oneself is a life-long project — a kind of challenge to *live well.* Like a strong marriage, good health and a good life do not 'just happen' as many might hope; we must be prepared to work at achieving this state. So in the serious desire to overcome the obstacles of anxiety, panic and agoraphobia, it is necessary to be committed to this cause.

The film *City of Joy*, based on the book by Dominique Lapierre, uses the principle that in life we have three options:

- to run
- to 'spectate'
- to commit.

Most people have known at some time the experience of running away from life's challenges. In my years of agoraphobia, I did my share of running, only to receive in return for that effort everincreasing fear and an all-pervading emptiness, to say nothing of a host of other accompanying negative emotions.

It is tempting too, for the fainthearted to 'spectate'. Why not, after all, let others do it all for us while we try to remain safe and comfortable? But this way of life, too, is profitless and only emphasises the dependency people have come to accept: the doctor knows best, the tablets will cure me, everything will be all right when . . . Being a spectator in life also leads us down an empty path.

But commitment — to oneself and to the world we live in — is the threshold we long for, the threshold to the wellspring of the goodness of life. Commitment to any worthwhile cause will always bring positive results. It sparks our motivation and kindles hope when hope seems to be flagging. Commitment is the tool that gets things done. We must, therefore, make commitment a priority and, through it, take responsibility for ourselves.

With commitment we can then begin to eradicate excessive tension by practising stillness with purpose. As its serenity enters our lives, from it will be distilled the answers we are seeking and the solution to the problem of this kind of fear.

A life free of problems is a life without experience and, perhaps, without meaning. The experience of agoraphobia in my life helped me towards richer personal development and a more profound understanding of life and of human kind. We are all 'amateur actors', feeling our way, learning by our mistakes and our successes; even the steps which sometimes seem to be backward eventually take us forward in the continuing growth towards completeness. And so we collect life's experiences as we might collect shells from the beach.

We should remember that, while sometimes those seashells are flung on to the sand in the midst of the storm, without fail, once the storm has passed, more shells will be gently laid there by the peaceful waters of a new day. As a child I found peace in Nessa's garden. Somewhere, in everyone's memory, is a garden of some kind where trouble is washed away by tranquillity. I use the example of the garden, not as an end in itself, but only to kindle within the reader's spirit the tiniest memory of stillness and the wish to seek further. For it is well to recapture that memory and realise its value. It could be just the glimmer of light necessary to help you on your way. It is necessary too, to grasp the fact that suffering, whatever it may be, is not necessarily something to be avoided or of which to be ashamed, but an opportunity for life enhancement. *Stillness meditation* is, in my experience, the skill by which that suffering can be more easily accepted, transformed and overcome.

I recognise my good fortune in overcoming fear. Although eight years seemed a long time to me then, it is nothing at all compared to those who have known fear for twenty-eight or thirty-eight years. But this doesn't mean that my understanding of the problem of fear is any the less, or that those who have suffered longer cannot change.

Here now, is a confession. During those years of fear I thought I would never forget one unpleasant moment. In the original telling of this story and in now reviewing it after twenty-five years, I have had to take my mind right back with some effort to recall the detail of eight years of that experience. A statement such as that, I think, holds sufficient conviction for the reader to know that anxiety, panic and agoraphobia definitely belong to my past.

It is my privilege to have shared all this with you. I trust that my story will continue to bring fear to greater awareness and provide that much-needed hope where required. To wish an easy road is to deny you adventure. I wish you, instead, a fulfilling journey upon which you will find a tranquil return to the truth and wholeness of yourself — and a future of contentment where all your dreams will be fulfilled.

I began this book by recalling a conversation with a stranger on a train. His thoughts seem a fitting expression to close with: 'People are scared, you know'! But it is generally because they are tense. People are tense, you know. But we don't have to be — there is a rewarding alternative!

APPENDIX: DR AINSLIE MEARES

Courtesy of Sylvia Black
(née Meares), April 1999

Ainslie Dixon Meares, BAgS, MD, BS, DPM, was an Australian psychiatrist, most famous as a pioneer in recognising stress as a major cause of illness and in teaching people how it could be overcome through meditation. He wrote of his work in thirty books, among them the international best seller *Relief Without Drugs* (Great Britain: Souvenir Press Ltd, 1968), and over one hundred medical papers.

Dr Meares was born in Melbourne, Australia, in 1910. He studied medicine at Melbourne University and graduated just as World War II broke out. He enlisted in the Australian Infantry Forces and became a regimental medical officer. Towards the end of the war he was stationed at an army hospital in Goulburn, New South Wales, where he treated soldiers who had become mentally disturbed by the trauma of their war experiences. This was probably the most significant point in Dr Meares' career because it was here that he made his decision to make psychiatry his life's work.

After the war he joined a practice at the Royal Melbourne Hospital, but quickly became disenchanted with the techniques of orthodox psychiatry such as psychoanalysis, electric shock treatment and drug therapy. Two years later he opened his own private practice.

He turned first to hypnosis. It was not the authoritative form of hypnosis where the hypnotist attempts to remove the patient's symptoms by suggestion that interested him, but hypno-analysis. This was considered to be a quicker version of psychoanalysis. In the hypnotic state the patient's inhibitions are reduced and the mind is therefore more open to revealing inner conflicts. However, Dr Meares soon discovered that sometimes patients would get better after hypnosis without their deep-seated problems ever being discovered. In this state their mental function had reverted to a biologically primitive mode of uncritical functioning and a state of calm, which Dr Meares called *atavistic regression*.

By now Dr Meares had come to believe that organic illness and psychological illness were not mutually exclusive — that in fact they were different manifestations of the same thing. Further, he was sure that there was one common cause, and that was anxiety. He reasoned that stress increased the levels of natural cortisone in the body which then inhibited the body's auto-immune system and left it open to illness.

To learn more about hypnosis and its effects on the brain he travelled all over the world studying various hypnotic states and their role in the lives of people of different cultures. He observed macumba in Brazil, voodoo in Haiti and fire-walking in Bali; he visited witch doctors in Africa and lived for a while with Zen Buddhist monks in Japan. But it was one particular yogi he met and sat with in the foothills of the Himalayas who proved to be a pivotal factor in Dr Meares' life. This man was 134 years old, meditated for sixteen hours each day and his inner calm was palpable. When asked if he were ever troubled by pain, his answer was that he did feel pain but that there was no hurt in it. He was aware of the warning signals of the pain and could respond accordingly, but he was not discomforted by it.

As the two men sat together sometimes they would not talk, but in the yogi's presence Dr Meares would find himself drifting into a state of reverie and afterwards would feel himself changed by this — he had taken on some of the yogi's calm.

Back in Melbourne, Dr Meares was determined to learn to meditate and through it to master pain. He started by lying on a low stone garden wall, the idea being to overcome discomfort, not to go to sleep. He learnt to shut out all thought and to allow his mind simply to drift. He found that the sensation of calm and ease lasted well beyond the period of meditation.

The next step was to overcome pain. He practised by piercing his skin with pins and laying burning string across his forearm. But the real test was to have an abscessed molar removed without anaesthetic (1963). It proved to be a much more difficult extraction than expected, with the dentist having to chisel away some of the jaw bone to get the tooth out sideways. Yet, while Dr Meares was aware of what was happening, he felt no pain; there was minimal bleeding and no post-operative discomfort. Other similar experiments followed with the same results.

It was time now to introduce atavistic regression (mental relaxation) to his patients without hypnosis. Dr Meares put what he had learnt from the yogi into practice. Speech makes people alert, so any communication he used had to be non-verbal. He, himself, had to exude calm, like the yogi, to create an atmosphere in which the patient, too, would feel calm. If the patient showed any sign of anxiety Dr Meares would respond with a gentle touch to the arm or a low murmur.

In the years that followed, Dr Meares successfully treated hundreds of patients for anxiety and pain by showing them how to achieve mental relaxation — his approach to meditation.

By 1975 Dr Meares sought to probe even further into the powers of the mind. He now wanted to see if by intensive meditation he could influence the effects of cancer. His colleagues in the medical profession saw this as an impossible and futile pursuit. He could not look to them for support or referrals and so he needed to advertise for patients who would be prepared to take part in his experiment. But doctors are not allowed to advertise, so he took the decision to formally retire from medical practice and concentrate entirely on his work in meditation.

Inevitably, patients were slow to make themselves available at first and those who did come were those for whom all other avenues of treatment had failed. They were terminal patients and Dr Meares was a last resort. But as word of his work spread, gradually the numbers built up and after ten years he was able to say confidently that intensive meditation could influence the growth of cancer. Nearly all his patients suffered less discomfort and pain and needed fewer drugs. Nearly all achieved an inner calm and a sense of peace, no longer concerned about death. Many patients exhibited a remarkable slowing of the growth of their cancers and lived considerably longer than expected. Some patients achieved remission.

Dr Meares died in 1986.

ABOUT THE AUTHOR

Pauline McKinnon was acknowledged by Dr Ainslie Meares as a prominent exponent of his unique approach to meditation, the major focus of her consulting work. In addition to her private practice, she conducts lectures and workshops in *stillness meditation* for various groups, including schools, community centres and hospitals and is a guest university presenter.

In writing *Quiet Magic* and *Help Yourself and Your Child to Happiness*, Pauline acted upon her concern for young people. In 1997 she began training others to teach this specific form of meditation to children and adolescents and also founded ESM Australia Inc, an organisation of professionals with a vision to integrate *stillness meditation* into formal education and health care. This has resulted in programmes being successfully introduced into some Australian primary schools.

Stillness meditation has allowed Pauline to balance her professional role with that of wife and mother and the pursuit of wider passions — which include the study of theology and philosophy and her ongoing enjoyment of singing.

For further information about ESMA please write to:

ESM Australia Inc.
C/- PO Box 151
Kew East 3102
Victoria
Australia